Buttonless

Buttonless

Incredible iPhone and iPad Games and the Stories Behind Them

Ryan Rigney

CRC Press
Taylor & Francis Group
Boca Raton London New York

CRC Press is an imprint of the
Taylor & Francis Group, an **informa** business

AN A K PETERS BOOK

CRC Press
Taylor & Francis Group
6000 Broken Sound Parkway NW, Suite 300
Boca Raton, FL 33487-2742

Library of Congress Cataloging-in-Publication Data

Rigney, Ryan.
    Buttonless : incredible iPhone and iPad games and the stories behind them / Ryan Rigney.
        p. cm.
    Summary: "If you own an iPhone, iPod, or iPad and are interested in gaming, then this book will be your absolute best resource. Written by an established video game journalist and with contributions from leading gamers, the book presents some of the most interesting iPhone and iPad games, along with stories of the people behind these games. It describes hundreds of titles, including well-known games and hidden gems. An excellent resource for serious gamers, the book provides insight into the development of games for the iOS platform. "-- Provided by publisher.
        ISBN 978-1-4398-9585-6 (pbk.)
        1. Computer games. 2. Mobile games. 3. iPhone (Smartphone) 4. iPad (Computer) I. Title.

GV1469.15.R54 2011
794.8--dc23   2011043514

Visit the Taylor & Francis Web site at
http://www.taylorandfrancis.com

and the CRC Press Web site at
http://www.crcpress.com

Table of Contents

Foreword

Back in 2008 when the App Store first opened, I was attempting to flex my start-up muscles by running a video game website aimed at parents and families. After spending nearly 20 years running magazines and websites like *Electronic Gaming Monthly*, 1UP.com, and the *Official US PlayStation Magazine*, I'd decided it was time to try and do something for people my own age. I was further motivated by having had kids fairly recently—and like any father of young children, I felt the need to talk about them ceaselessly and mold all kinds of decisions around the fact of my fatherhood whenever possible. In an attempt to shore up my slowly eroding gamer "cred," I was also appearing on a popular weekly gaming podcast that was aimed squarely at fervent, hardcore gamers.

As you can probably imagine, insights about video games gleaned from one of these professional environments didn't necessarily translate all that well to others. Though pretty progressive in the grand scheme of things, gamers don't deal with change as well as you'd think, while families tend to roll with whatever is of the moment. The gaming "establishment" loves Nintendo, PlayStation, and the Xbox—but more significantly, it loves what it finds comfortable and familiar.

Mario Kart is comfortable and familiar. *Halo* is comfortable and familiar. Controllers with four face buttons and two analog sticks are comfortable and familiar. What *isn't* is the idea that a company like Apple could come along and somehow threaten the establishment with a laissez faire attitude about supporting games while providing a completely different user experience and infrastructure.

I was vigorously berated at the time by my cohosts on the podcast and by the gaming community at large for suggesting that *maybe* we should take the iPhone more seriously as a game platform. I was admonished still further for intimating that perhaps Nintendo's stranglehold on the portable games market might be under threat. "It doesn't have any buttons," came the retort. "We don't want to play 'serious' games on a touch screen, it will never work," I was told, in spite of the fact that the DS has a touch screen. "Mobile gaming stinks," was the general sentiment, thanks to years of atrocious cell-phone games dictated by carrier stacks. This was before *Angry Birds*, of course. Before *Cut The Rope*, or *Anomaly: Warzone Earth*. It was before 2D Boy ported *World of Goo* to the iPad, or game-design auteurs from the 1980s and 1990s realized that the platform was absolutely *perfect* for resurrecting ideas that had lain dormant for decades.

What many people at the time underestimated was the killer one-two combo of portability and convenience. The Nintendo DS and PlayStation Portable aren't really pocket systems; they're backpack systems that take up far too much space, and require far too much messing around. You're not going to have one about your person at any given moment, and you have to make a conscious decision to leave the house properly equipped—there are chargers, carry cases, and all of the associated detritus and paraphernalia, and then on top of that you have to find some way to carry the games themselves. Bottom line? It's a huge pain. The iPhone changed all that; it's always with you (because it's an essential part of your life, being a phone, email, social, and media device), it's always charged, it's always connected, and it always has access to a wide selection of games. Plus, if you want *new* games, the App Store is just a screen tap away. In my opinion, people are fundamentally lazy (me especially), so something *that* convenient was bound to change our relationship with the entertainment it served.

We've had iOS devices in my house since the very beginning. My kids have grown up instinctively understanding how to swipe, pinch, and touch a glass screen to interact with the game characters they love. Although they've been raised on the classics, and are familiar with the all of the major games platforms, they are instinctively drawn to the iPhone and iPad. Given a choice between the Xbox 360 and the iPad, they tend to opt for the latter. On a recent vacation we packed a bag full of DS games, but they went unplayed for two whole weeks because both *Plants vs. Zombies* and *Swords and Soldiers* were far more satisfying for them when played on the iPad.

We are seeing a generational shift happen right before our eyes, and what's unsettling for many gamers is that it's coming from the last place they ever expected it. The future of games is upon us, and we'll look back on the first few years of iOS games as the experiences that changed our relationships with entertainment.

—John Davison
VP of Programming
GameSpot

Preface

The book that you're holding is the result of a strange obsession. Since 2009, I've spent an unreasonable amount of time and money purchasing, playing, and writing about games for the iPhone and iPad. What began as a hobby quickly turned into a daily part of my life, and before long I had accrued enough experience covering the iOS scene to land a job writing a weekly column about the App Store for GamePro.com.

Over the course of the following year, I wrote about and reviewed hundreds of iOS games. I interviewed many of the most interesting App Store developers, and my growing knowledge about the iPhone and iPad gaming market earned me writing gigs with magazines like PC Gamer, MacLife, and Macworld. One day, while sitting through a cousin's graduation ceremony, it hit me—I could write a book about this stuff.

The 67 games that you'll read about in *Buttonless* were not selected at random. I've purchased and played well over a thousand iOS games, and about a quarter of those were really worth something.

The games that populate this book are not merely good. They're the most interesting, well-designed, notable games on the App Store. Some of them were included because of their inventive mechanics or polished design. Others made it in because of their incredible popularity. But they all have one thing in common—they're worth your time and money.

Buttonless is not just a buyer's guide. Within the following pages, I hope to show you some interesting games that you might not have heard of, but my real goal is to share the stories behind these games. Games are created by people, not machines, and people struggling to create something awesome and original inevitably go through their fair share of trials while creating it.

To learn these stories, I conducted hundreds of exclusive interviews with the people behind the games I selected. I asked them questions about their creative process and the adversities they had to overcome, and pried for funny/interesting anecdotes from behind the scenes. I spoke with dozens of the most brilliant game designers in the world, and they continually surprised me with their insights and opinions about the ever-changing games industry that they've helped to shape.

If there's one thing I learned from those conversations, it's this: on the forefront of the mobile gaming revolution are real people, with stories that are crazy, stressful, hilarious, and (in some cases) heart-wrenching. These people have stories that are worth telling, and that's what *Buttonless* is about. I hope you enjoy it.

100 Rogues

Platform: iPad/iPhone/iPod Touch (universal app)
Price: $1.99
Developer: Dinofarm Games
Publisher: Fusion Reactions
Released: May 4, 2010

What Is It?

"Roguelikes" are games based on the 1986 PC game *Rogue*. Most roguelikes take place in monster-filled dungeons, and the player's goal is to retrieve some object of great importance from within the depths of the evil lair. One of the most important characteristics of a roguelike is that once the hero dies, he or she is gone forever. Even if a player has poured hours into the development of a character, getting surrounded by enemies and taking too much damage can result in the permanent death of that hero. Every decision players make becomes important when hours of real-world time can be wasted through simple mistakes.

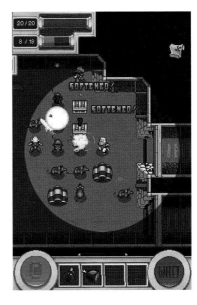

100 Rogues takes all of the aforementioned attributes and shrinks them into a tiny experience fit for mobile devices. Instead of taking each character you create on an epic journey that can potentially last for dozens of hours, each session of *100 Rogues* lasts an average of ten minutes. Your chosen character—whether a spell-slinging mage or a sword-wielding crusader—levels up and unlocks new abilities very quickly, and will likely live for only as long as it takes to sit through a commercial break while watching television (yes, iPhone games are the newest thing in mid-TV show entertainment). *100 Rogues* is a new spin on one of gaming's most versatile genres, and it works beautifully on iOS.

Behind the Game

100 Rogues was not intended to be an ambitious game. The game began as a simple clone of *POWDER*, a roguelike created by indie developer Jeff Lait (which happens to be available on the iPhone for free). Freshman developer Dinofarm Games had been commissioned by Fusion Reactions to make an iOS game, and it felt that it was up to the task. The game was scheduled to be completed in a little over three months. Seventeen months later, the game still wasn't complete.

But let's not get too far ahead of ourselves. To understand the troubled development of *100 Rogues*, you'll need the perspective of Wes Paugh, a programmer for Fusion Reactions who worked on the game. "When I was hired to work on *100 Rogues*, the game had been in development for three months, which was about 85% of the way through the initially estimated schedule," says Paugh. "The indication was that I was brought on to lend a quick hand with the last few stages of *100 Rogues* and to start a new project after that."

It soon became apparent that the "initially estimated schedule" wasn't going to be followed very closely, due largely to the fact that the scale of the game grew continually—no one working on the game had a clear idea of when features should stop being added. According to Paugh, the original designs for the game had essentially been forgotten and replaced with a feature list that required at least eight additional months of development. "It was like designing and building a spaghetti western film set and, when nearly done, deciding to build a functional town instead," says Paugh.

> ### Statistics
> - **Development time:** 18 months
> - **Total budget:** $40,000
> - **Times downloaded:** 100,000

Both Paugh and Keith Burgun, the game's design lead, remember the moment that the vision for the game became clear. Burgun had wanted to include a teleport ability in the game for certain enemy types, and Paugh was able to code it surprisingly easily. Paugh describes this as a watershed moment, in which *100 Rogues'* potential as a strategically rich game became clear. "Just like that, the player had a new, uniquely strategic enemy to face, and the game grew from an RPG in which you fought monsters with a bit higher stats each level into a game that required skill and strategy," he says.

Burgun agrees that it wasn't until *100 Rogues* had gotten relatively far into development that its final form began to take shape. "As the game's development went on, its design started to reveal itself to me," says Burgun. "This game was to be about tactical decision-making, using skill versus mobs of monsters." Burgun admits that in hindsight, there should have been a clear vision for the game at an earlier point of development, but that he got caught up in expanding its scope. "I fell into a 'more is better' trap to some degree with *100 Rogues*, but it was a learning experience, our first published game," says Burgun.

The team continued work on the game, but not without their fair share of tribulations. The game's original programmer had a falling out with the team's producer (George Morgan of Fusion Reactions), and at one point Paugh took a break from the game to finish up his education, leaving the game with no active programmer for a full three months. "The game would have been canned if not for the grace and sacrifice of our publisher," says Paugh. "Fusion Reactions was aware of our status as freshmen developers, and was prepared to accommodate the gross schedule slips because it understood that we knew what made a fun game, and would do whatever it took to achieve it."

> **Fun Facts**
> - *100 Rogues*' lead designer, Keith Burgun, has played drums for a video game music cover band—Dinosaur Lightning—for over ten years.
> - *100 Rogues*' name is a reference to *100 Worlds Story: The Tales of a Watery Wilderness*, an incredibly obscure NES game.
> - Keith Burgun runs an excellent video game design blog called Expensive Planetarium.

Finally, after 18 months of work, *100 Rogues* was released on the App Store. The game was finally in players' hands, but its troubles weren't over. In an update released in the fall of 2010, Dinofarm Games/Fusion Reactions inserted an iAd (Apple's in-app advertising application) into the game's score tally page, which appears after a character has died. It didn't go over well with fans. "Many players were absolutely livid that a paid app had an ad in it," says Paugh. "The accusations of greed were numerous and painful."

Paugh confesses that he still doesn't know whether the outrage over the in-game ad was unreasonable. "On the one hand, it was placed in a spot that didn't interfere with game play whatsoever, only appeared when you lost, and was visible less than 1% of the time when using the app," reasons Paugh. "On the other hand," he admits, "as a player, I would have been mad too."

The ad was removed within a week, but the damage had already been done. To this day, iTunes' reviews of the game still sometimes mention "the iAd fiasco," and posters on popular iOS gaming forums like those at TouchArcade.com regularly bring up the controversy as well. So was all that torment from users worth it? "All said and done, I think the ad made us $1.30," says Paugh.

Despite its remarkably problematic development process and the advertising controversy, *100 Rogues* continues to sell, in part because it was a huge critical success. Blogs and other game-review sites welcomed the game with high marks, and happy players helped spread the word. Games industry luminary and *Bioshock* creator Ken Levine even told Kotaku.com that he enjoyed playing *100 Rogues* before bed. "People clearly loved the game as much as we did," says Paugh. "And that's a great feeling."

With the experience of working as lead designer on *100 Rogues* under his belt, Burgun has this advice to developers: "Don't make your game unless it is something that absolutely has to be made. Meaning, there should be a game in your mind that you really want to play, but it doesn't exist yet. That's a good motivation for building a game."

Across Age DX

Platform: iPhone/iPod Touch (iPad version available separately)
Price: $3.99
Developer: Exe-Create
Publisher: FDG Entertainment
Released: February 11, 2010

What Is It?

Across Age looks and plays like a Super Nintendo action-RPG classic, and if it actually had been released in the 1990s, it would have stood toe-to-toe with the other greats of that era. I'd love to avoid comparing *Across Age* to *Zelda*, but there's just no getting around the similarities. Sure, *Across Age* has far deeper RPG mechanics (leveling up, upgrading skills, etc.), and the fact that players control two characters at once instead of just one is certainly a stark difference, but the moment-to-moment combat, dungeon exploration, and puzzle solving reeks of Nintendo's legendary adventure series.

The two-character mechanic that I mentioned is one of the most interesting aspects of *Across Age*. Players can switch between a melee character and a magic-user at any time, and the two can even be split up, allowing for interesting puzzle-solving challenges—including several that force you to send one character backwards in time to affect something in the present. The game is good about giving players a healthy balance of lightning-fast battles and slower paced puzzle-solving sections. It's designed to be played in larger chunks, but still manages to work as a mobile game thanks to its easy-to-use save system. *Across Age* is one of the meatiest, most interesting RPGs available for iOS devices.

Behind the Game

Thomas Kern and Philipp Döschl have always loved RPGs. Döschl names classic titles like *Phantasy Star, Ys, Final Fantasy*, and *Grandia* as some of his favorites from when he was a kid, and says that he'd always wanted to work on a Japanese-style RPG. "Every now and then we [Döschl and Kern] talked about what kind of RPG we could create, just to realize that such a project was not doable at that time," Döschl says.

In 2009, Kern and Döschl came across Exe-Create, a Japanese developer that had created *Across Age* for Japanese mobile phones. The two men convinced Exe-Create to work with them and their company, FDG Entertainment, to publish *Across Age* for iOS.

FDG did much of the work to redesign the game, changing the menu system, the way combat worked, and even elements of the game's story. Kern also set to work on composing a new soundtrack for the game, which had been one of his childhood dreams (the result is excellent, by the way). According to Döschl, Exe-Create was in charge of most of the technical side of things. It reworked the graphics and altered many of the areas in the existing version of the game.

One of the biggest challenges facing FDG was the language barrier; Döschl has minimal skills in speaking Japanese, and the Japanese team members were equally rudimentary in their English abilities. To overcome this, Döschl had to get creative. One of the things that Döschl wanted in the iOS version of the game was a cinematic for the opening and ending. "We understood very quickly that it would be very difficult and time-consuming to explain what the movie should be like, so we had to find another way," says Döschl. Döschl's solution was to begin gathering a collection of scenes from other RPGs and animes. He cut these scenes together to create a sort of cobbled-together, full-motion storyboard. This served as a reference for the new cinematic that would appear in the game.

At one point in development, Kern got extremely sick and had to leave production for nearly two months. The music was

---

Statistics

• **Development time:** 7 months

Fun Facts

• Döschl says that players should pay attention to some of the item-trading side quests if they want to get their hands on Ceska's best weapon—the "rune staff."

• Exe-Create has localized other games for America, including *The Lost Angelic Chronicles of Frane*, published on Steam in August 2011.

• FDG is perhaps best known for its *Bobby Carrot* franchise of mobile adventure games. There are a total of five entries, most of which have been ported to iOS.

almost done at that point, thankfully, but Döschl says that the gap his absence left in the team was significant.

Even after *Across Age* was finished, work on it wasn't complete. Many customers who bought the game from the App Store criticized its combat system, which requires players to wildly run into enemies in order to attack. Both FDG and Exe-Create thought it would be a neat way to avoid cluttering the screen with virtual buttons, but fan response proved otherwise. "We got a lot of requests to change it," Döschl admits. "So we added an attack button." Subsequently FDG continued to listen to players, and eventually the level of difficulty was adjusted to make the game easier and some of the more annoying traps that littered the maps were removed.

Angry Birds

Platform: iPhone/iPod Touch (iPad version available separately)
Price: $.99
Developer: Rovio Entertainment
Publisher: Chillingo
Released: December 10, 2009

What Is It?

500,000,000. Wait, no. Let me spell that out for you: five hundred million. That's how many times *Angry Birds* has been downloaded across all of the platforms on which it has been released (that's iPhone, iPad, Android, PC, Mac, PlayStation 3, and PSP, for those counting). It's not a "phenomenon" or a "runaway success" or any of those other descriptive buzzwords that people love to use. *Angry Birds* is the most ubiquitous game ever created.

For most of 2010 and 2011, the world was obsessed with Rovio's adorable but vicious avian mascots. You could go to a public place, look around at everyone poking at a smartphone, and (whether child or adult) there was a significant chance that the screen would be populated by those rascally green pigs and a variety of furious birds.

It wasn't always like that, though. I reviewed *Angry Birds* for TouchArcade.com on December 11, 2009—the day after the game's release. No other gaming site had yet noticed the game (no major gaming media paid attention to iOS gaming in those days), so I wanted to spread the word about what I saw as a hidden gem. In my review, I compared *Angry Birds* to *Boom Blox*, an overlooked Wii game created under the direction of Steven Spielberg. Like in *Boom Blox*, players of *Angry Birds* fling objects (in this case, bloodthirsty birds) at structures made of blocks in order to set off a physics-powered chain reaction that results in the destruction of a target hidden within the blocks.

As I later learned, *Angry Birds* actually draws much more heavily from *Crush the Castle*, a free-to-play browser game with noticeably less personality than Rovio's famous title. Regardless of its origins, *Angry Birds* has flung itself into pop culture. Its longevity has yet to be determined, but it sure has arrived with a bang.

Behind the Game

Way back in 2003, a trio of Finnish university students from Helsinki (Niklas Hed, Jarno Väkeväinen, and Kim Dikert) got together and decided to participate in a competition sponsored by HP and Nokia. The competition challenged participants to create a real-time multiplayer game (that is, not turn-based like *Words With Friends*) for mobile phones. The three men won the competition and joined together officially to form Relude (which they later renamed Rovio Mobile).

Mikael Hed is the cousin of Rovio cofounder Niklas Hed, and the current CEO of Rovio. He was there in March of 2009, whenever the first ideas for the game that became *Angry Birds* began floating around the Rovio offices. "We were doing work for hire, so our strategy was that it would take a number of titles before we could realistically make one hit," Hed says.

In order to facilitate the creation of some original games, Rovio began accepting fewer contracts in order to free up some of its own employees. It began holding meetings in which members of the team could propose game ideas. "Many of the proposals that we got were really well thought out," says Hed. "And then we had this one screenshot of this angry bird character just trudging around on the ground." According to Hed, everyone in the room loved the bird character, and the meeting devolved into a discussion about how to create a game around the character. "Prior to this meeting we had set up strict criteria to determine which game we would go with, but we threw that out for the angry bird character," says Hed.

The creator of the angry bird character was Rovio senior game designer Jaakko Iisalo. He had been drawing birds for another Rovio game, but after the positive reaction

> **Statistics**
> - **Number of games Rovio created before *Angry Birds*:** Over 30
> - **Number of those games you've ever heard of:** 0
> - **Times downloaded (across all platforms):** 350,000,000

to his character design, he jumped at the chance to design a new game based around his drawing.

Iisalo freely admits that *Angry Birds* is a product of its time—Rovio had done some research to figure out what sorts of games were popular and found that two-dimensional physics games were big, although they mostly existed as Flash-based web games.

Even after coming up with the idea to make *Angry Birds* a physics game, it took awhile before the famous slingshot was added. Iisalo says that in the beginning, players had to pull the birds in the direction they wanted to shoot. The game's designers agreed that this control scheme felt "somehow wrong," so they began dreaming up new solutions, including ones that Iisalo calls "completely weird," like one that he describes as a swing-type thing that players had to tap and release (I can't fathom how that would work).

Another element of *Angry Birds* that underwent several iterations was the story. Who are these birds? Why are they so angry at the pigs? "In one of the initial concepts, we had the tiny bird landing on top of the pig, then the pig sneezes (he had swine flu) and the bird falls off, gets mad, and tells his friends that the pig is teasing him," says Iisalo. "In hindsight, it's probably a good thing we didn't go with that!"

Angry Birds didn't become a worldwide phenomenon overnight. After its release in early December of 2009, it shot to number one in the Finnish App Store almost overnight, but Apple didn't feature the game until halfway through February of 2010. That was the spark that kicked off the *Angry Birds* revolution—from there the game pushed to number one in the UK, and other countries soon followed.

I spoke to Hed a little less than a year after *Angry Birds* was first released, and at the time Rovio had been able to expand to 23 employees. One of those employee's sole job was answering fan mail. Hed told me of one email they received from the mother of a 5-year-old boy who loved the game. "[She] sent us some scans and said that her son had drawn a level for the game, and we actually put the level in the game via an update," Hed says.

Since that time, Rovio has doubled its employee head count to over 50 people. It has released *Angry Birds* for every platform imaginable (Google's Chrome web browser, Facebook, Android, PlayStation Network, Mac, PC, and the list goes on), and Bloomberg reported in August of 2011 that the company has been seeking funding that would value the Rovio brand at over one billion dollars.

Everything has happened very quickly for a company that was largely an unknown identity before 2009. Rovio created over 30 unpopular games for various mobile platforms prior to its investment in the *Angry Birds* franchise, and even avid *Angry Birds* fans have to admit that *Angry Birds* fever can't last forever.

Fun Facts

- Many levels in *Angry Birds* are designed to look like specific objects. Iisalo says that one level looks like a "hamburger meal."
- The red bird does have a special power to unleash when players tap the screen—Rovio calls it the "war cry" (it does nothing).
- iOS publisher Chillingo claims that *Angry Birds* was "very different" before Rovio brought the game to it and took some of its suggestions for changes.
- Other iOS games by Rovio include *Angry Birds Seasons* and *Angry Birds Rio*.

Considering that Rovio chief marketing officer Peter Vesterbacka has said publicly that the company is "betting everything on *Angry Birds*," it's hard not to wonder—where will Rovio be in five years?

Babylonian Twins Premium

Platform: iPhone/iPod Touch (iPad version available separately)
Price: $1.99
Developer: Cosmos Interactive
Released: April 8, 2010

What Is It?

Babylonian Twins is a defiantly old-school platformer for people who crave a challenge. The game stars a pair of Iraqi princes on a quest to stop an evil wizard from destroying their kingdom. You won't be able to control both princes simultaneously, but you can switch between them at any point. This turns the inactive prince into a stone statue, which players can then hop onto (with the other twin) in order to reach previously inaccessible goodies or areas.

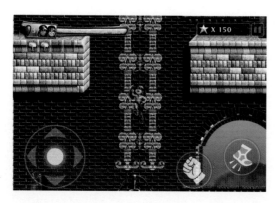

There's something oddly tricky about keeping track of both princes. Many puzzles require you to send the two boys to opposite ends of a level to trigger switches or collect items that will allow them both to progress. Levels are often quite spacious, both in height and width, making exploration and even backtracking a lot more fun than in other two-dimensional platformers in the App Store.

There's a rudimentary one-button combat mechanic (one twin wields a club, the other has a mace), but enemies are often extremely dangerous, and mace-happy players are likely to find their health drained very quickly.

Despite my insistence on calling *Babylonian Twins* a "platformer," the game really isn't about hopping from one floating platform to another; it's about exploring a beautifully designed artistic throwback to ancient Iraq. The fact that you get to listen to a wonderful soundtrack and solve fun puzzles while doing so is just a bonus.

Behind the Game

One of the many bad years for Iraq was 1993. Economic sanctions that had been implemented by the United Nations in 1990 were in full force, and the effects were devastating. The Iraqi literacy rate plummeted, the infant-mortality rate skyrocketed, and an embargo on the manufacturing and importation of chlorine (which the UN worried could be used to create chemical weapons) left the citizens of Iraq desperate for clean water.

Throughout these tough times the Iraqi people did what they could, and some found ways around the sanctions restricting imported goods. One example of a popular import was the Commodore Amiga, the successor to the Commodore 64. In the late 1980s Iraqis had begun importing the Amiga 500 (the low-end Commodore Amiga) in bulk, despite a cost of three to four times more than the standard retail price for the machine.

> **Statistics**
> • Estimated number of times Cosmos Interactive has raised/lowered the game's price: 150
> • Times downloaded (free): 460,000
> • Times downloaded (paid): 40,000

One early adopter of the Amiga was a young Iraqi named Rabah Shihab. After seeing a home video of the Commodore Amiga running *Defender of the Crown* and *Deluxe Paint* in 1988, Shihab saved hard-earned dinar for a full year before he was able to purchase an Amiga of his own. He and his brother played constantly, using games like *Speedball* and *KickOff* as an outlet for their competitive natures.

An absence of hard copyright laws at the time allowed Iraqi companies to pirate software and sell the copies at a high price, effectively making the country a no-man's-land for developers and leaving Iraqis like Shihab and his brother with no alternative to purchasing pirated games. Large-scale imports of the Amiga continued into the early 1990s, and by 1993 the Amiga's market penetration was relatively high compared to other computers.

Shihab went on to study computer engineering at the University of Baghdad. Inspired by other games, such as Team17's *Superfrog* and Konami's *Maze of Galious*, Shihab—who had been programming and creating games on his MSX computer since the age of 13—met with friends and fellow students Murtadha Salman and Mahir Alsalman, and together they set out to develop their own game. Shihab's goal was to create a game rich with Iraqi history, culture, and art that, as Shihab now reflects, "presented an image of Iraq as a country of something more than just wars and sanctions."

"Most people don't know much about Iraq and its history," Shihab says. "It is unfortunate that the small percentage of bad people affect the image of the greater majority, all of whom are peaceful, educated, smart, passionate, compassionate, and generous. We rarely hear the good stories from the media."

Because of his programming experience Shihab led the team of three, who informally referred to themselves as "the Mesopotamian team." Shihab designed the game, coded it using AsmOne, and fell into the role of project manager.

The game was created with very limited resources. "Imagine [having] no hard drive," Shihab says. "We had to constantly swap disks during each compilation. Add to that the fact that we had to save work constantly in case of power interruptions. We had to swap floppy disks many times."

"We had only one book, the *Amiga Hardware Reference Manual*," Shihab adds. "We had no Internet or game-developer reference books." The Amiga that Shihab used to create the game had only 512 KB of memory, an amount so small he had to use risky programming tricks to squeeze out all the power possible. This often led to crashes.

> **Fun Facts**
>
> • *Babylonian Twins*' music lead, Mahir Alsalman, had to share his music samples with the team by calling them and holding a phone up to his speaker.
> • There are three hidden bonus levels and several hidden treasures to find in *Babylonian Twins*. The treasures are based on real artifacts from Mesopotamian history.
> • Murtadha Salman created all of the original game's art using *Deluxe Paint* on the Amiga.

The finished product was *Babylonian Twins*, a title considered by many to be the first commercially viable video game created in Iraq. A puzzle platformer, the game follows twin princes of Babylon in a quest to protect their father's kingdom from an evil magician. Salman based the visual style of the game on art from history books, and Alsalman's soundtrack drew inspiration from traditional Iraqi music.

Shihab's coding prowess served him well, and the methods that he used to create the game made it run smoothly on the Amiga. "People have told me that this is the fastest-moving game on the Amiga," Shihab says proudly. "That's unfortunate, since it didn't come out for the Amiga."

They completed the game, but Shihab couldn't find a publisher. The UN sanctions were serving effectively as a legal blockade that prevented publication, so even if Shihab had found a company willing to publish the game, the likelihood of *Babylonian Twins* finding its way out of the country would have been extremely low. Shihab eventually negotiated with a Canadian publisher (he wasn't willing to name the publisher during our interviews), but that deal fell through as well. *Babylonian Twins* was a doomed project.

Years passed, and the Mesopotamian team moved on with their lives. Shihab moved first to Jordan, then to Dubai, where he started Cosmos Software with Auday Hussein, a longtime friend who had previously worked with the *Babylonian Twins* team. The company saw success with projects like virtual museums, and the pair moved to Canada. In the meantime, Salman had moved to Australia to continue his career as an architect, having spent a few years working on high-rise buildings in Dubai. Alsalman had finished medical school and became a brain surgeon in Baghdad before moving first to Jordan and then to the United States.

In 2007, Shihab's younger brother posted a gameplay video of *Babylonian Twins* on YouTube. The video went largely unnoticed until 2008, when members of the English Amiga Board discovered it. The online forum's members loved the game, and their positive response motivated Shihab to post a demo. The demo received huge praise and got Shihab thinking: the Apple App Store had recently launched and was successful, so he decided to begin work on an iPhone version of the game by himself. It didn't take long before he realized he'd have to take the project more seriously in order to see it come to fruition.

Shihab applied for funding from Telefilm, a Canadian government-funding agency that had cash and was willing to support him. With his new backers, he contacted Salman and Alsalman and asked them to work on the remake. "I got other team members involved," Shihab says, "but the core team remained the same." These other team members included programmers, a sound tester, and an artist, all of whom made it onto the new game's credit page.

Salman was taken aback and excited about the prospect of reviving *Babylonian Twins*. "When Rabah called me to tell me about reproducing the game, I was really in shock," he says. "I forgot about it completely. It was 16 years ago, but suddenly, all the memories of the Amiga days came back, and I found myself drawn to the idea of bringing our old work to life."

The newly reformed Mesopotamian team used email, instant messaging, and occasional phone calls to collaborate on the high-definition remake. After just a year, *Babylonian Twins* and the iPad-specific *Babylonian Twins HD* launched on the App Store. Critical and consumer response to the new *Babylonian Twins* was overwhelmingly positive.

Eurogamer praised the game's level design. The iPhone news and reviews site TouchArcade.com called the art "stunning" and the music "terrific," adding, "There are no outward signs that this is in fact a port, beyond a grand style of gameplay that harkens back to the golden age of the Amiga." Many iTunes users gave the game five-star reviews too. At the time of this writing, *Babylonian Twins* has enjoyed over half a million downloads.

After the game was finally published and the dust settled, the general feeling expressed by the team members was one of relief. "I spent all my spare time and weekends working on it for about eight months," Salman says, "but after we finished, it felt great. I would love to do it again."

An extended version of this story originally appeared in GamePro Magazine's *November 2010 issue as "Unpublished in Mesopotamia." You can also find the story online at GamePro.com.*

Battle for Wesnoth

Platform: iPhone/iPod Touch (iPad version available separately)
Price: $3.99
Developer: David White
Publisher: Kyle Poole
Released: November 23, 2009

What Is It?

For turn-based strategy-game fans, *Battle for Wesnoth* is like an open-source gift from God. Originally released for the PC/Mac in 2003, *Wesnoth* was designed to allow any player to create his or her own strategy-game campaign using the *Wesnoth* engine. Years of contributions from a talented community have made *Wesnoth* rich with content, and the iOS versions of the game include about 20 of some of the title's most popular user-created campaigns (which offer literally hundreds of hours of potential play time). The game has

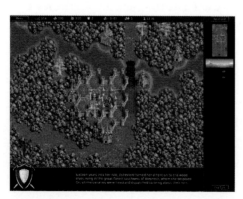

made its way to a variety of platforms, including the iPhone and iPad, since its initial release.

One of the coolest things about *Wesnoth* is that it supports a cross-platform multiplayer mode for players of the Mac/Linux/PC versions. Even nicer: you can also sync your saved games to the Cloud. That lets you play a few levels in a campaign on your iPad or iPhone while on the bus, then pick up right where you left off from the comfort of your desktop PC.

None of this would matter if *Wesnoth* wasn't a good strategy game, but it's phenomenal, even though its design is a bit of a hodgepodge of features from other popular strategy series. Without getting too technical, units move like they do in *Military Madness*, level up like heroes in *Fire Emblem*, and take advantage of terrain like those in *Advance Wars*.

Battle for Wesnoth has so much great content that it's almost enough to justify the price of an iOS device all by itself, especially if you're a strategy addict.

Behind the Game

The year was 2003. It had been three years since David White had graduated from college, and he was bored with his job. White worked as a programmer at what he describes as "a boring financial analysis–type company," and although he wasn't feeling particularly challenged by his job, he had refined his programming skills considerably along the way.

White decided that with his abilities, he should be able to write the code for a game. It wasn't his first attempt at game development; during his teenage years he had used his programming prowess to experiment with numerous game ideas, each of which failed in one way or another. He cheerfully attributes these failed attempts to "the unbridled enthusiasm of youth."

White wanted to make something that was inspired by some of his favorite childhood games, but he didn't want to sacrifice anything for the sake of nostalgia. "Rather than focus on games like *Sonic the Hedgehog*, which are widely known and played, I decided I would take inspiration from more obscure, forgotten games, and try to breathe new life into their best concepts," White says.

> **Statistics**
> - **Development time:** 8 years (and counting)
> - **Total budget:** It's open-source!

Obscure is certainly the right word for the games White chose to look to for inspiration: *Warsong* and *Master of Monsters* are both turn-based strategy games originally released for the Sega Genesis. If you were looking to a Genesis strategy game for inspiration the most obvious choice would be one of the *Shining Force* games, but White was only interested in borrowing the best ideas from *Warsong* and *Master of Monsters*, and then improving upon them. "I also felt there were some nice things that could have been done that each of them missed out on," says White. "Over the course of just a few weeks I came up with an idea for basic game mechanics, and in just one week I wrote a basic prototype."

White admits that although his programming skills are up to par, he's not a one-man band. "I am a terrible artist, and worse musician," he says. "And I didn't know anybody who I felt could reliably contribute these pieces."

White decided to release an early version of the game with his placeholder art and no sound to speak of. *Wesnoth* version 0.1 had rudimentary AI, but it served its purpose by demonstrating the game's core mechanics. Putting his game up on the Internet quickly proved to be a far more significant move than he'd thought it would be.

Shortly after release a Spanish artist named Francisco Muñoz contacted White, offering to contribute improved artwork to the game. White accepted Muñoz's offer and worked with him for the next couple of months. During that time, White began to correspond with others interested in contributing to the project. Less than two months after the initial release he decided to open up an official chat channel and online forums for the game, which were open to anyone who wanted to help out.

At that point *Wesnoth* had essentially gone open-source. Dozens of contributors spent hours of their time contributing art, code, music, and sound effects. Others helped out by play-testing the game and suggesting ideas. "Some people arrived to contribute just one or two things and then left," says White. "Others became amazingly committed to the project." Members of the community wanted to create their own stories in the game, so White programmed in that ability. When the community wanted to play *Wesnoth* as a competitive multiplayer game, White worked that into the code as well.

As more and more users became interested in the project, White embraced them, delegating large responsibilities to those contributors dedicated enough to oversee specific aspects of the game's development. "I appointed 'lords' of music and of art, then of 'balance' and multiplayer maps—people who could make final decisions over their areas of responsibility," he says.

By 2006, *Wesnoth* had taken on a life of its own. "I realized that development would continue whether or not I continued to contribute," White says. He slowly became less involved with the project he started, but still acted as the lead developer. He had the power to settle disputes between contributors, and he still provided ideas occasionally and worked on implementing features. "*Wesnoth* was a living project," he says. "It was mature enough to play as a finished product, but still evolving and being improved."

In 2009, White was approached by Kyle Poole, a software developer who had made a name for himself creating the critically acclaimed *Kyle's Quest* series of games for Palm mobile devices. Poole wanted to port *Wesnoth* to iOS, and he had set up a plan to donate a portion of his proceeds to Wesnoth Inc., a foundation White had set up to help fund the continued development of the game. White was skeptical about the whole idea, but gave Poole the go-ahead. "I was open to any attempt, knowing full well that success was not necessarily likely," he recalls.

Poole had worked previously as the lead developer on *Reign of Swords*, an iPhone game that played somewhat similarly to *Wesnoth*. Poole is surprisingly frank when it comes to his opinion of the quality of *Wesnoth* in relation to his game. "The game design and game play was better than *Reign of Swords* in every way," Poole says candidly. "I thought it would be a great game to have on the iPhone."

Poole began work on the iPhone version of *Wesnoth* and quickly found that White had been correct in his assumption that porting the game would be a difficult process. It took six months of full-time work on Poole's part to get *Wesnoth* to run properly on the iPhone, with much of that time spent optimizing the game's code so it would run quickly on the device. "I didn't know what I was getting myself into," he admits.

White was impressed with Poole's work, calling his port "an excellent job." He was even more impressed when Poole continued to support the game after launch, delivering five massive updates to the game, each of which added new user-created campaigns that offered hours of content. "Kyle didn't just port it and leave," boasts White. "This built enthusiasm in the iPhone community around *Wesnoth* and was very successful in building sales."

Fun Facts

- *Battle for Wesnoth* is available for free download at wesnoth.org.
- Kyle Poole quit his job and moved to Vietnam after falling in love with the country on a business trip. He is now married and lives there with his wife and daughter.
- Poole also created *Firestorm*, a Game Boy Advance emulator that was the first emulator to be threatened with a lawsuit (Nintendo was upset).
- Other apps by Kyle Poole include *Shadow Era* and *Kyle's Quest 2.*

Blobster

Platform: iPhone/iPod Touch (iPad version available separately)
Price: $.99
Developer: Divine Robot
Publisher: Chillingo
Released: July 13, 2011

What Is It?

Blobster is an iPhone/iPad-exclusive platformer with a control scheme designed from the ground up to work well with a touch interface. The game opens with a few short comic book panels that tell of the evil perpetrated by the "Big and Powerful Corporation" (not a very subtle reference to BP), which has been polluting the once-serene land of Blobtopia.

Touching either side of the screen will move Blobster left or right, and players can persuade the stretchy fellow to go airborne by touching him and pulling back to create a sort of *Angry Birds*-esque slingshot effect.

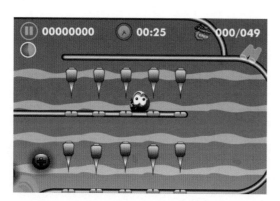

Levels are colorful, spacious environments in which your goal is to collect a dozen or so "blobules" (they really get their money's worth out of this "blob" gag), which are located at several different specific parts of the level. You'll have to fling your way past enemies, occasionally collecting upgrades and keys that will allow you access to new areas of the environment.

I had a lot of fun with the game's arcade mode, but it's also worth playing through just to unlock survival mode. This is a very fun, endless mode where you're tasked with trying to make it as far as you can before falling to your inevitable watery doom.

Blobster is a well-designed platformer in its own right, but what makes it a great iOS game are all the things it doesn't do—like not complicating things with tons of on-screen buttons or ham-fisting in some sort of three-star performance rating system. It doesn't follow the blueprint that many other Chillingo-published games do, so platformer lovers should give it a chance.

Behind the Game

One morning in February of 2010, Henrik Jönsson woke up with a fully formed idea for a game. The game idea centered on stretching a piece of goo to fling it across an area. Without getting out of bed, Jönsson cracked open his laptop and called his business partner Nils Andreasson to tell him about the idea.

By the end of March, Jönsson and Nils had a working prototype built around Jönsson's game idea, and they set about gathering feedback from a variety of unlikely places. "The prototype tested really well with random people in the pub," says Jönsson. This was a sign that things were headed in the right direction, as Divine Robot's last game hadn't fared nearly as well in the pub test.

Initially the game was built around flinging the piece of goo infinitely through a procedurally-generated environment. Jönsson figured they could finish the app in around six weeks. His prediction was a little off target. Three months into the project, Divine Robot decided to implement an arcade mode with more traditional, linear levels. "As there was a certain environmental disaster happening that summer, we decided to make the background story of the game about saving the environment—and poke a bit of fun at those responsible," says Jönsson.

By July, Divine Robot had a build of the game that it was ready to show off to potential consumers. It began beta testing in August. "The initial feedback showed the levels we had designed were too hard, and they made a lot of players frustrated," says Jönsson. "We went back to the drawing board and put together another set of 20 levels—which proved too easy. Third time round we did better and by then we had designed well over 100 levels, most of which were discarded."

> **Statistics**
> - **Development time:** 18 months
> - **Total budget:** $160,000
> - **Times downloaded:** 200,000

In January, Divine Robot brought the game to Chillingo, which agreed to a publishing deal but recommended another six months of polishing and development. At this point, the game had gone from an expected six-week development cycle to an eighteen-month time frame. Jönsson says that most of the levels had to be redesigned once again, with an emphasis on more enemies and power-ups.

This was probably a bit of an annoyance for Divine Robot's Jaana Nykanen, who was pregnant with twins during *Blobster*'s last phase of development. "It was quite a sight to see her designing those evermore complex puzzles with her MacBook sitting on top of that great big belly," laughs Jönsson.

Jönsson attributes the game's prolonged development to a number of factors, including several investment discussions that wound up not materializing. "We squandered a lot of time there," he admits. "The whole indie mobile-development world is full of gold diggers and big talk, but few actually get down and create something that works and makes money."

Jönsson says that things have changed since work on *Blobster* began. "We now have a very lean production pipeline and can create a title like *Blobster* in less than a third of the time." *Blobster* hit the number three slot on the top charts at release, and Jönsson says that the team has ambitious plans for continual updates in the works.

The Blocks Cometh

Platform: iPhone/iPod Touch
Price: $1.99
Developer: Halfbot
Released: February 16, 2011

What Is It?

In *The Blocks Cometh* you play as a strangely nimble fellow who has been trapped in a *Tetris*-like world in which blocks constantly plummet from the sky. Luckily, you're equipped with a few abilities that will help you survive—at least for a time. Using a virtual D-pad and two on-screen buttons, you can jump, double-jump in mid-air, and shoot a blaster (the latter of which is quite helpful for breaking blocks to get yourself out of otherwise sticky situations). However, there's one more tool in your hero's arsenal, and it's by far the coolest: wall jumping.

As blocks fall from the sky you can leap to meet them in mid-air, enabling you to propel off their sides and leap once more. Skilled players can mix double jumps and wall jumps to avoid touching the ground for minutes at a time. It's a dangerous practice, of course, as a mistimed wall-jump can essentially ensure death by crushing, but that's part of the fun!

Players can choose to play the game safely by leaping from box to box only when absolutely necessary—but brave, high-flying players will be rewarded with higher scores (and more fun, in my opinion).

The Blocks Cometh has all the makings of a great "play it anywhere" game. Each game lasts mere minutes, and it's fast-paced enough to offer something satisfying in a truly short time frame.

Behind the Game

Derek Laufman and Melvin Samuel originally met while working together at a console game studio in Ontario, Canada. After a string of layoffs left that company in shambles, both men decided to leave their jobs in order to pursue other interests. Although they went their separate ways career-wise, Samuel and Laufman kept in touch since they belonged to the same gym.

Laufman says that he and Samuel talked regularly about the possibility of creating a two-person game studio, and after an entire year of freelance work the two decided to take the leap. They spent a long night trying to come up with a suitable name, and after settling on Halfbot ("we liked the way it rolled off our tongues," explains Laufman) they began setting up their office in one of Samuel's spare bedrooms. Samuel's place was chosen in part because he had just gotten a new puppy and they wanted to watch after the dog while working.

Laufman says that the first order of business for the newly formed company was to decide for which platform they would develop their games. "We were torn between the iPhone market and the Flash market," Laufman says. "Both were easy platforms to get into if you were an indie developer, and that really appealed to us."

After listening to advice from friends with experience developing for iOS, and reading about both platforms, Halfbot decided to go with Flash development as its first choice. "It seemed fairly simple," says Laufman. "Develop a game, throw it up on Flash Game License (www.flashgamelicense.com), and then watch the bids start rolling in."

Here's a little primer on how the business of making Flash games works: Flash Game License is a website designed to connect developers with Flash game portals. Flash game sites like armorgames.com or addictinggames.com pay developers money to get the right to put logos on the games and host them at their addresses. Flash Game License is like eBay for these Flash game portals—sponsors like Kongregate and Armor Games get into bidding wars over certain games. Some games are more popular than others, and bids can reach over $10,000 in some cases. "FGL was *the* site that almost every new Flash developer used to market his or her game to the Flash portals," explains Laufman.

Laufman and Samuel had heard stories about developers pulling in as much as $25,000 for a single Flash game, but were realistic enough to realize that such a success wasn't the most likely outcome for them. Still, they decided that as long as they could get some decent bids (between $5,000 and $10,000), it would be worth their time. "We did some quick math and decided that if we could develop a game for Flash in a month, we could easily be supporting ourselves in the Flash game market," he says.

The first title Halfbot developed was a little shooter/platformer called *I Don't Come in Peace!*. The game took about six weeks to develop—two weeks longer than their original four-week goal—but Samuel and Laufman were happy with what they had created. They put the game online at Flash Game License and waited for bids to come in. Sure enough, bids were made within the first day, but they weren't what Halfbot had been expecting. "They were pretty sad," Laufman says. "$300, $500, and $800 were the bids on the first day. We had read in the FGL forums that a lot of portals, especially the smaller ones, often tried to lowball Flash developers, so we weren't entirely shocked to see these numbers on the first day."

Numbers like that simply aren't enough for established developers like Samuel and Laufman. "We have families to support and mortgages to pay, and we can't afford to be accepting bids that low," Laufman says. The bidding eventually reached around $1,500, but never went any higher. Halfbot wasn't off to a good start, and things weren't about to get better.

The next few months were spent developing Flash games for a popular kids' site, Moshimonsters.com. That work kept Halfbot afloat, but the team wasn't happy with the situation. "These weren't the games we wanted to make, and the money really wasn't that good," Laufman admits. "This was quickly becoming a market that couldn't sustain us."

Feeling creatively drained, Laufman and Samuel decided to challenge themselves to create a working game in just six hours. Forty-five minutes in, Laufman had developed the idea for a game about a guy avoiding falling blocks, and four hours later Halfbot had a working prototype for *The Blocks Cometh*. After another four weeks of polishing, the team had a completed game that was ready for the Flash market. *The Blocks Cometh* was the company's best-performing game yet, and the response from fans and friends was extremely positive.

Halfbot's positive experience with *The Blocks Cometh* couldn't make up for the other drawbacks of developing for the Flash market. Halfbot created one more title for Moshigames.com (a game called *Peppy's Stunt Bike*), and then called it quits on Flash development.

Near the beginning of 2011, Halfbot decided to move to iOS in the hopes that it might be more financially viable than the Flash game market. They decided to kick things off by porting *The Blocks Cometh* to the iPhone, but that changed when they found out that *someone else* had already ported the game.

Two weeks into working on *The Blocks Cometh*'s iOS port, Halfbot discovered that a company called Edison Game had already released *The Blocks Cometh* for iOS. The company had stolen all of the artwork from Halfbot's game and created an almost perfect replica of it. It made one tiny change—the main character had been stolen from another game, *League of Evil* by WoblyWare.

Edison's rip-off game cracked the top 100 on sales charts after being featured by Apple in its "New and Noteworthy" section. Edison was raking in money that belonged to Halfbot, and there was little Halfbot could do about it. "We started to panic," says Laufman.

Halfbot emailed Apple to have it remove the offending app but didn't hear back for days. Desperate, Laufman decided to reach out to media outlets to spread the word to gamers about the fraud. "We didn't have any real connections in the media at that point," says Laufman. "So we just had to cross our fingers and cold email as many media outlets as we could get our hands on."

The emails were sent out at 2:00 a.m., and Laufman got his first response five hours later. Jim Sterling from Destructoid.com was on the case, and within a day his article about Halfbot's plight had blown up—it became one of the top stories on Reddit, and Twitter lit up with people tweeting that others should avoid buying Edison's clone.

Five full days after sending an email to Apple, Halfbot received a form letter from the company letting it know that Apple was looking into the situation. Laufman shot back some questions about what measures Apple would be taking but didn't ever hear back. The next day, Apple actually featured Edison Game's rip-off again in their "What's Hot" section. Laufman and Samuel were furious, but the game was finally pulled from the App Store after another two days of tense waiting. "To this day, we haven't received any further communication from Apple on the matter," Laufman says. "We'd say that was probably one of the most frustrating parts of this entire ordeal. We just wanted to be reassured that Apple was on our side, that it was doing everything in its power to rectify the situation and that possibly it was going to ensure that the crooked developers were going to be punished in some fashion. But we never got anything like that. It was really disappointing."

Halfbot finally finished the official iOS port of *The Blocks Cometh*, and the game launched straight onto the App Store's top sales charts, thanks in part to the fact that Apple featured the genuine version in its "New and Noteworthy" section. Unfortunately, sales of the game soon stagnated, and the game slowly slipped off the charts. Laufman blames the rip-off for the slow sales, saying that App Store customers may have already purchased the Edison Game version. "Whatever the reason, it seemed that the rip-off had ultimately affected our sales of the game," he says sadly. "It was a little heartbreaking really, and after seeing the game jump in the charts right off the bat and then sink so fast, it did a number on us emotionally."

Laufman says that although Halfbot's introduction to the App Store was a bit of a nightmare, there is a silver lining to the story. The popularity of Jim Sterling's write-up about Halfbot's game earned it a massive following of fans and exposed tens of thousands of people sympathetic to its plight to the game. "We have way more industry connections than we ever had and we have so many amazing supporters, both in the gaming media and gamers alike," Laufman says. "You can't buy publicity like this."

Broken Sword
Director's Cut

Platform: iPhone/iPod Touch (iPad version available separately)
Price: $4.99
Developer: Revolution Software
Released: January 23, 2010

What Is It?

The original PC release of *Broken Sword* (it was called *Circle of Blood* in the United States) is considered one of the best point-and-click adventure games ever made, so its remastering and re-release on the iPad and iPhone is a big deal. Dave Gibbons (most notable for his work on *Watchmen*) contributed to the game with new art and animation for the *Director's Cut* version. Other additional content allows players to take direct control of one of the main characters, Nico, for the first time.

Broken Sword follows French journalist Nico Collard and an unsuspecting American tourist, George Stobbart, as they investigate a series of crimes that are somehow connected. Murder, exploding cafés, and new story elements (particularly one following the story of Nico's father) give the game a sense of suspense that compels you to keep playing.

The iOS versions of the game feature high-resolution graphics and other minor enhancements like a few unique puzzles, but the best addition is the new hint system, which makes it easy for players who aren't accustomed to point-and-click adventure games (or glance-and-poke games, in this case) to jump right in without feeling confused.

If you have the option to choose between the iPhone and iPad version, go with the iPad. These environments were designed with a bigger screen in mind.

Behind the Game

All Charles Cecil wants to do is create fantastic adventure games.

After founding Revolution Software in 1990, Cecil led his team in the creation of two of the most critically acclaimed point-and-click adventure games ever: *Lure of the Temptress* in 1992 and the beloved *Beneath a Steel Sky* in 1994. Both were published by (the now defunct) Virgin Interactive. After both games found success, Virgin approached Revolution with demands for another, even bigger game. "Virgin said that it wanted to up the ante," says Cecil. "It wanted a game that was really cutting edge."

Cecil and his wife met up with Sean Brennan, the COO of Virgin Interactive, for a friendly dinner. "We were talking about heroes and antiheroes, and Sean had just read *Foucault's Pendulum* by Umberto Eco," says Cecil. "At that point almost nobody knew about the Knights Templar. I started researching them and I was absolutely blown away by the story."

As Cecil learned more about the Knights Templar, an idea for a game began to form. What could serve as a better backdrop for a game than an ancient legend filled with conspiracies and hidden secrets? Cecil's mind began to race with the possibilities. "You have clues that they would have left, you have power, intrigue, everything that would suit a game extremely well," he says.

Revolution soon began work on the new game, which it dubbed *Broken Sword*. Since the story behind the game was inspired by both fact and fiction, Cecil decided to take a relaxed approach to historical accuracy, weaving plenty of mythology into the game's historically-based tale. This philosophy carried over into every aspect of the game's design, including the city layouts. "It's not about realism, it's about believability," he says, quoting a long-held game developer axiom. "And these people [the Revolution team] knew how to take believability and push it so that elements of the layout were not accurate but looked absolutely fantastic."

After discussing the influence of the legends surrounding the Knights Templar on *Broken Sword*, Cecil was quick to remind me that his game was released seven years before Dan Brown's megapopular novel, *The Da Vinci Code*. Cecil carefully informed me that "our [Revolution's] fans are absolutely adamant that Dan Brown must have played *Broken Sword* because there are so many similarities in terms of the plot."

"Now I would never dare make such a claim because his lawyers are much better paid than mine," chuckles Cecil. "But I'm very happy to accept the word of the fans, who absolutely believe he must have been inspired by a number of our ideas."

Broken Sword's marketing team didn't share Cecil's confidence in the game until much later in the development process. According to Cecil, that was in part because of the way adventure games are developed: they don't really come together until the last few weeks of development.

In the United States, a lack of confidence in the game wasn't the only issue that Cecil had to deal with when working with Virgin's marketing team. The team decided to change *Broken Sword*'s name to *Circle of Blood*, believing this title would appeal strongly to an American audience. When asked why that happened, Cecil laughed and suggested that I should ask the marketing team myself. "I have no idea, really," he said. "It didn't make a lot of sense."

When *Broken Sword* was finally released, the original PlayStation had just launched. Cecil contacted Sony to see if it had any interest in the game, but the reception he got was not particularly enthusiastic. "Publishers were absolutely obsessed with the idea that the PlayStation gamers would only want to play visceral, three-dimensional games," explained Cecil, with a hint of disbelief in his voice.

Eventually Cecil was able to convince Sony to publish the game on the PlayStation, and his bet paid off. The PlayStation version of the game received glowing reviews and even went on to sell about a half-million copies. "In those days this was absolutely exceptional," Cecil says proudly.

Cecil claims that the success of PlayStation was a double-edged sword. "The rush to create PlayStation-type games—the visceral games, the three-dimensional games—alienated a huge portion of the market who basically went away and only came again for Wii and DS," says Cecil. "I admire Nintendo enormously for building the market, but all it's really doing in many cases is bringing back the people who had left in the mid-1990s when games changed so radically to follow the perceived wisdom of the PlayStation era."

"As a developer, we were much closer to our audience than our publishers were, and we had a very strong sense of what we thought would work, and we were proved right."

Over a decade after creating the original *Broken Sword* game for PC, Cecil began pitching a full-fledged remake of the game, which he wanted to release on Wii and DS. Ubisoft agreed to publish the game, and Revolution began work on the new title. Cecil was delighted at the chance to revisit the story he'd crafted in the mid-1990s. "What was fantastic was being able to take a game that was released in 1996, and, in 2008, to look back at the weaknesses and look back at the story flaws and address them," he says. "It was an extraordinary opportunity to add background and to tweak elements of the story that we didn't feel quite made sense."

Although Cecil says that work on the remastered versions of the game for DS and Wii was overwhelming at times, the game was very well received upon release. Six months later Apple approached Revolution, saying that it thought the game would work very well on the iPhone.

Cecil was flattered by Apple's request, and the idea of doing an iOS port appealed to him. He had been impressed by the tactility that the DS touch screen offered, and knew that the iPhone's capacitive touch screen could make things even more interesting. "It goes one stage further when you're actually touching the screen with your finger," he explains. "You're exploring the environments in a really exciting way."

Within a matter of months Revolution had ported the *Director's Cut* version to the iPhone. The iOS version of the game has gone on to become extremely successful, with about a quarter of a million copies downloaded across both the iPhone and iPad platforms.

Cecil gives credit for the game's success to its original development team, which had been together since the company was founded to create *Lure of the Temptress*. "About half of us are still working at Revolution," he says. "It was a supremely talented group of people. I only realize that now by looking back and seeing what those people produced at that time."

Canabalt

Platform: iPad/iPhone/iPod Touch (universal app)
Price: $2.99
Developer: Semi Secret Software
Released: October 1, 2009

What Is It?

Despite its origins as a Flash game, *Canabalt* became a massively influential example of how to design a great iPhone game. It popularized an entire genre of similar "endless-running" games on the App Store, including big titles like *Monster Dash*, *Grim Joggers*, and *Jetpack Joyride*.

The core concept behind *Canabalt* is pretty easy to grasp from the moment you begin playing. You have limited control over a man who is sprinting for his life across the rooftops of a crumbling, monochromatic city. Tapping the screen will cause the man to jump, and your goal is to time those leaps well enough for him to avoid falling to his doom.

Although the extremely limited controls would lead you to believe that *Canabalt* is an all-too-easy "casual game," there's actually an interesting element of risk management—players have some level of control over their own speed. The man in the suit will build up speed automatically as he runs, but banging into crates will slow him down. If he gets going too fast, it can be difficult to react to incoming hazards in a timely manner. On the other hand, if he goes too slowly players will earn points more slowly and risk not having enough momentum to clear certain jumps successfully.

Savvy players will intentionally hit obstacles occasionally to keep their speed at a manageable pace. It's an interesting idea, especially since in most games like this players can't control the level of difficulty. Take *Tetris*, for example: as you progress, the game becomes more and more difficult, until eventually it reaches a point where no human could possibly react quickly enough to move blocks into play. *Canabalt*'s crates offer a creative solution to this problem.

Behind the Game

The Experimental Gameplay Project (www.experimentalgameplay.com) is a website started by a collection of indie game developers interested in sparking creative game development. Each month the site posts a different theme, and participating developers must design and complete a game in no more than seven days.

Canabalt is indirectly the result of one of these challenges. The theme that month was minimalism, which worked quite well for Adam Saltsman; he had a good bit of experience creating mobile games, so the theme got him thinking about one-button games. The thing that led Saltsman from the concept of one-button gaming to *Canabalt* was the original *Super Mario Bros.*, which he had been playing at the time. "In *Super Mario Bros.* it's easy to spend a lot of time just running to the right, holding the right arrow on the directional pad as well as the B button for run, while intermittently tapping the A button to jump," says Saltsman. "It was a pretty short leap to imagine a game where you were running automatically, and all you had was a jump button."

A short leap, indeed. The next idea that struck Saltsman was "What if the complexity is in the environment, instead of in the controls?" It's not an entirely original concept, and Saltsman says that the idea was in part a reaction to EA's *Mirror's Edge*, which didn't entirely satisfy him. "I had really high expectations for [it], but the clumsy controls were a big disappointment for me, personally," says Saltsman. "I wanted to make something that was about rhythm, flow, speed, and flight, and all these pieces seemed to fit together really well. Plus, jumping through windows is awesome."

Statistics

- **Development time:** 2 weeks
- **Total budget:** $30,000
- **Times downloaded:** 250,000

Saltsman's initial take on the game's jumping mechanic was quite different from the one that made it into the final version of the game. "The first course I took was to make the use of the one button as difficult as possible," he says. "So the first version of the game had *Tony Hawk*–style jumping. That is, you held the jump button to charge up the jump, then let go to actually leap. The length and height of the leap would be dependent on how long you charged for."

Saltsman sent an early version of the game with these mechanics to his friend Edmund McMillen, who most know as one of the cocreators of *Super Meat Boy*. In Saltsman's words, McMillen "chewed me out for having stupid controls." Saltsman decided that McMillen was right and switched the game back to a *Super Mario Bros.*–style control scheme.

Saltsman says that in retrospect, he's very happy that McMillen intervened. He recognizes now that *Tony Hawk 2*'s control method worked for that game because it's a slower-paced game, whereas *Canabalt* focuses more on speed. The "hold to charge" control method wasn't going to work well for *Canabalt* for a multitude of reasons—the biggest being that every jump would need to be planned. Last-second jumps would fail, more likely than not.

Fun Facts

• There are 19 unique messages that can appear when a player dies in *Canabalt*.
• Other things cut from *Canabalt* during its development include branching paths in levels and the ability to slide.
• You can play *Canabalt* for free online at http://www.canabalt.com/.
• Other apps by Semi Secret Software include *Gravity Hook* and *Steambirds*.

Another major influence on the design of *Canabalt* can be attributed to indie developer Farbs, creator of a game called *Captain Forever*. "One of the many cool things about *Captain Forever* is if you stumble across a massive, hostile enemy, you can just run away," says Saltsman. "If you run far enough away, it just kind of disappears, and you encounter something else instead. At the time this kind of blew our minds, as it goes against our traditional ideas of progress and challenge in games. If you could just avoid all the dangerous things, where's the fun? And yet, *Captain Forever* was phenomenal."

The concept of being able to simply avoid danger at will led to the inclusion of crates in *Canabalt*. Saltsman made it so that intentionally running into crates would slow players down, allowing them to set their own pace. "While this seemed to run counter to a lot of ideas about games and game challenges, the fact that player-determined difficulty worked so well in *Captain Forever* gave me the confidence to add it to *Canabalt*."

For the game's soundtrack, Saltsman got in touch with Danny Baranowsky (most famous for his excellent work on the *Super Meat Boy* soundtrack). Baranowsky volunteered to do the music for *Canabalt* for free, and subsequently created the much-beloved *Canabalt* theme (called "Run") in a single evening. "He's awesome," notes Saltsman.

One thing that came up several times during my interview with Saltsman was the opening segment of *Canabalt*, which sees the main character running down a long hallway and exploding through a window onto the rooftops. Saltsman says this was inspired by an experience he had working at a company in Austin. "They [the company] got this big office down on a river," he says. "I had a window looking out onto the river, and every Friday this party boat, like a two-story paddle boat, would go creeping down the river right by my window. It was slow torture."

According to Saltsman, the office he was working in had a long hallway with a big window at the end. "When the party boat would drift slowly past my window, I would fantasize about sprinting down the hallway and crashing through the window, ostensibly to freedom," says Saltsman. He suspects his fantasy had a subliminal effect on *Canabalt*, and given the number of times he used the word "window" in our interview (I counted ten), I'm inclined to agree.

All told, the original Flash version of *Canabalt* was finished in just a few days. Saltsman's friend and fellow Semi Secret Software employee Eric Johnson ported *Canabalt* to the iPhone in a little under ten days. The developer has continued to support the game since it launched in 2009, and it has since been updated to support the iPhone 4's Retina display, Apple's Game Center multiplayer service, and the iPad.

Compression

Platform: iPhone/iPod Touch (iPad version available separately)
Price: $2.99
Developer: Little White Bear Studios
Released: December 24, 2009

What Is It?

At first glance, *Compression* appears to be little more than a clone of *Dr. Mario* with a steampunk skin. Pairs of colorful blocks rain from the top of the screen, and lining up or

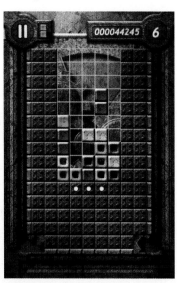

stacking three blocks of the same color will earn you points and remove those blocks from play.

It all looks like a played-out puzzle-game concept, but things get interesting whenever the walls begin to slowly close in towards the middle and the floor starts to rise to meet the ceiling. Take too long to clean the level of blocks, and you'll quickly run out of space to play. The play field will get more cramped every few turns, and the moving walls and floor will slide blocks around to new positions, requiring you to think ahead and plan the block placements strategically.

In addition to the "classic" mode there's also an interesting variant called *Blocked* that introduces unmatchable metal blocks and bomb power-ups to destroy them. That's available as a separate in-app purchase, and it's totally worth the 99-cent asking price.

The game's soundtrack has a dark, industrial sound that fits the unusually gritty visual style (unusual for a puzzle game, that is), and I found that it really adds to the sense of urgency created by the constricting walls. *Compression* is excellently implemented *Dr. Mario*–style gameplay with a claustrophobic twist.

Behind the Game

Little White Bear Studios is a small studio made up of just two employees—a husband-and-wife duo named Craig and Lindi Kemper. Craig Kemper describes himself as a programmer, "with just enough Photoshop experience to fool people into thinking I'm an artist as well." Lindi is a codesigner who contributes puzzles and artwork. She also acts as a sort of critical filter for Craig. "All decisions have to pass her inspection, as she represents the average App Store customer," claims Craig.

When LWB Studio began developing the app that would eventually become *Compression*, Craig knew he wanted to make a "block-dropping" game—essentially, a game that's in the same genre as *Tetris*. Being the programmer that he is, Craig rewrote *Tetris* just to see what it would take to program a block-dropping game. "[It] actually provided a lot of info about the basic aspects of a block-dropping game," says Craig. "Lindi and I played *Tetris* for a day and made observations about why it was fun."

> ### Statistics
> - **Development time:** 4 months
> - **Total budget:** $1,000
> - **Times downloaded:** About 6,300 (not including free downloads)

The next step for Craig was to systematically strip away all the parts of *Tetris* that make it what it is. He wanted to see what a block-dropping game looked like in its most basic state and whether or not that could be fun.

Craig played with his modified version of *Tetris* for a bit, but eventually decided to implement new ideas. Instead of filling up a line to make blocks disappear, players of this new game had to match three blocks of the same color. "So we had this simple block-dropping concept," says Craig. "It was okay, but not anything remarkable."

It's worth mentioning that earlier in the development of *Compression*, Craig had fooled around with an idea involving triangular blocks entering from the sides of the screen. A day after this occurred to him, TouchArcade.com ran a preview about a game called *Unify*. "It was extremely similar to our idea, except that it used rectangles instead of triangles," Craig says. *Unify* was months ahead of us in development. We didn't want to look like a copycat, so we scrapped the idea."

Now that Craig had his color-matching mechanic in place, he decided to revisit the concept of elements in a puzzle game coming in from multiple directions. "I didn't want it to turn into *Unify*, so I decided to make the game board move in multiple directions, instead of the pieces," he says. "The walls would move, causing chaos on the game board. That was something I hadn't seen before, and *Compression* was born."

Both Craig and Lindi Kemper were in love with the idea of moving walls. Craig combined the wall-compression mechanic with the block-dropping prototype he had already created. *Compression*'s final form began to emerge.

You may have noticed that throughout the process of developing *Compression*'s mechanics, Craig never mentioned Nintendo's *Dr. Mario* series, which has a very similar matching system to the one he developed for *Compression*. There's a reason for this—he'd never played it. Neither of the Kempers had ever seen *Dr. Mario* in action until they stumbled upon a video of it while doing research for *Compression*. When he did discover the game, Kemper says, his heart sank.

Craig had unintentionally developed a *Dr. Mario* game variant, and he knew it. "People were always going to compare it to [*Dr. Mario*] and think that's what we based the game on," he says. This struck him as being particularly annoying, but he took it all in stride. "We based it on *Tetris*, and then removed all the *Tetris*-specific bits of it. Who knows, maybe that's what Nintendo did too."

As Christmas of 2009 neared, development on *Compression* wrapped up. The game was ready to be released, but the Kempers were wary of the yearly App Store freeze, a planned period each year around Christmas when Apple temporarily halts the app approval process, leaving any apps submitted after a certain time to wait until January to be vetted. Updates can't be pushed out, the sales charts are no longer updated, and no new games are released. In effect, the App Store stops.

Little White Bear Studios submitted the final version of *Compression* to the App Store on December 21. The team fully expected their game would be approved at some point after the App Store resumed operations in January, but they were in for a surprise. Apple had frozen the App Store, but not before mass approving about 10,000 apps in a single day. *Compression* was among the apps shoved through the door.

This move was disastrous for all 10,000 of the approved apps. Such an incredible oversaturation of the marketplace, combined with the fact that the sales charts were no longer being updated, doomed *Compression* to be effectively dead on arrival. "It was a launch nightmare," says Craig. "On Christmas day, our other apps sold a combined total of 655 paid copies. *Compression* sold seven copies. About four months of work, and the game made five dollars on the biggest sales day of the year."

The next few months saw Little White Bear Studios struggling to market the game. The game was featured by Apple on a couple of occasions, and the release of the iPad version helped spark a few sales, but *Compression* wasn't even close to making its mark on the App Store sales charts, and no amount of post-release updating or promotion could save it.

Compression was not a financial success, but it did benefit the Kempers in other ways. The game was an undeniable critical hit, garnering positive reviews and the adoration of the few thousand gamers who purchased it. Ultimately, Craig sees *Compression* as a learning experience. "*Compression* was a test of our skills on all levels, but also a test of our ability to move on to other things when it failed to perform. If your game isn't selling, even after an update, a sale, a free version, whatever . . . let it go. Move on to something else. You can't force customers to like your game. Learn from it and make something new."

Cow Trouble

Platform: iPhone/iPod Touch
Price: $.99
Developer: CosMind & Blue
Released: March 3, 2011

What Is It?

"Drop balls. Tip Cow." These are some of the first words you'll see while playing *Cow Trouble*, and they do a good job of summing up the game. See, Farmer Diddle's cows

apparently got stuck in some clouds while attempting to jump over the moon, and it's now your job to knock them out of the sky with some well-placed beach balls. It's almost exactly like real farming!

The game plays out similarly to other physics puzzlers in the App Store, with balls that bounce around at different angles depending on the angle of the surfaces you drop them on. If you're good, you can sometimes use a single ball to take out several cows at once. In fact, you'll have to get clever to succeed even at the game's earliest stages.

As you progress you'll unlock different types of balls (like bombs and baseballs), and some balls have a special power that can be used while in midair (does it sound like *Angry Birds* yet?). *Cow Trouble* is easily one of the most challenging physics puzzlers on the iPhone, especially if you're going for 100% completion. Even from the earliest levels, most players will have to restart levels repeatedly in a trial-and-error fashion to figure out exactly how things should be done.

None of that distracts from the game's charm (or its strange sense of humor), though. It's a puzzler designed for more experienced players, especially those who may have felt unchallenged by the simplicity of titles like *Cut the Rope.*

Behind the Game

Justin Leingang (a.k.a. CosMind) and Aaron Pendley (a.k.a. Blue) met and became friends while working on Nintendo DS games for a small game studio. After a few years, the two went their separate ways, with Leingang directing the creation of *Treasure World* for the DS and Pendley heading over to Vigil Games to work on *Darksiders* as an engineer.

After completing these projects, each decided to venture out on his own as an independent developer, and around this time Leingang dreamed up an idea for a game that he thought would be perfect for the iPhone. He summarizes his thought process far better than I could: "[It] came from a wacky daydream I had about cows jumping over the moon, getting stuck in the clouds, and having to be knocked back down in the only logical way imaginable: whacking them from above with balls," he explains.

After discovering that Pendley was also leaving the traditional games space, Leingang contacted his old coworker with a proposal to team up and turn his daydream into a real game. "I wrote a rough prototype and let him play it," says Leingang. "From this we both immediately knew that the concept could be fleshed out and bloomed into an engaging video game design. We gave each other a huge running, jumping high-five and formed CosMind & Blue, LLC."

Shortly after Leingang and Pendley formed their corporation, though, Pendley had to move out of state. This put something of a damper on things, as it's obviously much harder to collaborate with someone who is living hundreds of miles away. "Instead of working a few minutes away from one another, we were suddenly forced to rely completely on the magic of v-chat for interfacing," Leingang says.

> ### Statistics
>
> - **Development time:** 6 months
> - **Times downloaded (when it was free for a day):** 59,000
> - **Times downloaded (paid version):** 4,400

Leingang admits that one of the biggest challenges facing the two was their shared, over-the-top sense of humor, with otherwise serious discussions constantly devolving into double entendres and other jokes. "Cows and balls and Diddles and chickens and beach babes . . . it's almost impossible to not start cracking up when trying to converse seriously about creating something with stuff like that involved," laughs Leingang.

From the beginning, Leingang and Pendley were realistic about their chances at success. They knew that they needed to create a successful game within a reasonable time frame, although they also understood that success was even more important than getting the game out the door quickly.

After six months of work, *Cow Trouble* hit the App Store. CosMind & Blue had met its goal by producing a great game in a reasonable time frame, but the game was by no means a success. According to Leingang, they missed their hoped-for sales by "a long, long shot."

Leingang believes that *Cow Trouble* is just too complex for the majority of iOS gamers. His theory is that the game's design allows for "too many meaningful choices to make during play." Despite the game's disappointing performance, Leingang has an upbeat perspective, saying that he and Pendley learned a lot from the experience. "Of course we're both bummed about *Cow Trouble*'s poor performance in the App Store," he says. "However, we're both very understanding about why it's performed poorly. But, that's what makes the App Store market a wonderful environment for the time being. If there were some very clear keys to success, the big money men (publishers) would simply build them into all their video games and pay the big bucks to tell everyone that their games exists and are the best (i.e., large advert campaigns) and nobody else would ever be able to succeed."

Fun Facts

- In one early build of *Cow Trouble*, players knocked cows off their clouds by launching fireworks from the ground.
- The company that Leingang and Pendley both worked for before heading out on their own was The Fizz Factor, which only did licensed games before shutting down in 2009.

Cut the Rope

Platform: iPhone/iPod Touch (iPad version available separately)
Price: $.99
Developer: ZeptoLab
Publisher: Chillingo
Released: October 4, 2010

What Is It?

Although there's certainly a lot of rope cutting in *Cut the Rope*, there's also a surprising amount of air blasting, bubble popping, and gravity switching, all in the name of getting a piece of candy into the hungry maw of a cute little critter named Om Nom. Like *Angry Birds*, *Cut the Rope* is a physics-based puzzle game, but it's less about destruction and more about figuring out precisely how to navigate a level using the tools given to you. *Cut the Rope* was released at a point in the iPhone's life when it was rare to see a game with a really slick presentation. It set a new standard with its gorgeous, glossy art style and skillfully crafted physics mechanics that make the game play flawlessly on iOS.

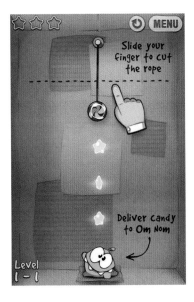

Many iOS games use a three-star scoring system to rate player skill, but *Cut the Rope* uses its stars in a more interesting way. In each level players can choose to take the easy route and simply head for the exit (Om Nom's candy hole). Alternatively, players who crave a challenge can take a more difficult path (or paths) to collect the three stars that are scattered about. It's an interesting system that adds both an extra layer of challenge and replay value, and it's probably part of the reason that the game is the multimillion-selling success it is today.

Behind the Game

The first title ever created by Zeptolab was *Parachute Ninja*, a tilt-controlled platformer that sold about 300,000 copies and briefly appeared on the App Store's top sales charts. The game was sort of a hodgepodge of tilt and touch-screen game mechanics; players tapped to deploy a parachute while in midair, and touching or pulling certain objects was often necessary to progress.

A lot of ideas made it into the final version of *Parachute Ninja*, but just as many were cut. One of the things dropped was a rope mechanic that had originally been pretty central to the idea behind the game. "One of the original names for the game was *Yo-Yo Ninja*," says Zeptolab chief creative officer Semyon Voinov. "The idea was that a rope would be used as a safety device while he jumped from one platform to another."

The rope idea got trashed because Zeptolab found that it was just a bit too hard to control, but the team had already put in the hard work to program a realistic rope. Voinov says that even though the prototype of the rope was little more than a solid color line on the screen, it was really cool to watch and interact with.

Statistics

- **Development time:** 4 months
- **Number of days after the game's release before it hit the one-million sales mark:** 9
- **Times downloaded:** 9,000,000

After *Parachute Ninja*, Zeptolab again turned to its rope mechanic and began coming up with various prototypes centered around it. The small company created a handful of game ideas, but eventually settled on a game mechanic that centered around transporting a single object or character from point A to point B.

According to Voinov, there was much debate about the specifics of this idea. They weren't sure if they wanted to be transporting a character from one place to another or what the motivation would be for moving the objects, but eventually they settled on the idea of delivering food to a stationary creature (which they later named Om Nom). "We felt that the concept of feeding some creature with some food is a nice concept to build an emotional relationship, because there's definitely something warm and enjoyable about it," Voinov says. "It evokes a parental feeling when you feed a creature."

To further exploit the parental feelings brought on by delivering food to Om Nom, the Zeptolab team intentionally designed their creature to have the facial characteristics of a young child. Then, to make sure that Om Nom wasn't too cutesy for more experienced players, they gave their creation a row of sharp teeth. "I liked the idea that it [Om Nom] would be a monster; it kinda sounded cool, although maybe that's just the kid inside me talking," laughs Voinov. "The nice thing about monsters is that they're not too childish and they're not too adult. Both adults and kids like monsters."

This sort of marketing-driven thinking drove much of the design of *Cut the Rope*. Zeptolab was determined to make a game that appealed to the widest possible audience, and nearly every decision it made was in service of this goal. Voinov says that from a purely financial standpoint, the decision to include a character like Om Nom was one of their best ideas. "We hadn't thought about that much then, but now I think that characters are also a great way to build a brand," he muses. "If the character had just been a block, we probably wouldn't be able to sell any plush toys."

Voinov says that one of the most common questions Zeptolab gets is "Why is Om Nom sitting in a box?" He responds, "We didn't really have a logical explanation for that back then, but now looking at the idea, I think it comes from childhood. I think many kids have this experience where they find this living creature like a hedgehog or a bird that has fallen out of a nest, and they put it in a box, and they try to observe it or feed it. It's something that applies to many people's childhood memories."

> **Fun Facts**
>
> - Om Nom's name wasn't mentioned anywhere in *Cut the Rope* until the first update, when it was added to the instructions included in the first level.
> - Why did Zeptolab choose Chillingo? "They have *Angry Birds*," says Voinov.
> - Before *Cut the Rope*'s success, Zeptolab's employees all worked from home. They now have office space.
> - Other apps by ZeptoLab include *Parachute Ninja* and *Cut the Rope: Experiments*.

Cut the Rope began to near completion, and Zeptolab's employees started showing the game to friends and family members while searching for a publisher. The initial response to the game was mixed. Voinov says that even his own girlfriend wasn't very keen on the game at first.

Luckily Zeptolab was able to strike a publishing deal with Chillingo, who saw the game's potential. As a part of its agreement, Chillingo provided some valuable feedback on certain elements of the gameplay (Voinov didn't get too specific) and Zeptolab made it to the polishing stage. The team wanted the game's art to look particularly clean, so extra care and time was taken before Zeptolab felt it was ready for release.

Since its release in October of 2010, *Cut the Rope* has become a moneymaking machine. The game is just as much a regular in the top ten sales charts as *Fruit Ninja* and *Angry Birds*, and has sold millions upon millions of copies. Zeptolab had obviously hoped for the best, but it wasn't ready for the explosive success that the game enjoyed. "It was really hard for us to believe that at some point we knocked *Angry Birds* from its number one position," says Voinov. "It even felt unreal." ZeptoLab had no time to celebrate. Immediately after launching and landing in the top ten, the company set to work on updates and bug fixes.

In its first year, *Cut the Rope* sold a little more than nine million units. ZeptoLab is clearly excited about those numbers, but Voinov is making sure the company is handling its sudden profitability with care. ZeptoLab desperately wants to become more than a one-hit wonder, and it's handling the money from those millions of sales accordingly.

"When people hear those numbers they think that we're driving Ferraris here, with bling-bling on our necks," Voinov jokes. "But that's not really true, because Apple takes its part of the pie, then the publisher takes its part, then we pay taxes, and then we pretty much put it on the company's account. We're not putting that in our pocket. What the success of *Cut the Rope* allowed us is freedom. After all, money is a measure of freedom in our capitalistic world."

Dark Nebula
Episodes One and Two

Platform: iPhone/iPod Touch
Price: Free–$1.99
Developer: 1337 Game Design
Released: October 14, 2009

What Is It?

Dark Nebula is a lot like Illusion Labs' *Labyrinth* series in that you control a small metal ball by tilting your iDevice, but it could more accurately be described as a puzzle-heavy adventure game. There's a shocking amount of variety in *Dark Nebula*'s level design, especially in *Episode Two* in which the sheer number of different hazards you'll encounter (from crushers to turrets and even giant boss monsters that you'll have to fight) is astounding.

Players who try for fast level-completion times will find that often the biggest challenge in *Dark Nebula* is keeping the ball under control when it's rolling at high speeds. This isn't a critique of the game's controls—those are excellent. It's more that *Dark Nebula* is a game about fine-tuned movement through treacherous areas. Especially in *Episode Two*'s boss battles (in which you're given a weapon to defend yourself), accuracy is key, and players with shaky hands won't do very well.

Dark Nebula is so polished that for many gamers who picked it up in October of 2009, it was like emerging from a dark room into one that was fully lit. The differences in quality between it and many of the games that came before it is striking.

Behind the Game

Anders Hejdenberg is no stranger to the games industry. The Swedish developer is credited on over a dozen games, and even worked as the lead designer on EA's *Battlefield 2: Modern Combat*. He kept working there for a short while after his work on the *Battlefield* series was done, but ultimately became dissatisfied with the industry, which he saw as being fueled by a desire for money rather than innovation or a passion for design. Hejdenberg left, taking what he describes as a long vacation.

Time passed, and Hejdenberg began to feel the itch to get back into game design. Remembering his aversion to the politics involved in working on big-budget games, he decided to do things in a new way. "I had bought the iPhone just a couple of weeks after its launch, and I was very impressed by what it could do," he says. "By complete coincidence, my friend had just left his job to work as an iPhone programming consultant, and I was thinking about various games he could potentially create for it."

During a sleepless night Hejdenberg had an idea, and within a month he had hired his friend to create what would eventually become *Dark Nebula: Episode One*. "The months that followed were truly amazing," says Hejdenberg. "The magic I had felt starting out in the industry was back, and making games was fun again. There was no publisher telling us what to do, there was no creative director interfering with the creative process—it was just pure bliss."

During development of the first episode of *Dark Nebula*, a big part of the challenge was nailing down the game's controls. Hejdenberg was hesitant at first to use tilt controls, because in his experience games using this method simply didn't feel right (mind you, this was before the release of *Tilt to Live*). "We thought it was the accelerometer's fault, but it turned out that the controls were just not implemented very well," he says.

Episode One was eventually completed, and the game got plenty of attention from magazines and blogs but sales didn't exactly skyrocket. Despite this, Hejdenberg knew that he wanted to make a second episode. "We were having too much fun," he explains.

Hejdenberg didn't want his sequel to be just more of the same, so he and his team dove into *Episode Two* with bigger ambitions. They added a combat system, bigger levels, and boss fights. This allowed for much greater overall variety in game design, as Hejdenberg's team could include enemies, bigger puzzles, and vastly more elaborate level design.

Despite having ambitious plans for the sequel, Hejdenberg believed he could finish the game in just five months. That was all he had money for, anyway. "We ran into some problems," says Hejdenberg. "We wanted a lot of new things for the second episode, and some of those things took a lot longer than we had anticipated."

After only a few months into the development of *Episode Two*, Hejdenberg was running dangerously low on cash. This led to some serious belt-tightening on his part. "I lived on homemade bread and potato soup for weeks on end and prayed that my shoes wouldn't fall apart in the rough Swedish weather, because I couldn't afford a new pair," he says.

Episode Two was still months away from being in the shape that Hejdenberg wanted, but he wasn't going to cave and release an unfinished product. "For us there were only two options, really—we either release a great game or we release nothing at all," he says. "We had spent too much time in the past working on titles that didn't turn out as well as they could have, and if we were going to cut corners when working on our own game, we could just as well go back to the regular games industry."

Episode Two ended up taking almost ten months to complete—twice the time Hejdenberg had hoped for. But a clever marketing move on Hejdenberg's part saved him and his team from financial ruin. "I had been in contact with another developer that had released its game for free over a weekend and got almost 50,000 downloads between Friday and Sunday," he says.

At this point, sales of *Dark Nebula: Episode One* were bringing in only about $60 per day, so Hejdenberg decided to take a risk and offer the game for free one Friday. iOS developers have access to daily reports that cover download figures of their titles. These reports are generated once every 24 hours, so Hejdenberg had a short—but tense—waiting period ahead of him before he could view the results of his price change.

On Saturday, Friday's report came in, and Hejdenberg was blown away. The number of downloads on Friday alone had surpassed 50,000. At this rate, he figured, they'd have over 150,000 downloads by the time the weekend was over.

Sunday arrived, and Hejdenberg was able to see how the game had faired on Saturday. The game hadn't been downloaded 50,000 times again. It had been downloaded 250,000 times. The weekend wasn't over yet, and Hejdenberg was already getting calls from very upset IT guys who ran the servers hosting the high-score leaderboards for *Dark Nebula*. "He said that the load was so high on the server that their other customers couldn't reach their homepages," says Hejdenberg. *Dark Nebula: Episode One* had become the number one downloaded free app in 25 countries—including the biggest market, the United States.

By the end of the free weekend, *Dark Nebula*'s first episode had been downloaded over one million times. There were now at least a million gamers aware of the fact that a second game would be available soon, and even after Hejdenberg switched the price of the game back to 99 cents, word-of-mouth resulted in the game continuing to sell at a much higher rate than it had before. This was exactly what the team working on *Dark Nebula: Episode Two* needed. "*Episode Two* was saved, and we had enough money to make it just the way we wanted it—without cutting any corners," says Hejdenberg.

Upon release, *Episode Two* became the second-most highly rated iPhone game of 2010, surpassed only by Rocketcat Games' *Super Quickhook*. Apple added the game to its iPhone Hall of Fame (a list of its favorite apps), and *Game Developer* magazine included 1337 Game Design in its annual list of the best game developers in the world (in the number seven slot, right after huge names like Nintendo and Blizzard).

When asked what he considers to be his biggest success, Hejdenberg replies, "Being part of a game series that was made without compromises."

Dirt

Platform: iPhone/iPod Touch
Price: $.99
Developer: Broken Kings
Released: February 2, 2011

What Is It?

Dirt is one of the most unsettling, thought-provoking games I've ever played. Without giving too much of the plot away, I'll say that you play as the pickaxe-wielding spirit of a deceased family cat. The entirety of *Dirt* takes place underneath the grave in which the cat has been buried. Tapping the screen will cause the cat to move and dig up blocks directly in front of him, and turning your iPhone will shift the world's gravity in different directions. As you dig, you'll uncover multicolored gems and unlock short story segments that depict scenes from the cat's life. You'll also occasionally stumble across artifacts that contribute in some small way to the larger story behind the game.

Dirt's soundtrack does a lot to create a creepy atmosphere, and terrifying encounters with other beings who live underneath the earth's surface keep the experience tense throughout.

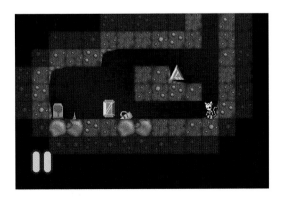

For most players, *Dirt* will only take about an hour to complete, but by the end of that hour you'll have been told a genuinely moving story in a way few games have ever attempted. It's worth far more than the measly dollar that Broken Kings is asking for it, so anyone interested in seeing how games can be used as a storytelling medium should consider *Dirt* a must buy.

Behind the Game

When Stephen Gazzard gathered four friends together to create a game studio, he was aware of the challenges that lay ahead.

Broken Kings was to be a five-person studio that produced games quickly on a virtually nonexistent budget. All five people (Gazzard, his wife, two best friends, and the girlfriend of one of his friends) moved into the same house to keep expenses down, and the team laid out a shoestring budget—a total of $4,000–$5,000 per month for the five of them. "The idea was that if we worked only weekends, but worked incredibly hard, we could pump a game out each weekend," says Gazzard.

> **Statistics**
>
> • **Development time:** 4 days
> • **Total budget:** $2,000
> • **Times downloaded:** 65,000

After reading the stories behind all of the other games in this book (some of which took months or even years to complete), you'll know that this was an insane idea. But Gazzard was confident and had no shortage of innovative ideas to make the plan work.

One of the women on the team filmed the rest of the group at various key points in the development process, with the idea being that they'd upload the footage—essentially a video dev diary—to YouTube. The hope was that the team could grow a fan base organically by giving off a personable vibe.

By the time Broken Kings had begun work on *Dirt*, it had already produced two other games by following its unique "weekends only" method. The first game had gone over schedule a little, and working on the second game had been a bit of a drag. "The second one, *Smoothie Operator*, ended up being picked more because we couldn't find something that we all agreed upon than out of any particular passion," says Gazzard. "It was a compromise, and this was a big mistake."

The team was tired when work on *Dirt* began, and they had decided collectively that the third game should be more of a "toy" than a game. Gazzard cites *Minecraft* as a major source of inspiration.

Gazzard and his team had their Friday morning meeting and agreed that the game should be about digging and discovering artifacts. Before work on the game had even begun, the group agreed that the game should be called *Dirt*. Some Broken Kings fans pointed out that there was already a series of racing games on consoles called *Dirt*, but Gazzard didn't particularly care. "We had already reserved the name on iTunes, and damned if we were going to change it," he said.

Halfway into the weekend, work on the game was coming along nicely. One of the team members, Josiah, was a big fan of *Shadow of the Colossus* (a PlayStation 2 game that received near-universal acclaim). "He loved to tell us about all these things that were in the world, that you could discover, but that the game designers never actually told you were there," says Gazzard. "You could just ride from colossus to colossus and never know about all these hidden little gems."

The members of Broken Kings decided that they could do something similar—hide little gems throughout the game that, when combined, could tell a sort of story. The team was already on day two of development (remember, they had planned to finish the game in three), and they now had to integrate new art elements into the game and rearrange much of the game to make it more conducive to telling a tale. This was made more difficult by the fact that the team hadn't fully considered how much of a change this would be. "We still didn't realize that our game was no longer about digging," says Gazzard.

Sunday night arrived, and once again the team was behind schedule. Half the team had planned to go on a trip Monday, so Gazzard and Josiah spent all Monday finishing the game. *Dirt* was done, and it was submitted to the App Store on Tuesday morning. "I think *Dirt* was the game that the five of us anticipated the most," says Gazzard. "We put so much of ourselves into it, creatively and emotionally, that of the four games we completed, it stood out the most."

> **Fun Facts**
>
> - The team's video dev diaries can be viewed on YouTube. Search for "broken-kings."
> - The creepy, talking worm that sometimes appears when you're exploring in *Dirt* is named "Teddy."
> - Each of the colored gems is somehow related to one of the human family members . . . consider that a hint.
> - Other apps by Broken Kings include *Castle Conflict* and *Skwerl.*

An interesting, but sad side note: Gazzard insists that the story in *Dirt* is not based on the death of an actual pet, but the team did have a cat that lived in the house with them at the time. Shortly after Broken Kings ceased operation, she passed away from cancer. "She had been my pet cat since I was seven years old and so I have been afraid to play *Dirt* since then," says Gazzard. "The fear of her death was in me at a low level then; I was still denying that the lump on her stomach could really kill her. I think if she had already been gone, I would have been unable to complete *Dirt*."

Broken Kings didn't last for much longer after work on *Dirt* was complete. The team had a financial backer lined up, but that deal never went through, and the members of the team simply ran out of money. Gazzard calls the experience "a glorious two months," but admits that the short-lived studio put him in quite a bit of debt. He now does contract work, and says that it would be difficult for the five original Broken Kings members to get together again.

Doodle Jump

Platform: iPhone/iPod Touch (iPad version available separately)
Price: $.99
Developer: Lima Sky
Released: March 15, 2009

What Is It?

Doodle Jump will always be known as one of the first games on the iPhone to grab the attention of a mass audience. The simple game about hopping captured the attention of

over ten million people willing to drop 99 cents on the game and inspired an army of derivative "Doodle" games (none of which were very good).

The appeal of *Doodle Jump* is difficult to explain. The tilt-controlled game probably wouldn't be so addicting were it not for its excellent scoring system, which practically screams at players to "DO IT AGAIN AND DO IT BETTER" at the end of each run. Then there are the simple, poorly-drawn power-ups and monsters that have become iconic in the years since the game's release. Jumping on springs is still as exhilarating as the feeling you get from jumping on an actual trampoline, and collecting the elusive rocket-pack power-up has sometimes caused me to make rocket liftoff sounds with my mouth (I wish I were joking).

The more recent addition of a multiplayer mode has provided yet another reason to play this trifling game for hours. I've played *Doodle Jump* in bed until my arms hurt, and I've lost possession of my iPod for hours as friends and family members borrowed it to play one more round. I can't explain it, but I and ten million other people can't get enough of *Doodle Jump*.

Behind the Game

Sometimes people ask Igor Pusenjak if *Doodle Jump* is the first game he's ever created. "Actually," he tells them, "it's my last game."

It was 2008, and for Igor and his brother Marko the App Store appeared to be an excellent opportunity to make some money while doing something fun together. The two men had traditionally made their living by doing web development and had no formal experience with game design, so they decided to test the waters by releasing an incredibly simple "bubble wrap simulator."

Despite its inanity, Lima Sky's *Bubble Wrap* app sold thousands of copies at its 99-cent price point. With increased confidence in the App Store, Igor and Marko began App Store development full time.

The Pusenjaks's approach to App Store development was unique—they pumped out dozens of apps in mere months. It's a strategy that many developers might call spamming, but Lima Sky sees things differently. "One of the things we tried to do with all of our projects prior to *Doodle Jump* is have a really short turnaround time and release the equivalent of pilots like in the TV show industry," explains Igor. "We'd release a first decent playable version and if the reactions were good we'd continue working on it. If not, we'd move to something else."

This sort of approach to game development would only be possible on the App Store, but it certainly makes sense for an iOS developer. Lima Sky's "treat it like a TV pilot" policy led to the release of numerous strange titles that haven't sold very well, including some educational apps built around memorizing different flags and a whole mess of matching games.

> **Statistics**
> - **Development time:** 3 months
> - **Updates between March 2009 and September 2011:** 48
> - **Times downloaded on iOS:** 10,000,000

One of the first actual games that Lima Sky released on the App Store was *Eat Bunny Eat*, a simple game starring a bunny that has to catch carrots as they fall from the sky. According to Igor (the art/design side of Lima Sky's two-man team), the game wasn't a massive success, but it did earn the company a small following. Lima Sky began thinking about releasing a sequel to the game, starring the same bunny character.

Since the new game would be constructed around a bunny character, the Pusenjaks quickly dreamt up a game idea centered around jumping ever higher. Marko set to work coding the game, but Igor ran into some issues while animating the bunny character. "I was having trouble coming up with something that I actually liked," he says. "I couldn't get the platforms to look good. The bunny movements didn't look very good."

Since the game needed placeholder art to use with his code, Igor drew up a quick sketch (or a doodle, as some might call it) of a strange creature with four legs, a green T-shirt, and an anteater-like snout. Marko used the temporary art in his prototype.

Igor is openly critical of his own abilities as an illustrator, but says that he and Marko began to fall in love with the "doodle" art style after seeing it in motion. Soon he abandoned efforts to develop better art based on the bunny character, instead choosing to adopt the doodle style. *Doodle Jump* was born. A few months later it was released on the App Store.

Doodle Jump's art style eventually became one of the most iconic things about the game, but Igor says that initially not everyone was thrilled with the way the game looked. "One of the typical comments was, 'You know, it's fun, but I don't know about the art,'" he laughs. "Then as time went on we've seen people develop sort of emotional connections with the art and begin loving the characters and the art in the game."

As I mentioned earlier, the months following *Doodle Jump's* meteoric rise to the top of sales charts on the App Store saw the release of a number of *Doodle*-inspired games with brazenly uninventive titles like *Doodle Kart*, *Doodle Army*, and even *Doodle God*. "Doodle game" soon became something of a trope. It became a common joke that lazy developers could simply slap the word "doodle" on their games and it would immediately become a chart topper. This didn't go over very well with the Pusenjak brothers, who felt that their brand was being unfairly exploited. "I feel really frustrated," Igor admitted when I asked him about the situation. "The easiest thing to do now is to say, 'Hey look at these guys, they've been so successful with *Doodle Jump*. Let me make a doodle something because doodle is a generic name and I can do whatever because I'm describing my art style.' So not only is it hurting us in a way that the art style is not so unique anymore, but it's becoming a joke. People are sick of doodle this and doodle that games."

Things came to a head in early 2011, when Lima Sky began contacting other App Store developers with "doodle" games in an effort to enforce its trademark and force other developers to drop "doodle" from their games' names. The ensuing events wound up backfiring on Lima Sky in a PR disaster that PocketGamer.co.uk called "Doodlegate." "It's not an episode that I'm proud of in any way," sighs Igor. "We were being portrayed as this big evil company when really we're just two guys."

Lima Sky eventually stopped pursuing other developers using the doodle name in their games, but the episode had already left a negative imprint on Lima Sky and Igor,

---

Fun Facts

- The main character in *Doodle Jump* is named Doodle the Doodler.
- Other apps by Lima Sky include *Animath* and *Bubble Wrap*.
- Lima Sky's *Bubble Wrap* app is the only "officially licensed" Bubble Wrap app on the App Store (Bubble Wrap is a trademark owned by the Sealed Air Corporation).
- Set your name as "Ooga" in *Doodle Jump* to be able to play as one of the pygmies from *Pocket God*!

who was the public face for the company throughout the controversy. After the ordeal was over, Igor wrote an open letter that attempted to explain his side of the story. "At the end of the day, I am a game developer, just like many of you," the letter read. "I want to spend my days creating great games and not dealing with the legal issues."

All of this is especially interesting when you consider that many people believe *Doodle Jump* itself to be a clone of another iOS game—*PapiJump*. *PapiJump* is a nearly identical game that was released months before Lima Sky even began work on *Doodle Jump*. It too stars a small character bouncing ever higher on small floating platforms.

I asked Igor about the similarities, and although he admits that the similarities between the two titles are "huge," he says that he and his brother hadn't heard of it until after *Doodle Jump* was released. "I've looked at it afterwards because I've seen so many people mention it, and I think we did a better job," he says.

Igor may have a point there. Since *Doodle Jump*'s release in early 2009, Lima Sky has supported the game with dozens and dozens of free updates that added new content and addressed bugs. Some updates have added new items to the game, while others have offered entirely new ways to play (online multiplayer via Game Center was probably the biggest thing added to the game postlaunch).

In the second half of 2011, Lima Sky finally released an iPad-specific version of the game. As with the iPhone version, their plans for it don't end with the 1.0 release. For the Pusenjak brothers, *Doodle Jump* isn't something that they want to create and be done with. It's a living product that they're putting everything into. This concept seemed strange to me until I asked them if they could tell me how much time they'd put into the development of the game. "That's my favorite question," Igor laughed. "We're still making it."

"Unlike the traditional sort of console, CD, and DVD kinds of games, we don't see iPhone games as a finished project. They're like websites. If you have a website that has static content, nobody comes back to it. A good website is one that's alive and changing all the time."

This sort of philosophy has been successful for other game developers (*World of Warcraft* is probably the best example of a living, changing game), and it has certainly been successful for Igor and Marko, who almost overnight went from being average, middle-class web developers to multimillionaires behind one of the most iconic mobile games ever created. "It's insane. We're just out of our minds," Igor says. "I don't really believe it, still. It's like someone will pinch me in the morning and wake me up."

Doom II RPG

Platform: iPhone/iPod Touch
Price: $3.99
Developer: iD Software
Released: February 8, 2010

What Is It?

Doom II RPG looks like a cleaned up version of *Doom II*, but it's no first-person shooter—it is entirely turn-based. When you're not moving, nothing else in the world moves either. When you take a step it counts as a turn, and everyone else (namely enemies) gets a turn to move too. As you might expect, many of the weapons and enemies will be familiar to fans of the old *Doom* games.

When you're taking turns battering a monster you'll see its HP bar going down; you'll

gain XP, level up, and find items and equipment hidden in the environment.

Doom II RPG's combat system allows it to be a strategically rich game. You have a chainsaw for whenever you're right up next to an enemy, and you also get guns that allow you to hit enemies several tiles away—so you'll have strategic options for positioning yourself and switching weapons to take out as many enemies as possible, while limiting the hits you take.

There are fully functional, traditionally-styled *Doom* games in the App Store, but the fact that this one is turn-based suits the iPhone incredibly well. You're using an on-screen D-pad, but it's not like you have to be quick and twitchy. I'm not even that big of a fan of the *Doom* franchise—but *Doom II RPG* is awesome.

Behind the Game

Katherine Anna Kang is a film producer, video-game designer, and entrepreneur. She has been CEO and president of multiple companies, and she's a cofounder of Armadillo Aerospace, a company built to invest in space tourism. She's also married to John Carmack, a video-game industry legend perhaps most widely known as the man responsible for *Doom*.

The original *Doom RPG*, released in 2005, was a major hit. It won multiple "game of the year" awards for its category and sold fairly well. Kang, who was a producer on the project, followed it up with both games in the *Orcs & Elves* series, which were also well received. "We always knew that *Doom II RPG* was going to happen," says Kang. "The original was a hit with critics and fans alike, and it was our most profitable mobile game yet."

Several years had passed since the first game had been created, but Kang's team at id Mobile still weren't entirely sure that they wanted to revisit the *Doom RPG* universe. Kang says that about half of the team wanted to continue working on the *Orcs & Elves* series, while the other half was ready to do *Doom II RPG*. At the time, Kang worried that mobile technology couldn't handle the things the team wanted to do with a second game in the series. "We wanted to do something really spectacular," she says. "The *Doom* name has so much history and such a large fan base that we didn't want to do anything but a stellar job."

Kang also admits that she enjoyed the freedom of working within the *Orcs & Elves* universe, which was an original series. Whereas the *Doom* universe already had the bulk of its story set in stone, *Orcs & Elves* was a fresh world waiting to be populated by a writer like Kang. She had even created an interesting female protagonist to build the game around. "In the end, the powers that be decided we were going to do *Doom II RPG*," Kang says. "When the decision was made, our wheels started turning." The team was able to create a story that didn't conflict with the recently released *Doom IV*, and work on the game began in earnest.

As Kang wrote *Doom II RPG*'s story, she regretted being unable to use the female protagonist she had dreamed up for *Orcs & Elves 3*. "I had a talk with John [Carmack], and after a few 'discussions' he agreed that my idea could work," Kang says. "I wasn't confident

> **Fun Facts**
>
> - The earliest prototypes for *Doom II RPG* were actually designed with more traditional handset devices in mind.
> - Some enemies can be seen in the official trailer for *Doom II RPG* that don't show up in the final version of the game.

that millions of *Doom* fans would be crazy about playing as a female character, so we created three protagonists for the player to choose from: Major (the female Marine), Sarge (the classic *Doom* Marine), and a scientist (our resident geek)."

As Kang wrote dialogue for the three characters, she became more attached to each of them. She recalls being sad that players wouldn't get a chance to know each of them, since they'd have to play through the game multiple times to see it from the perspective of each character. It didn't take long for the team to come up with the idea to do a comic book to complement the game's story. id Mobile artist Jonathan Lane did the art, and Kang handled the writing. It was a creative solution that allowed players to meet each of the playable characters before making a choice once the game began. "The more he put our ideas into images, the more excited I became," says Kang. "Perhaps it was a bit extravagant, but most of us thought a comic book would be really cool."

Kang says that originally the plan was to design the game so that each character had his or her own secrets and Easter eggs spread throughout the levels. Unfortunately, the team wasn't able to implement much of it due to budgetary and time constraints. "We had to make do with having fun by other means—mostly text based," says Kang. "We had fun with names and characters, and gave nods to various id games and characters. In fact, there's a big separate story going on in there where a *Wolf RPG* character makes an appearance along with a descendant of a *Wolf* hero."

Kang credits artist and level designer Matt Ross for making *Doom II RPG* as funny as it is. "It's Ross who is solely responsible for memorable scenes like the one near the beginning of the game where the monster gets his head chainsawed off. More often than not, if the humor is sick and/or crude, it will be his," she laughs.

Throughout the process of creating *Doom II RPG* Kang was pregnant with her second child, and she says that she was sick "every single day." Miraculously, the game had just been finished by the time she needed to be rushed to the hospital for an emergency C-section.

Kang says she's happy with the way the game was received (it was met with universally positive reviews), especially given the limited resources used to create it. "Like all the games we developed, I always wish we had more time, more money, and more staff," she says. "In the end though, I think we did a great job and we're proud of what we were able to do with what little we had."

Edge

Platform: iPad/iPhone/iPod Touch (universal app)
Price: $2.99
Developer: Mobigame
Released: January 4, 2009

What Is It?

Edge wasn't originally designed with the iPhone in mind, but plop the game into the hands of anyone with an iDevice and he or she will never know the difference. Using swipe controls, players guide a rainbow-colored block through a world made of cubes. The world itself is constructed out of drab, gray blocks, but any moving objects (including the block that players control) flash constantly like six-sided strobe lights. Slowly sliding a finger across the screen will make the block gradually teeter onto its side in one of four directions, whereas a quicker stroke on the screen will cause it to tumble at high speeds across the geometric terrain that constitutes each level.

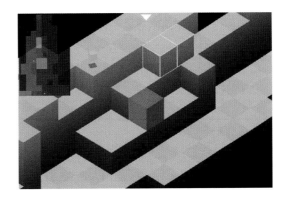

The block itself has extremely limited abilities. It can roll, or climb up and hang onto short walls, but that's about it. Most of the puzzles involve rapidly navigating across moving or floating platforms, with the ultimate goal of making it to the teleporter at the end of each level. Players will be confronted with typical platforming challenges like switches that need to be pressed to activate a series of events, etc., but the real challenge of the game lies in the player's ability to manage the momentum of the cube to finish each level at the maximum possible speed (while at the same time collecting each of the glowing pixels that are scattered across the levels). It's a simple-looking game that benefits greatly from its implementation of some truly original ideas and a fantastic soundtrack.

Behind the Game

How do you create a game that can be easily grasped by a player of any age? It's a question that has plagued game developers since the earliest days of the industry, but Matthieu Malot came up with an answer—blocks. Every kid plays with blocks. They're simple, and they're safe: parents can give blocks to babies and feel confident that they won't be able to swallow them. It's a tangible, physical toy that even the youngest child can make sense of, making it the perfect basis for a kid-friendly game.

To prepare themselves for the design challenges ahead, Malot and David Papazian (who wrote the code for *Edge*) bought Rubik's cubes. "When you work on a game with cubes, you need cubes," explains Papazian. "We could simulate some situations and think concretely thanks to those."

Most of *Edge*'s fun lies in the way that players control the cube; its speed changes with the length of the swipe, which gives the player room for finely tuned movement. The unfortunate aspect of this is that it's difficult to grasp the appeal of *Edge* without actually playing it, making it a challenge to convince gamers to buy the game if they've only seen screenshots. Malot and Papazian agreed that the best course of action would be to attempt to sell *Edge* to a handset manufacturer who could preload the game onto its devices.

Statistics

- **Total cost of development:** $130,000
- **Time spent in development:** 2 years
- **Times downloaded:** 2,000,000+

For 18 months Papazian and Malot worked tirelessly on *Edge*. Money was tight for both of them—Papazian depended on his father for the occasional loan and Malot had no source of income at all. "In France there is a kind of insurance program for unemployed people," explains Papazian. "It was the only source of income for Matthieu during that time."

Things began to look up in mid-2008 when the two members of Mobigame approached Sony Ericsson and convinced the company to buy the game for a sum that Mobigame was extremely happy with. In September, *Edge* won the Milthon award for best mobile game of the year in France. "We were ready to release it," says Papazian.

Mobigame may have been ready to release the game, but its potential publisher was not. Sony Ericsson began major cost-cutting programs in late 2008, reducing its global workforce by over 50% and shuttering R&D centers around the world. The deal was off.

Papazian and Malot quickly began working on porting *Edge* to the iPhone, and it was finally released on Christmas Eve, 2008. Unfortunately, the game's official release was not the end of Mobigame's troubles.

Five months after *Edge* was released, Papazian received an email from Timothy Langdell, owner (and sole employee) of a company called The Edge. Langdell informed Papazian that he believed Mobigame's title was an infringement on his trademark. He also insinuated that *Edge* was a clone of a title called *Bobby Bearing*, which Langdell had developed in the 1980s under his company's brand. Langdell wasn't going to let Mobigame off easy, either. He wanted monetary compensation.

Games journalist Simon Parkin wrote extensively about the Mobigame-Langdell dispute for Eurogamer.net. In his article, "The Edge of Reason?," Parkin published many of the emails that Langdell and Papazian sent back and forth. The letters paint Langdell as something of a bully—a money-hungry trademark troll out to take Mobigame for all it was worth.

In his excellently written four-page piece Parkin chronicles the whole story far better than I can, but the short version is that Mobigame was forced to pull *Edge* from the App Store, returning months later with alternate names like *Edgy* and *Edge by Mobigame*. Eventually, Langdell picked and lost a legal battle with Electronic Arts (he was after the company for the use of the word "edge" in its game, *Mirror's Edge*). Langdell was stripped of his trademarks, and Mobigame's *Edge* returned to the App Store. "Tim Langdell is crazy," says Papazian. "I can't find other words. He caused us a lot of damage, and our game was removed for more than a year from the US App Store."

Papazian told me that he worked with EA and Future Publishing (owners of *Edge Magazine* and former victims of Langdell) after his case was made public, and that the eventual takedown of Langdell was something of a group effort. He calls the two companies his "most important allies."

"For legal reasons I cannot explain exactly what we did," Papazian explains, "but the result was that EA won a lawsuit against Tim Langdell in the United States and all his precious trademarks were cancelled. Now there is no threat to *Edge*."

Since its release, *Edge* has sold millions of copies and received numerous awards—it was a finalist in three separate award categories in the 2009 Independent Games Festival. There are plans for a PC/Mac version of the game, as well as a full-fledged sequel with a cross-platform multiplayer mode.

> **Fun Facts**
>
> - *Edge*'s soundtrack is available for free download at Mobigame.net.
> - It took two years to create *Edge*, but only one month to port it to the iPad.
> - *Edge* has been preloaded onto millions of Java-based Samsung phones.
> - Other apps by Mobigame include *EDGE Extended* and *Perfect Cell.*

Enviro-Bear 2010

Platform: iPhone/iPod Touch
Price: $.99
Developer: Blinkbat Games
Released: July 8, 2009

What Is It?

Enviro-Bear 2010 isn't like a lot of the other games on this list. The controls are intentionally designed to be incredibly arduous, gameplay mechanics aren't explained to players in any clear way, and the entire thing takes place in a "posthuman" world in which bears drive cars.

You play as the elongated right arm of one such car-driving bear. Yes, you read that correctly: players have control over just one of the bear's arms, and all tasks (holding down

the gas pedal, steering, eating fish, etc.) must be completed using that arm. Plus, you have to switch between tasks quickly—fending off badgers at one moment, and slamming on the brakes to avoid trees the next.

Although nothing about the world of *Enviro-Bear* is spelled out explicitly, there is quite a lot of depth. Clever players will find numerous ways to interact with the environment. For instance, crashing into a large rock will cause a smaller chunk of rock to chip off and land in your car. You can then use the rock as a weight on your gas pedal so that you can focus on steering around trees as you seek out food.

The ultimate goal is for the bear to eat as much as possible in preparation for winter. A banner commanding players to "HIBERNATE!" will appear on the screen when you've eaten enough, and you'll have to search for a cave to safely drive into. The entire thing is nonsensically hilarious, but that's sort of the point.

Behind the Game

Enviro-Bear 2010 began as a response to a challenge: TIGsource.com's Cockpit Competition. The challenge required developers to create a game centered around cockpits in less than a month. There are plenty of things that developers could do with that concept: you could imagine a space-flight sim, a game about driving trains, or some sort of Air Force training program.

But Justin Smith's brain operates a little bit differently from yours or mine. "The original plan was to have squirrels driving a car through a postapocalyptic wasteland, attacking other squirrel cars to take their nuts," says Smith. "You would be able to board the other cars pirate-style and swashbuckle with enemy squirrels. The car would be controlled by multiple squirrels, each on a different instrument."

Apparently, multiple squirrels were too much to deal with in a single month. Smith had what he describes as a "panic attack," and refined his somewhat insane game idea into something slightly more reasonable. Only slightly. Says Smith, "I thought, what's easy? Bears!"

Smith calls the month that followed a boring process, and wanted to focus more on the postmortem of the game in our interview. To make a long story short, he managed to finish his game within the deadline, and *Enviro-Bear* took home TIGSource.com's first place prize. Following the release of the PC version, Smith set to work on getting the game compatible with iOS. This took almost exactly one more month.

> ### Statistics
>
> - **Development time:** 2 months
> - **Total budget:** Living expenses
> - **Times downloaded:** About 50,000

Once the game was released on the App Store, Smith saw most of his sales within the first month—things dropped off sharply after that. He credits this to a sort of "15 minutes of fame" effect and notes that much of the game's success is due to "hilarious trolls" on several online forums. "Some of the App-Store reviews people left were comic genius," says Smith.

He's not joking about that. I ventured into the App Store to read some of the top user reviews from those who had purchased *Enviro-Bear,* and I wasn't disappointed. "This game is impossible to control and I can never tell what's going on," claimed one customer.

"Badgers keep eating my fish and I don't know what's happening. This is the greatest game ever made. One million stars."

"Some games make you realize the actual power of the iPhone, both through their rich interactivity and high-quality graphics. This game combines that with a bear driving a car," read another. Other reviews were just as humorous. One reviewer claimed that the game cured his "mega AIDS" and landed him a job as a rocket scientist. Another said that it was a perfect simulation of life in Russia. "It raised my grandmother from the dead," one review concluded.

With endorsements like that, you'd think that *Enviro-Bear* would have no trouble selling thousands of copies, and you wouldn't be wrong. According to Smith, however, the types of customers buying his game are not the ones you'd expect. "I was totally blindsided by how popular the game is with the four-to-six-year-old demographic," he says. "I made a colorful, simple game with animals, but I made it for adults."

Smith says that although he is very pleased with how the game looks, he believes himself to be a terrible artist. His decision to create his own art for the game is a reflection of his indifferent approach to the project. "There's plenty of good artists looking for collaborations out there," he says. "I just thought the game was going to be a complete failure and didn't want to drag anyone down with me."

Smith is happy with the way the game has performed, but players shouldn't expect to see many updates from him in the future. "It's a tough game to mess with," he explains. "My code is so bad, it's like going to Chernobyl every time I open the project. I can only expose myself to it for short stretches of time, then I have to decontaminate."

> **Fun Facts**
> - In the game, golden fish do nothing. "Gold has no value in a posthuman world," Smith explains.
> - The first game Smith ever created was an Atari-ST title called *Frolik*.
> - *Enviro-Bear*'s music was composed by a hotel manager from Bali, Indonesia.
> - Other apps by Blinkbat Games include *Skullpogo* and *So Long, Oregon!*.

EpicWin

Platform: iPhone/iPod Touch
Price: $2.99
Developer: Supermono Limited
Released: August 18, 2010

Where Is It?

There's always been a problem with task-managing software—if you're busy enough to need to have a task manager in the first place, you're probably also too busy to take the time to fill out and update some clunky task-managing app. Busy people have very little incentive to waste their time with such things.

EpicWin is a creative, gaming-based solution to this problem. It takes task managers to the next level by turning your life into an RPG in which the quests are your daily tasks and goals. You set the "quests" and decide how many experience points each quest is worth based on the amount of time or effort is needed to complete it. Earning XP will allow you to gain levels, and you'll occasionally be "rewarded" with in-game items (which are usually pretty hilarious—anyone else want a "helm of questionable appeal?").

Let's say you need to take out the trash. That's a small task, with a value of maybe 50 experience

points. A class paper or work presentation would be worth more. It's up to you to decide, so it is possible to cheat: you could say that flushing crayons down your toilet is worth 300 experience points, but those using *EpicWin* to help get things done are unlikely to abuse it in this way.

EpicWin uses incentives that gamers playing RPGs have known about for years: there's something intrinsically addictive and even endorphin producing about seeing an XP bar fill up over time. It's a manufactured, fake feeling—but it feels good nonetheless. It exploits the human mind in a way that's, frankly, pretty fun.

Behind the Game

Rex Crowle was a game developer with an obsession, albeit not one related to his own game. It was around 2004, and Crowle was working at Lionhead Studios on the team headed by the legendary Peter Molyneux. He and another Lionhead employee (Tak Fung) had been competing for high scores in an online game called *Progress Quest*, a "zero-player RPG" (you'll learn more about that on p. 103).

Progress Quest is, in a way, a parody of the way that characters in role-playing games constantly become more powerful as the game progresses. It strips out all of the actual gameplay and mechanics of those games and reduces it to a text-only simulation. "The only interaction a player had was to turn it [the game] on and keep it running," Crowle explains. "The game played itself—listing, in text form, what was happening in the game world. 'You have picked up an amulet of healing.' 'You have been bitten by a high-school troll.' All while the numeric stats above adjusted accordingly."

Progress Quest ranked every active player in the world, and score was determined almost entirely by how long the game had been running on a player's computer. As a result, serious *Progress Quest* players had to keep their PCs running for weeks at a time in order to maintain their high positions on the game's global leaderboard. "A crash or reboot could see you tumbling hundreds of places down the table," says Crowle.

> **Statistics**
>
> • Number of experience points I give myself for remembering to floss: 100
> • Number of experience points I give myself for going a complete day without biting my nails: 300

About five years later, Crowle was riding a train from London to the rural farm he grew up on. He says that the familiar ride is one of the only times he isn't exposed to an Internet connection, and it gives him time to think. "I'd been thinking a lot about my productivity and how I could better stay on top of everything," he says. "I'd tried using to-do list software, but there was never enough incentive to fill out all my tasks and format them into those different contexts and projects." Crowle says that he has no trouble with getting things done, but the problem arises when he forgets to document what he's done or what he needs to do next. "I started thinking about quests in games—how I love ticking everything off in all the side-quests, and generally making sure I'm keeping that quest-log pruned," he says.

Crowle got out his laptop and began making mock-ups of a to-do list presented in the style of a quest log from an RPG like *Diablo* or *World of Warcraft*. He began thinking about how his idea could translate to an app on a phone, and even drew a design for the dwarf character that appears in the final version of *EpicWin*. A few days later, Crowle was still hard at work on the idea. He had designed an entire flow chart that explained how the app would work. "By that time I really felt like the app had great potential," he says. "I was past my usual 48-hour cycle of thinking of an idea but losing interest by the following day." Crowle decided that he needed to find a collaborator to make the project come to life.

Crowle remembered his old friend and former coworker, Tak Fung. He thought about their shared obsession with *Progress Quest* and decided it would be an excellent starting point for his own game. Fung (who started Supermono Limited) had already established himself as a talented iOS developer with the release of *MiniSquadron* in late 2009. If there were any doubts about his abilities after that, he could point critics to the beautiful and inventive *Fox vs. Duck*.

Crowle convinced Fung to meet him in a cramped coffee shop in London, and he pitched the idea by showing him screenshots of his designs on a scratched-up first-generation iPod Touch. Fung thought that the idea seemed fun, so he agreed to help Crowle.

Taking *EpicWin* from concept to reality wasn't very difficult for Crowle and Fung. Crowle had designed much of the game already, so the biggest issue was figuring out how to code it. For Fung, that wasn't a problem—but problems did arise for Supermono once *EpicWin* was released. The team had hired a few beta testers to try and find issues with the app, but no one spotted one particularly horrendous bug until immediately after the game went live on the App Store. Crowle and Fung didn't hear about the bug until they were at the launch party, which they were throwing for themselves at a local pub. "If the app was exited before it finished loading then it would freeze up and never load again without being reinstalled," explains Crowle. "It was a total disaster."

Supermono rushed to fix the game, but Apple took a frustratingly long time to put the update on the App Store. There was an agonizing period where *EpicWin*'s disappointed customers were sending dozens of emails to Supermono to complain about their broken app. It was a horrible few days, but just as the fix was approved, Apple featured *EpicWin* as App of the Week in most of the European App Stores.

One of the most interesting post-launch things that happened to *EpicWin* was when proponents of "gamification" began using Crowle's creation as their go-to example of how to do gamification correctly. According to writer Nicolas Lovell, gamification is about using game-like mechanics to improve a business process, customer experience, or profits.

Fun Facts

- Crowle created many of the trailers for Media Molecule's *LittleBigPlanet* series.
- The comedic teaser trailer for *EpicWin* (created by Crowle, obviously) was immensely popular, garnering over half-a-million views on YouTube.
- Crowle hints that one day *EpicWin* might have an actual RPG game added in: as you leveled up in the task list, the gameplay would become easier. It may happen!
- Other apps by Supermono include *MiniSquadron* and *Fox vs. Duck*.

His article "The Ten Rules of Gamification" appeared first on GamesBrief.com and later on Gamasutra.com. Anybody can see how *EpicWin* embodies these rules: it literally turns your life into an RPG. But despite all the free press his game was getting, Crowle wasn't entirely happy with the attention. He describes being approached by multiple marketing companies that wanted him to add sponsored items to his game. "That all felt a bit uncomfortable to me," he says. "I wanted people to use *EpicWin* to help themselves do whatever they wanted, not be specifically rewarded for buying ten gallons of a popular energy drink or enrolling in a particular gym." Turning down the marketing agencies' offers meant turning down a decent amount of money, but Crowle didn't want to sacrifice the game's integrity.

EpicWin has since been updated to support syncing with Google Calendar, and an Android version is nearly complete as of the time of this writing.

Flight Control

Platform: iPhone/iPod Touch (iPad version available separately)
Price: $.99
Developer: Firemint
Released: March 5, 2009

What Is It?

I've always associated *Flight Control* with *Canabalt*. Although the games couldn't be more different from a gameplay perspective, both are landmark titles that demonstrate the value of using the iPhone's touch screen to make something simple and accessible. Instead of trying to force a weird control scheme or an inappropriate genre like a first-person shooter onto the device, the developers of both games examined the tool at hand (the iPhone touch screen) and decided to use it the way it was meant to be used. They understand that one shouldn't use a screwdriver as a hammer.

Flight Control is fairly simple: planes fly in from the side, and you use your finger to draw a path that guides them to their appropriate landing strips, which are color coded to match different plane types. The trick is to avoid letting two planes cross paths and collide with each other. Eventually you'll have a

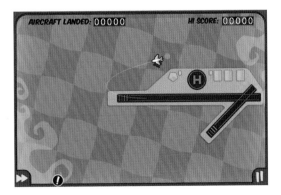

dozen or more planes on the screen at once, all of which are commanded by pilots with no sense of self-preservation. It's a time-management game in some ways, and, in others, a strategy game where you have to think one step ahead to prevent a collision in others. As the game progresses, you'll begin to have to think three or four steps ahead, to the point that sometimes you'll be directing planes to fly in loops just so they'll be out of your way.

One of the best things about *Flight Control* is its multiplayer support. You can play with others using Wi-Fi or Bluetooth on the iPhone, but the iPad has the best multiplayer experience, thanks to its supersized maps and same-device multiplayer. Cooperative play gives birth to a lot of fun scenarios, and it works really well as a tabletop multiplayer experience. It's an incredible demonstration of how the iPad can be used in ways that the iPhone simply can't.

Behind the Game

Firemint began life in 1999 as a company called ndWare. At first, the company had but one employee—CEO Robert Murray. Slowly, Murray gathered a team, and ndWare began developing work-for-hire games for mobile platforms; its first game was *Nicktoons Racing* for the Game Boy Advance, which received positive reviews.

For the next few years, ndWare developed whatever mobile titles it could get its hands on. This included some truly odd titles, like *Soul Daddy BKB*, a side-scrolling beat-'em-up that featured gang fights "in the hood."

In 2004, ndWare became Firemint. The company spent the next few years growing and pumping out dozens of mobile versions of popular titles—like *Need for Speed: Most Wanted* and an adaptation of Pixar's *Ratatouille*. By late 2008, the company had over two dozen games under its belt. Murray decided that it was time for a change.

After shipping its last commissioned game (*Back at the Barnyard: Slop Bucket Games* for the Nintendo DS), Firemint had set to work on its first original game—a racing-simulation game called *Real Racing*. This was unlike anything the company had done before, and it knew little about how the sales environment in the App Store worked. Despite this, the game was planned from the beginning to work on iOS.

Eight months after the team had started working on *Real Racing*, Murray began thinking of a few game ideas built around the iPhone's touch screen. Over a one-week period during his Christmas break, Murray single-handedly created the first prototype for the game that would eventually become *Flight Control*. "The most significant challenge in creating *Flight Control* was in actually doing it," says Murray. "I gave up my holidays and committed myself to finishing a game that week. It wasn't easy; it was intense."

Murray had a second motivation for creating and finishing *Flight Control*; it would allow the company to go through the process of publishing a game on the App Store before setting

Statistics

- **Development time:** 3 weeks
- **Total budget:** $50,000
- **Times downloaded on iPhone alone:** 4,500,000

loose its true baby (*Real Racing*). By creating a simple, low-risk game, Murray could test the App Store's waters with no major financial risk to his company.

Murray says that at first, he had no feel for how successful *Flight Control* would be. Everyone who played the game seemed to enjoy it, but that wasn't enough to ease Murray's concerns. He worried about whether the game was too simple, but felt confident that the game's core line-drawing mechanic was good. "At the core of it, I just loved the feeling of drawing on the touch screen," he says. "It was immediate and intuitive."

After Firemint's holidays were over, Murray brought his prototype into the office and two other team members on board, resident artist Jesse West and his wife, Alex. The trio managed to finish up work on the game in just a matter of weeks, and *Flight Control* 1.0 was released on the App Store in March of 2009, a full three months before *Real Racing*. You know the rest.

Flight Control was successful beyond Firemint's wildest dreams. Instead of simply providing Firemint with experience and knowledge about the App Store publishing process, it pushed the company into the spotlight. Firemint transitioned overnight into a confident, financially secure developer with real name recognition. "It gave us both the confidence and financial support to really go out on our own," says Murray.

> **Fun Facts**
>
> - You can actually stop aircraft by holding your finger down on them.
> - *Flight Control* started out using a "vector graphics" art style. It wasn't until later in the project that its charming, retro art was added.
> - Flightcontrol.cloudcell.com has lots of tips for improving your *Flight Control* game.
> - Other apps by Firemint include *Real Racing 2* and *Spy Mouse*.

Since the release of *Flight Control*, Firemint has become one of the most respected iOS developers in the world. *Real Racing* was just as much of a critical and sales success as *Flight Control*, as was *Real Racing 2*, which followed a year later (first for the iPad, then for the iPhone about six months after). Firemint has ported *Flight Control* to both the PlayStation 3 and the DS, and it actually knocked *Angry Birds* from the number one sales slot in the App Store in September of 2011 with *Spy Mouse*, an original game using a line-drawing mechanic similar to the one in *Flight Control*.

In January of 2011, Firemint acquired Infinite Interactive, the creators of the massively popular *Puzzle Quest* series. Only three months later, Firemint itself was acquired by EA. The company now employs over 60 people. It's safe to say that just three years after going independent, Firemint won't be doing any more work-for-hire games any time soon.

Forget-Me-Not

Platform: iPad/iPhone/iPod Touch (universal app)
Price: $1.99
Developer: Nyarlu Labs
Released: March 22, 2011

What Is It?

Everything about *Forget-Me-Not* evokes memories of a 1980s arcade. The graphics are extremely simple and pixelated, and the art style makes heavy use of primary colors.

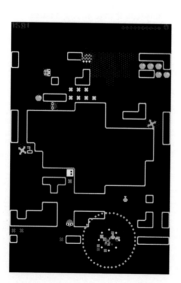

Similarly, the audio is over-the-top with its bleeps, bloops, and other retro-sounding squeals and purrs. Its mechanics also seem to draw from games of that era, and it's likely to elicit comparisons to *Pac-Man* (if Pac-Man had an automatic weapon). Like Namco's classic game, *Forget-Me-Not* has you zipping around a maze, collecting items (flowers) and dodging baddies. Once you gather all of the flowers in a level and collect a key, the exit will open, allowing you to travel down to the next stage.

Your laser fires constantly as you gather flowers. That may sound like a concession to the iOS platform (similar to the way cars in *Real Racing* constantly accelerate so the player doesn't have to hold down an on-screen button), but it's actually an intentional design decision that makes the game more interesting. Much like in *Pac-Man*, the sides of the levels wrap around, so if there's a hole in a wall on the side of the screen you can enter that hole and pop out on the opposite side of the level. Likewise, if your bullets go into that hole, they will come out of the corresponding hole on the opposite side of the screen. This creates some interesting scenarios in which you can potentially shoot yourself in the back. However, if you've already collected the level's key, it will drag behind you and block any incoming bullets from behind.

Another weird gameplay element that's even more hidden and less obvious is the wall-grinding mechanic. If you're traveling next to a wall and swipe into it, your character will begin grinding against the wall. If you do this long enough you'll build up a sort of charge that will allow you to ram into enemies and kill them. It's features like this that make the game far more complex than it appears to be on the surface.

It's a good thing that *Forget-Me-Not* isn't an actual arcade game, because if it were, I'd be desperately in need of some more quarters.

Behind the Game

Brandon Williamson says that *Forget-Me-Not* is a game he has wanted to make since he was a kid. It all began in the late 1980s, when the 8-year-old Williamson was subscribed to *Compute!'s Gazette*. The *Gazette* often printed lines of code that readers could type into their computers to make a working game. Two such games were *Crossroads* and *Crossroads II: Pandemonium* by Steve Harter. The *Crossroads* games were only distributed in this way, making them cult classics.

The games had extremely rudimentary graphics. Creatures on screen were represented by text characters joined together to make tiny creatures that wandered around mazes shooting at each other. Williamson was particularly fond of the two-player mode, which allowed players to either cooperate or compete with each other. "The innovative thing about the *Crossroads* games is that the player is really just another creature in the maze," Williamson explains. "Enemies will not only attack the player but also each other, and some kinds of enemies have alliances with others. It feels like a miniature ecosystem. If you just sit there not doing anything, the game world keeps on going regardless."

Having to type in the code himself got Williamson interested in programming. He was too young to fully grasp how the whole process worked, but he became fascinated with the process of making games. "Type all this stuff into the computer and out comes a game! That's pretty magical," he says.

As Williamson grew up, he began trying to make games on his family PC. He didn't have too much success, but did manage to create a few simple maze games—nothing on the level of Steve Harter's games, but they were working games.

Around that time he discovered *Nethack*, a descendant of *Rogue*. *Nethack* was the first roguelike that he had ever played, and he was impressed with the fact that the levels in the game were procedurally generated—they were different every time he played. "I love that," says Williamson.

In 2008, Williamson began tinkering with making home-brew games for the Nintendo DS. He particularly liked the touch screen of the DS, and eventually made two games (*Magnetic Shaving Derby*—which he later ported to iOS—and a game called *Snowride*).

His home-brew DS games were popular, and Williamson met others in the home-brew community who hooked him up with an iPhone developer called Tin Man Games. Williamson did freelance coding work for a few of Tin Man's iPhone titles, which gave him experience and the confidence to make his own stuff for the iPhone.

Williamson didn't exactly have a plan for an original iOS game, but he began thinking about things that he wanted his game to do. He created a system that would generate levels automatically (the same way that *Nethack* did) and programmed in a feature that allowed levels to wrap around, which meant that characters could go into one side of the screen and pop out on the other end. "It's so weird and unrealistic," says Williamson. "But it makes things somehow feel very dynamic."

Then Williamson began thinking about *Crossroads* and the "ecosystem" of monsters that made it so interesting. He became determined to add something similar to his own game.

Old arcade games were undoubtedly the biggest inspiration for Williamson during his work on *Forget-Me-Not*. He was so dedicated to re-creating an old-school arcade experience that he intentionally duplicated less popular elements of the games. "I wanted it to sound all bleepy, and over-the-top, and somewhat annoying like an old arcade machine," he says.

Throughout, Williamson was completely alone. He loves working on games as a hobby but says that he finds it difficult sometimes. "The hardest thing about it was just finding the motivation to keep going," he admits. "I work alone and don't know anyone in real life who is into games to talk about it with . . . being in a bit of a vacuum like that, it's easy to get disheartened—I tend to start feeling down about my work after awhile."

Williamson only worked on the game for about four weeks, but the time spent working alone began to make him feel depressed. He sent the game to a friend to see what he thought of it, and told the friend that he didn't think the game was even worth selling. "I thought people would be disappointed with the game and wanted to avoid a lot of 'not worth two dollars'–style reviews," he says.

Fun Facts

- It is possible to kill the ghost that appears when you take too long to finish a level. Williamson says it's "quite hard," though.
- Although the names of the enemies in *Forget-Me-Not* aren't listed in the game, Williamson has named all of them. He says his favorites are the "Mean Turners."
- Williamson says that wall-grinding isn't vital to playing the game, but that better players should learn to use it.
- Other apps by Nyarlu Labs include *Magnetic Shaving Derby*.

Luckily, Williamson's friend was able to talk some sense into him. He insisted that it was a good game, and Williamson took his advice and released the game for $1.99. IndieGames.com picked up the game's trailer and promoted it, and *Forget-Me-Not* became one of the best-reviewed iOS games on Metacritic. It didn't sell incredibly well, but Williamson was happy with the critical feedback. "The world of marketing and selling things doesn't interest me much, I just want to make cool stuff," he says. "I'd like to think that this shows in my game, and that's why lots of people are liking it."

Frogatto

Platform: iPad/iPhone/iPod Touch (universal app)
Price: $.99
Developer: Lost Pixel
Released: July 21, 2010

What Is It?

Frogatto is a side-scrolling platformer that handles like a *Yoshi's Island* game, albeit one with wall-jumping mechanics (which should be familiar for fans of games like *Super Meat Boy* or *N+*). Like Yoshi, Frogatto can lick up and spit out enemies, but he can also dispatch them by hopping on their heads Mario-style.

   Frogatto is not the most mechanically complicated game in the world, and most

of the challenge lies in finding clever ways to deal with groups of enemies so you can hop and wall-jump your way to the end of the level. Along the way, you'll get to enjoy some of the best modern pixel art you've ever seen—it looks particularly gorgeous on the iPhone 4's Retina display.

   In addition to its basic story mode, *Frogatto* also comes with several minigames. "Run" and "Climb" are fun, but the best is "Coin Race," in which you hop around levels attempting to collect all of the coins before time runs out.

The iPhone and iPad versions of *Frogatto* are very good—even great. Still, it's fair to say that the (free) PC and Mac versions play a bit more smoothly thanks to their use of physical controls, as opposed to the virtual D-pad solution used for iOS. However, if you'd like to support Lost Pixel by paying for *Frogatto* and getting a cool pocket-friendly edition, I highly recommend giving the iOS version a try.

Behind the Game

Although *Frogatto* is technically the first and (thus far) only iOS game to be released by developers Lost Pixel, the work of many of its studio members has been featured once before in this book. That's because most of Lost Pixel's team met while working on *Battle for Wesnoth*, the open-source strategy RPG by David White (which I covered on pp. 28–31).

Team member Ben Anderman recounts the way that the *Frogatto* team was formed. It all began when White saw some artwork that had been contributed by *Wesnoth* fan Guido Bos. "He [White] thought it looked cool, and thought it was a shame it wasn't being used, so he went off and created a prototype [of *Frogatto*] and sent it to Guido," says Anderman.

> **Statistics**
> - **Development time:** 2 years (and continuing)
> - **Total budget:** $0—it's open source!
> - **Times downloaded:** Over 9,000

This effectively launched a splinter group of *Wesnoth* contributors who began to focus on *Frogatto* instead. While Anderman worked on getting the game up and running on the Mac, a number of recognizable *Wesnoth* names began streaming in to contribute as well. Richard Kettering (*Wesnoth*'s art director) helped out with programming, Ryan Reily was brought in to lend a hand with music and sound, and Guido Bos continued to make new art.

Most of the Lost Pixel team members have never met each other outside the Internet. Richard Kettering has met David White and Ryan Reily in person, but the rest of the team worked from their own homes, sending in their contributions to the project via email.

The Lost Pixel team worked on *Frogatto* for two years before they decided to put a playable version of the game out. This ended up being pretty close to the version that players can currently buy—but Anderman says the team doesn't consider the game a finished product. "We did our best to get a playable release out there, with no blaring loose ends, because it's very, very hard to

> **Fun Facts**
> - *Frogatto*'s signature art style changed three times from inception to launch.
> - Ben Anderman is an avid unicyclist.
> - Originally, Frogatto had the ability to attack with his fists.

keep motivation up after two years with no feedback," he says. "But there's a lot more required to get *Frogatto* to the point where it's what we would consider a full game." Anderman says that the team has plans for a lot more content, including a multiplayer mode, and new levels, enemies, bosses, and more.

Fruit Ninja

Platform: iPhone/iPod Touch (iPad version available separately)
Price: $.99
Developer: Halfbrick Studios
Released: April 20, 2010

What Is It?

In its original form, *Fruit Ninja* was as casual as casual games can get. Fruit shoots up, you slash it with your finger. If three fruits fall or you accidentally touch a bomb, you get a strike. Three strikes and it's game over.

As time has gone on, the game has retained its casual quality while at the same time evolving into something with a lot more depth. Now there are weapons to unlock and different modes, including the fantastic arcade mode, which is a timed version of the basic, endless mode.

Halfbrick has also changed the fundamental mechanics of the game over time. Now, if you manage to cut three fruits in a single swipe you'll get bonus points. The change lends a risk-reward element to the game that encourages players to wait whenever they see a fruit appear, in case more fruit pops up and allows for a juicy, well-timed strike that will award additional points. Meanwhile, the addition of unlockable skins and achievements contributes to the "one more game" fever that the game has always been so good at inspiring.

Fruit Ninja is a parent's best friend. It includes a special casual mode in which it's impossible to fail, which is perfect for kids. Both kids and adults will also learn a few things about fruit thanks to the sensei character, who pops up to share random fun facts about fruit after each game.

Because of its simplicity, *Fruit Ninja* manages to appeal to a ridiculously wide audience. I've seen people age 2 and 52 play and love *Fruit Ninja*, something that few games achieve. There's something intrinsically fun about *Fruit Ninja*'s juicy, squishy physicality.

Behind the Game

Before creating *Fruit Ninja*, Halfbrick game designer Luke Muscat was working on another game, a racing title for the Xbox Live Indie Games Channel and PSP called *Rocket Racing* (now called *Aero Racer* because of a legal issue). *Rocket Racing* began as a side project for a few members of Halfbrick's team but it eventually grew into something much bigger, and the company had high hopes for it. Unfortunately, the game flopped in a big way. According to Muscat, the game was received well enough critically, but it was a commercial disaster. "We were so invested in it, so we were excited about it," says Muscat. "And when it came out it didn't do much for us and it was really disappointing, because we were proud of the game." Muscat believes it was the hardcore, technical nature of the game that made it such a failure. "Clearly making a hardcore racing game for PSP minis didn't work out, so I figured lets do the exact opposite of that," says Muscat. "So my new goal was to make a really casual, easy to play, kind of literal game."

Around this time Halfbrick held a round of "Halfbrick Fridays," days on which studio employees got a chance to stand up and pitch a game idea to their peers. Traditionally the studio had focused mainly on doing contract work, so Halfbrick Fridays were a chance for its team to do something truly original. Muscat wanted to participate in the upcoming round of pitches, so he tried to think up a game that would work well on the iPhone.

For this particular Halfbrick Friday, Halfbrick CEO Shainiel Deo had laid down a ground rule—each game had to exist completely within a single screen. That meant no scrolling, zooming out, or anything of that sort. For Muscat, this limitation worked perfectly. Muscat sat down at his desk with a blank sheet of paper and pretended that it was an iPhone. He began dragging his finger over the "screen" in a variety of gestures and shapes, trying to imagine different ways that game players would interact with the device. "I had done quite a bit of work on DS games," he says. "I worked on *Avatar: Enter the Inferno* and *Marvel Superhero Squad* so I was fairly familiar with what works and doesn't work on touch screens." It was at this point that Muscat suddenly remembered an old infomercial he'd seen for the Miracle Blade World Class Knife. In the ad, the excitable Chef

Tony throws a pineapple up into the air and cuts it to show how sharp his crazy knife is. Muscat had purchased a set of knives for himself, and now he began thinking about ways to fit a fruit-slicing mechanic into a game. "The thing that was sort of exciting to me about it was that it was really kind of simple, but had this G-rated gore about it that I liked the idea of," says Muscat. "All our first concepts were of watermelons just because they seem to have that sort of good, hardish shell and are quite soft and juicy on the inside. I really wanted it to be kinda splattery and gory yet G-rated. Very viscerally satisfying to do."

Friday arrived, and Muscat was ready with his pitch. He tells me that the company had limited pitches to five minutes because entire days were being lost to drawn-out presentations by overly excited employees.

When it was Muscat's turn to speak, he got up and showed a PowerPoint presentation with only five slides. On the first screen were the words "Ninjas hate fruit, slice them with your finger." He explained the game's three-strike mechanic and walked off stage. The whole thing took fewer than 40 seconds.

A few people showed interest in the game, but the prevailing reaction from others in the company was "wait, that's it?" Two people agreed to work with Muscat on the game, but they both left the company soon after, leaving Muscat with a game idea and nothing else. Subsequently Muscat and his team had to start looking for contracts in order to keep the company afloat, but the games industry in Australia wasn't doing well and the team wasn't able to find a contract worth a reasonable amount of money. "We were just kinda sitting in our little areas like, hmmm . . . this is looking dire," laughs Muscat. "We just lost a bunch of money on *Rocket Racing* and there's no contracts, so at that point we're like, okay, what if we try some iPhone games?"

Muscat and a peer named Joe Gatling drew up a plan to create two complete iPhone games in six weeks apiece. They came up with more than a dozen game ideas and began knocking out prototypes using Adobe Flash, never spending more than a single day on one prototype.

After creating a good number of these prototypes, Muscat and Gatling picked half a dozen of their favorites and emailed them out to every employee in the company. One of these prototypes was *Fruit Ninja*. The email asked their fellow Halfbrickers to play the games and rank them.

Fruit Ninja came out on top overwhelmingly. Muscat and two other Halfbrick employees began working on the game almost immediately, and within just six weeks the first version of *Fruit Ninja* was released on the App Store. After about a week the game was doing quite well in Australia (it was in the top five), thanks to aggressive advertising and timely reviews from gaming sites. The game wasn't topping charts in other countries, but the team was stoked with the game's performance, so they stayed late one Friday night

Statistics

- **Development time for fruit splatters:** 2.5 weeks
- **Development time for arcade mode:** 3.5 months
- **Times downloaded (all versions across all platforms):** 60,000,000+

to drink beers and celebrate. "We were scanning the charts, watching the game move up or down by one spot," says Muscat. "It's kinda this weird spectator sport. Like if you'd trained a horse and then watched it race."

By 11:30 p.m. most members of the team had gone home to sleep, while the remaining few who were still in the office were "fairly well drunk." Muscat was getting ready to walk out the door when Deo came out of his office with what Muscat describes as a stunned look on his face. "I've got this email sitting in my in-box, and it's from Apple," Deo said. "It says 'urgent: we need some key artwork to use for *Fruit Ninja* for the App Store.'"

The email didn't explicitly state that *Fruit Ninja* was going to be featured by Apple, but that was the message being sent. It was a scenario that the team had hoped and prepared for, but they had no idea that the call from Apple might come at such an inconvenient hour. Panicking, the still-inebriated Halfbrick employees called both *Fruit Ninja*'s artist Shath and head marketing guy Phil, and got them to come back into the office to create a banner that Apple could use to promote the game. That took until 1:00 in the morning, but it was well worth the time.

> ### Fun Facts
>
> - The famous first trailer for *Fruit Ninja* was filmed on a $20 budget. The guy in the ninja costume is Stephen Last, the game's programmer.
> - The instructions in the game's "about" screen are actually a haiku written by Muscat. He says that a grand total of zero people have noticed.
> - *Fruit Ninja*'s achievements include several references to quotes from *The Simpsons*.
> - Other apps by Halfbrick Studios include *Age of Zombies* and *Jetpack Joyride*.

The next week Apple featured *Fruit Ninja*, and sales exploded. The game was propelled into the top ten on almost every country's chart and became just as much of a staple in the top ten as *Angry Birds*. For Halfbrick, *Fruit Ninja* is more than just a commercial success. It's a game that the team's family members can actually get into. "It's really hard," says Muscat. "We made this hardcore racing game [*Rocket Racing*], and Shainiel takes it home to his kids and they're going to play it for all of 30 seconds before they realize that they can't figure it out."

Things are different for *Fruit Ninja*. Muscat says that he gave the game to his grandmother, who had never even seen an iPhone before. She played the game for a bit and loved it, managing a score of 45 in classic mode on her first attempt. "One of the most exciting things about *Fruit Ninja* is having the people that we're close to invested and excited about the stuff we're making," Muscat says. "In the end, they're the support group. They're the people who keep us going and keep us working."

Fruit Ninja's effect on Halfbrick has been incredibly positive as well. The company no longer has to do work-for-hire projects; this is something that Muscat is particularly pleased with, as contract work can often be grueling and unfulfilling. "A lot of the guys here are the same guys who'd work on our early licensed titles," he says. "And they'd get slammed in reviews, but we'd get rushed to push out a game in six months and meet ridiculous publisher expectations and change things at the last minute for them. So then you work for six-and-a-half months, and then the game comes out and it gets reviewed terribly and no one particularly likes the game, and these guys who are extremely talented are going through that. That's tough to go through."

Thanks to *Fruit Ninja*, Halfbrick has risen to superstar status in the iOS world. They've become A-class developers with the ability to do what they want, when they want, without reliance on publishers. With just the tiniest hint of pride in his voice, Muscat says that things have changed for the better. "Now I feel like the games we're making are Halfbrick games, whereas before they were just games that Halfbrick worked on."

Garage Inc.

Platform: iPhone/iPod Touch (iPad version available separately)
Price: $.99
Developer: TransGaming
Publisher: Breakthrough Entertainment
Released: January 6, 2011

What Is It?

Garage Inc. is like *Diner Dash*, but targeted towards male gamers and set in 1920s Chicago. The main character is Angelo Marito, who's in a bit of a bad spot. At the beginning of the tale Marito's cousin Sal offers to loan him a large sum of money to help him start an automobile repair shop. Marito accepts, and begins building a small empire.

At first you'll be dealing with just one car at a time, but soon the shop will grow and you'll hire mechanics with different specialties (electrical work, mechanical work, etc.) to deal with the range of problems your customers have. For example, if a customer needs to get a car's headlights fixed, you'll want to put an employee with electrical experience on the job. But if they're all busy on other cars, you'll have to do some shuffling to make things work. By presenting scenarios like this, *Garage Inc.* tests your ability to quickly sort out and manage sticky situations.

The gameplay is broken up with fully voiced, animated cutscenes, which tell a strikingly dark tale. It's a gorgeous art style, and there's an era-appropriate swing soundtrack that fits really well with the tone of the game. The story mode is occasionally interrupted by minigames, which use the touch screen to allow you to do things like connect wires or repair a car door. It's nothing you haven't seen before, but it gives the game a nice sense of pacing.

Despite the fact that *Garage Inc.* is essentially a skin of *Diner Dash*, the game is really worth playing just for the story. And once you're done with that, the endless mode will keep you occupied even further.

Behind the Game

Breakthrough Entertainment, a publisher, originally pitched the idea for *Garage Inc.* to TransGaming as a collection of car-fixing minigames. Breakthrough hadn't thought about including characters or a story in the game, though, and as a result had gotten turned down by the Canadian funding agency it had pitched it to. "They contacted us saying something like, 'Hey, we have this concept. There's something here, but it needs to be made better so that we can pitch it to another funding agency and this time get money,'" says TransGaming manager Wojtek Kawczynski.

TransGaming was busy working on a Wii game at the time (*In the Mix Featuring Armin van Burren*), but it put together a quick pitch that set the game during Prohibition. "We liked the setting and the cars," explains Kawczynski.

Garage Inc. was to be a blend of minigames and *Diner Dash*–style management. Or, as the game's publisher puts it: "*Diner Dash* for dudes." When TransGaming finally had the time to work on *Garage Inc.*, it began by hiring a summer student to do research on the Prohibition era. "She actually did an amazing job of finding a bunch of historical facts/dates/language that allowed us to set the game in a very specific time period and anchor it around real events," says Kawczynski.

Kawczynski calls the process of working with an external publisher "tricky." "We were lucky in that we had a lot of freedom to do what we thought was right but there were a few issues that we didn't agree on," he admits.

Kawczynski mentions cutscenes (motion comics with full voice-overs) as one such issue. Breakthrough thought that gamers playing something like *Garage Inc.* wouldn't want cutscenes, and TransGaming had already created them. As a result, the iPhone version has no cutscenes, whereas every other version of the game (including the iPad version) does.

Statistics

- **Development time:** 9 months
- **Number of people working on the game:** 10
- **Times downloaded across all platforms:** 500,000

Fun Facts

- The character "Many" is based on the summer student (Amanda) who worked for TransGaming.
- TransGaming has handled the Mac ports of numerous big-name games like *Dragon Age II*, *FIFA Soccer 12*, and *The Sims: Medieval*.

TransGaming was worried that it was taking too big of a risk by reworking a traditionally female-focused genre for a male audience. "It could have spelled disaster," says Kawczynski. Luckily, the risk paid off. *Garage Inc.* has sold about 500,000 units across all available platforms, enabling TransGaming to enter its next project with increased confidence (and funding).

Geared

Platform: iPhone/iPod Touch (iPad version available separately)
Price: $2.99
Developer: Bryan Mitchell
Released: August 8, 2009

What Is It?

In each level of *Geared*, players are confronted with a number of different stationary gears. Your goal is to get those gears moving. Luckily, there's always one gear in the level that is already moving, and you can use it to power the others.

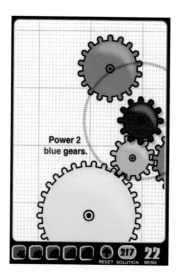

In your toolbox you'll have access to a variety of different-sized gears, and you'll have to drop these into the environment carefully to connect all of the gears in the level together. Sometimes that can be pretty tricky, and often you'll have to do some experimentation to figure out which order you should follow to make everything connect and work properly. This only gets more challenging as you progress: each level requires you to be a bit more precise than the previous one with the placement of your gears, and as you go along new puzzle elements are added in (like one that prevents you from placing gears on certain parts of the screen).

Geared is a single-player game, but it's well suited to collaborative gameplay. I've pulled out *Geared* on my iPad several times when among friends and had hours of fun as everyone in the group leaned over the device and made suggestions about how to solve a puzzle. In this way it's a lot like Valve's *Portal* series (although admittedly *Geared* is much simpler than that mind-bending game).

Behind the Game

Bryan Mitchell's father is the owner of a construction company called Omnibuilt. In April of 2009, both Bryan and his brother were working for the company when his brother had the idea to create a game for the App Store. Although Bryan had attended a high school with an emphasis on computer science, he hadn't done much programming in the five years since then. As such, he had no experience with Objective C or Open GL, the languages that iPhone games run on.

Bryan's brother offered him about one week's pay ($500) to create the game for him. In return for his initial investment, they agreed on a 50-50 split of the proceeds generated by sales of the game.

Bryan enjoyed working closely with his father and brother, but was happy to leave the 120-degree, non-air-conditioned buildings of the construction site behind. His father was enthusiastic about the idea, so he allowed Bryan to spend his workweeks in the company offices, where Bryan could concentrate on creating the game.

After about seven weeks, Bryan had refamiliarized himself with the basics of programming and completed his first game: *Spaceballs*, which was essentially an outer-space take on PopCap's popular *Zuma* series. It was a difficult process, especially since Bryan had never completed a game before. "I was determined to get it done," he says.

Sales of *Spaceballs* looked promising at first, but the game quickly dropped off the charts and out of view of consumers. "We made something like $80 the first day it was released," says Mitchell. "That really excited us. But by the next day it had dropped to $40. Then $20. And eventually it was doing only a couple of sales a day."

Disheartened, Bryan went back to working for his father, but kept spending the occasional night working on apps. His brother still believed that the app thing could go somewhere, so they retained their original agreement for the next couple of games and apps that Bryan created, with his brother investing a few hundred dollars in return for a 50% revenue share.

The next game Bryan created was also a sales flop, and he began to see his hobby as a way to pass the time rather than a viable profit model. "I no longer saw a potential there for success," Bryan says. "And that's when I made the biggest mistake I ever made, and hopefully will ever make."

> **Statistics**
> - **Total number of downloads for *Geared* (including free days):** 6,000,000
> - **Profits generated by *Geared*:** $500,000
> - **Budget for *Geared 2*:** $50,000

Bryan needed money for rent, so he asked a friend to invest some money. None of his games had generated more than a couple hundred dollars at that point, but one friend was willing to invest $200 in exchange for a 10% stake in the game he was currently working on. That game was called *Geared*.

Near the end of July of 2009, Bryan submitted *Geared* to Apple for approval. Once approved, the game made $300 on its first day, and continued to make similar amounts for the next week. Bryan only received 40% of the revenue, but he was making more from the game than he was from his day job at the construction company.

Bryan got a $1,250 loan from his father and used the money to buy advertising for *Geared* in the form of banner ads on TouchArcade.com. At the end of that week, Touch Arcade reviewed the game and Apple featured the game in its "What's Hot" list on iTunes. Immediately afterwards, *Geared* shot to the number one position and began making as much as $12,000 every day.

Everyone was happy, but Bryan's relationship with the friend who had invested $200 began to break down. They began to fight when it was revealed that the friend hadn't made any effort to tell friends or coworkers about *Geared*. Bryan argued that the friend should have been more invested in the project, and the friend reasoned that he wasn't required to do anything according to the contract the two had written up and signed. "That's when our relationship fell apart and all communication ceased," Bryan says.

The friend eventually filed a lawsuit stating that the agreed-upon percentage of profits wasn't being paid to him, beginning a complicated legal process that lasted for over a year. The lawsuit has since been resolved, and Bryan cautiously states that he's not allowed to say any more about the matter. "I still feel very taken advantage of, but at least it's all over," he says. "It's a mistake to learn from, and we're all moving forward."

For *Geared 2*, Bryan estimates that he invested about ten times as much money into advertising, but got less out of it than he did for the $1,250 he put towards marketing the first game. "When you advertise, you're really just advertising to Apple," he reasons. "It's like a big 'Hey Apple, please love my game!' If they do, you're gold."

Fun Facts

- The original name for *Geared* was *Gears*. Bryan didn't change the name until he began the submission process and saw that *Gears* was already taken.

- Bryan says that the artwork in *Geared* has changed in "almost every update." He has slowly polished and improved it over time.

- In Bryan's first iOS game, *Spaceballs*, players can unlock all the game modes by alternately tapping on the two top corners of the main menu.

- Other apps by Bryan Mitchell include *Anthronome: Tap Challenge* and *Geared 2*.

Godville

Platform: iPad/iPhone/iPod Touch (universal app)
Price: Free
Developer: Godville
Released: July 18, 2010

What Is It?

In *Godville*, you're given the ability to create a single "hero"—a stock medieval adventurer with a lust for loot and quests—and then monitor that hero's progress by reading his diary, which is essentially a Twitter feed. The diary is regularly updated with commentary from the hero as he goes on quests, haggles with traders, and spends a shocking amount of time in pubs. It's a strange, original genre that the game's developers call a zero-player game.

As a player, your interaction with your hero is relatively limited. You can use "god power" to encourage or punish your hero for the actions he takes on his own, although the results of your influence can vary wildly. If your hero writes in his diary that he has entered battle with a monster and taken damage, encouraging him may allow him to recover some of his health. At other times, encouraging him might only cause a flower to sprout up next to him.

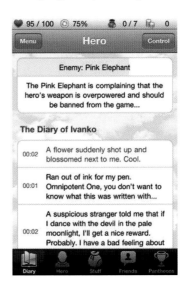

Since most of the events, diary entries, and items in *Godville* are player-created, the game is often pretty hilarious. Updates that I've encountered include gems like "Rescued a rabbit. Had a nice dinner," and the more elaborate and referential "Came across a bunch of flamboyant vampires arguing over some underage girl with a few overgrown wolves. Looked like a lame show, kept walking."

Godville barely qualifies as a game, but the hive mind of players contributing to it has made it into one of the funniest interactive experiences on any handheld.

Behind the Game

Dmitry Kosinov and Mikhail Platov wanted to create a zero-player game, or a game with no actual gameplay. Admittedly, this is a small genre. Kosinov and Platov name *Progress Quest* (another free-to-play, online ZPG) as the title that made them aware of the existence of such games. *Progress Quest* got them thinking—they could make their own ZPG if they wanted. Other games in the genre weren't very good, so it wouldn't be an entirely difficult task. "We were slowly nurturing various ideas," says Kosinov. "And in 2007 we finally felt ready to give it a try."

> ### Statistics
> - **Development time:** 4 years and continuing
> - **Total budget:** Living expenses
> - **Times downloaded:** Over 100,000

Both men had a shared love for Terry Pratchett's book *Small Gods*, which is a comedic, fictional look at organized religion. In the book, there are just as many gods as there are people, and these gods are easily angered. The central theme of the book asks, what happens when belief in God is replaced by mere religious ritual?

Kosinov and Platov wanted *Godville* to be set in a similar universe, where each player worked as a "small god," each with his or her very own follower. The concept of playing as a god who had a very small influence on the world struck the duo as something that would fit perfectly with a ZPG, so development on *Godville* began.

The first version of the game was entirely in Russian (the native language of both men) and was available exclusively as a web browser. The game continued to exist in this state for a couple of years, but eventually the team was approached by a group of English-speaking Russians who volunteered to help with translation duties.

A couple of months later, GodvilleGame.com was live. An iPhone and iPad version soon followed, and an influx of English players and contributors flooded the *Godville* servers.

One thing I asked the team about was the game's name, which makes it appear to be a clone of one of Zynga's many "ville" games (*FarmVille*, *CityVille*, etc.). Kosinov was quick to remind me that Zynga is a fairly young company. "Back in 2007 when we released our first version, there were no *FarmVille* or other 'ville' games," says Kosinov. "We chose the name mainly for two reasons: it explains the idea of the game, and it just sounds good in both Russian and English."

In July of 2010, three years after work on the game had begun, an iOS version of the game was ready to launch. This opened it up to an entirely new audience of mobile gamers.

As *Godville* began to attract more and more players, Kosinov and Platov began to worry about how they would be able to afford the server fees. "We started this project for fun," admitted Platov. "All of our friends were saying that we'd never break even with it."

Their friends had a point. The game was free to play and had no advertising to speak of, so the team needed to develop some sort of profit model. When I interviewed the team for GamePro.com in 2010, they didn't seem thrilled by the prospect of introducing ads to the game. "*Godville* has never been ad-supported and we hope it will never be," Platov told me.

Eventually, things reached a point where the two men had to purchase more servers to keep the game functioning. They decided to introduce a donations button that players could use to support operational costs. Some players did indeed donate, but it wasn't enough to make the game sustainable.

After a bit of thought, Kosinov and Platov stumbled upon a solution. They added an option to purchase "charges" (with real money) that replenish players' ability to use their god powers. It was an elegant solution, because it doesn't interfere with a player's gameplay experience in any way, and at the same time it's easily accessible if a player happens to be in a spending mood. "We're still considering them as a way for players to show their gratitude to the project," says Platov.

The introduction of in-app purchases was a success; Kosinov and Platov were able to hire another person to keep the game's Android version up-to-date. Although they say they're not swimming in money, they now feel confident that they'll have the ability to continue working on the project without fear of having to shut things down on a moment's notice. "We can't wait to see how everyone will react to the things we have up our sleeves," says Kosinov.

Halcyon

Platform: iPad only
Price: $1.99
Developer: Zach Gage
Released: November 23, 2010

What Is It?

Halcyon doesn't look like much; one glance at the screenshot below might lead you to believe that the game is nothing more than lifeless lines and arrows plastered on a screen. In actuality, it's a surprisingly rich twitch-action game: arrows come in from the side of the screen and your job is to use lines drawn with your finger to connect and direct same-colored arrows towards each other. So, for example, if a purple arrow is flying in from the top line and another purple arrow flies in from the opposite direction on the bottom line, you'll want to draw a line connecting the top arrow to any part of the bottom line. As soon as you do, that top arrow will rocket across the screen on the line you've just drawn and slam into the other purple arrow, destroying both of them.

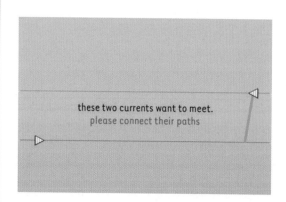

these two currents want to meet.
please connect their paths

In order to win, you'll want to prevent arrows of different colors from hitting each other. As the game's pace picks up, dozens of arrows will fill the screen. Arrows on a crash course with different-colored arrows will light up red, like the planes in *Flight Control* do when they're in danger of colliding.

Halcyon is really a test of reflexes more than anything else, but it works because it keeps you engaged. Music is also a big part of *Halcyon*, because when the arrows collide, they strike a note. Since many arrows collide in rapid succession, you'll actually create a make-shift song. On top of this, each level is intentionally designed to look like a harp, so when you run your finger across the screen to draw a line you'll pluck the virtual strings and create other notes. All of these elements combine to make the game a calming, musical experience.

Halcyon is one of my favorite examples of a game that couldn't be done on any platform other than the iPad. Given the speed and precision that the game demands, drawing the lines with a mouse would be nearly impossible—it's a testament to some of the unique things that are possible with a touch interface.

Behind the Game

Zach Gage is an artist who focuses on the relationship between people and technology. This has manifested itself in a number of different ways. One program that Gage has created is called *Can We Talk?*. It's a chat program for having serious conversations.

In the tutorial video for *Can We Talk?* Gage explains that chat has never been perfect for having serious conversations because it's hard to tell if the other person is paying attention to the screen. *Can We Talk?* records whether users are looking at the screen and whether they've covered the chat with another window. This information is relayed to the other person, so each user knows whether messages are being ignored or simply haven't been read yet. "Being born in 1985, I was around just before the massive public adoption of the Internet, and my adolescence mirrored the adolescence of the Internet as it related to public culture," Gage explains.

Gage notes that in recent years, people have begun to spend significant portions of their lives online. "Most of my conceptual art focuses on what this means," he says. In short, his biggest interest is examining the "strange rules" that govern online communication. He's a sociologist for the 21st century. Gage's interest in rule systems carries over and mixes with his passion for creating games. "Instead of finding strange systems to explore and manipulate, I create them," he says. "Instead of making their way through a story, in my games, players (hopefully) learn a small set of rules and then discover how limitlessly those rules can be applied, given the right amount of skill and time."

When Gage bought an iPad, he says he was floored by the device. He sees it as "what laptops were meant to be" and believes that in just a few years people will be using tablets as replacements for their regular computers. "I knew I had to make a game on it," he says. "But what?"

Gage first experimented with making a *Pong*-style two-player game, but wasn't satisfied with that prototype. His next attempt was another two-player game where players built bases and launched missiles at their opponents' bases. "That week, Erik Svedäng released *Shot Shot Shoot*, and I realized he had absolutely nailed the game I was trying to make," Gage says. "It was very sad, but also really wonderful, and I played the hell out of his game."

The night after Gage purchased and played *Shot Shot Shoot*, he lay in bed thinking about how Svedäng's game is about shooting missiles and getting them around your opponent's missiles. "I woke up with the idea for *Halcyon*, fully formed, built it in three hours, and discovered that it totally worked," Gage says.

According to Gage, *Halcyon* is an inversion of the gameplay in *Shot Shot Shoot*. Unlike Svedäng's game, missiles in *Halycon* only appear in a set number of spots, and players need to guide them into each other to succeed.

Gage also likes to think of his game as a hybrid between *Flight Control* and *Tetris*. At first, this sounds like a confusing juxtaposition, but it's a fair comparison. *Flight Control* is about guiding small objects into certain positions on a map, using lines drawn by players' fingers. *Halcyon* takes that concept and applies it to a playing field that has a limited number of rows, just like *Tetris*. "*Tetris* severely limits the amount of options the player has for the moment, but that allows a huge increase in the amount of thinking you can force the player to do about the state of the field," Gage says. "*Halcyon* limits the field in a similar way."

After spending three hours creating the prototype for *Halcyon*, Gage gathered his things and went over to the home of Kurt Bieg, a close friend and talented sound engineer. Gage had already added notes to each of the strings, so he and Bieg spent the rest of the day discussing how to fit a complex, interesting musical system into *Halcyon*. "We actually got something real close to the final version done that evening."

Although Bieg and Gage were able to create a game in a matter of days that was close to the 1.0 release of *Halcyon*, they spent the next couple of months tweaking difficulty and sound samples in the game so it would be perfect on the day of its release.

Gage half-jokingly calls the game a "really temperamental beast." Gage adds, "Looking back, it's hard to believe how fast it all happened."

Hand of Greed

Platform: iPhone/iPod Touch (iPad version available separately)
Price: $.99
Developer: Brainium Studios
Publisher: Appular
Released: April 23, 2010

What Is It?

Hand of Greed is a game that's completely focused on challenging your sense of timing and the nimbleness of your fingers. The game stars you as a master thief, and in each level you're confronted with a single-screen area filled with spinning blades, saws, and other pointy objects that might cause harm to a would-be thief. Just underneath this wall of sharp objects there reside numerous gold nuggets and gems, which you can pick up with a single touch. Your job is to figure out the patterns of the moving blades so you can slip a finger in at just the right moment and retrieve your reward without getting sliced, chopped, or otherwise mutilated.

As time goes on, more dangerous and complex traps get added into the mix and things become extremely difficult. Also, players are penalized for taking too long to collect all of the loot on the screen, providing an incentive to keep players tapping as quickly as possible.

You'll almost want to cringe whenever you do mess up and touch one of the blades in *Hand of Greed*, thanks to the powerful audio and visuals that depict virtual blood squirting from your finger. The effects do an excellent job of keeping you on edge the entire time you're playing, and after a long session you may find yourself just as tense as you would have been if your fingers actually were in danger of getting cut.

Despite its casual, twitch style, *Hand of Greed* is one of the hardest games on the iPhone. If all robberies were this dangerous, the prison system would host a lot more fingerless criminals.

Behind the Game

Farhad Shakiba and Jake Brownson met while in college. Shakiba, who had moved to the United States from Iran during his teenage years, says that he and Brownson had wanted to start a business together for years before finally opening Brainium Studios in 2008.

With Shakiba's artistic abilities and Brownson's programming know-how, Brainium had an early hit on the App Store with *Jumbline*, a word game that challenges players to create words with a pile of jumbled-up letter blocks. With one success under its belt, Brainium Studios was making enough money to support itself, and Shakiba and Brownson were motivated to begin their next project.

Shakiba spent a lot of time dreaming up fun and interesting ways to interact with the iPhone's touch screen. From the start, Brainium made it a policy to make games well suited to the touch screen—that meant no virtual joysticks or clumsy on-screen buttons. "I am a visual guy and ideas generally come to me as a moving vision of the final implementation," Shakiba explains. "I imagined a game where the user would have to touch the screen while avoiding moving and spinning blades. It was as simple as that." Shakiba kept the idea in the back of his mind, but he had trouble thinking of ways to build an entire game around such a simple mechanic.

> ### Statistics
> - **Development time:** 7 months
> - **Number of times Shakiba played and failed level 3-1 before deciding to lower the difficulty level:** 159
> - **Times downloaded:** 100,000+

Soon after thinking of the blade idea, Shakiba and Brownson began discussing plans for their next project, which they decided they wanted to complete within a relatively quick development cycle. They had exceeded their projected time frame with *Jumbline*, so they wanted to create a game in under a month, if possible.

Shakiba mentioned the spinning-blades idea to Brownson and he loved it, but encouraged Shakiba to think of ways to turn it into a full-game concept. It all came to him one morning while taking a shower. "The thought popped in my mind, that the blades should spin over a ground covered with gems," he says. "The game would be called *Hand of Greed* because you'd be role-playing an individual partaking in the act of being greedy and picking up riches endlessly." Shakiba was immensely satisfied with the idea, sold Brownson on it, and *Hand of Greed* was born.

It didn't take long for Brainium Studios to realize that its one-month development cycle simply wouldn't be possible. The two men agreed that they should spend extra time developing the game's visual style so that it would stand out from other games in the App Store, and so that its setting would make sense for the mechanic. Shakiba says they could have taken the easy route by slapping on doodle graphics, but they wanted to create an immersive experience that added weight and meaning to the potentially mindless task of touching jewels on the game board. These weren't the only things that took up more time than the team had planned for. "We spent a lot of time trying to make the game menus interesting," admits Shakiba. "I'm not sure that was a good business decision."

By the time *Hand of Greed* made it to the App Store, it had been in development for nearly eight months. Shakiba and Brownson had created the game they wanted, but it had come with its fair share of trials. "I can safely say that I was both emotionally and mentally exhausted in the last half of the project," Shakiba says. "It really felt like running those last few miles on a long run, on a steep uphill slope."

One of the biggest challenges that the developers faced while creating the game was adjusting the level of difficulty. Shakiba became so good at the game that he lost perspective on how it would play for newcomers, and Brainium ended up hiring a team of testers to help with the fine-tuning. Shakiba says he suspects that without the adjustments Brainium made in response to tester feedback, less than 5% of *Hand of Greed* players would have made it past the fifth level.

> ### Fun Facts
>
> - *Hand of Greed* was originally going to include boss battles against special blades, but they weren't incorporated due to time constraints.
> - Shakiba says that the feel of *Hand of Greed* was greatly influenced by 1990s PC hits like *Baldur's Gate* and *Planescape Torment*.
> - The hand in the main menu is a heavily processed picture of Shakiba's hand.
> - Other apps by Brainium Studios include *Jumbline 2* **and** *Wordsearch Star.*

Hard Lines

Platform: iPad/iPhone/iPod Touch (universal app)
Price: $.99
Developer: Spilt Milk Studios
Released: June 8, 2011

What Is It?

In *Hard Lines*, you control a snake-like character represented by a single, one-pixel-thick line, directing its movements by swiping up, down, left, or right. In many cases you're out to destroy other lines by cutting ahead of them and forcing them to run into you. As in the megapopular Nokia cell-phone game that we all know and love, you can die either by running into the wall or by running into your own body. It's the same here, but in this game you'll most likely die by running into other lines because the arenas are generally big enough so that you can avoid walls.

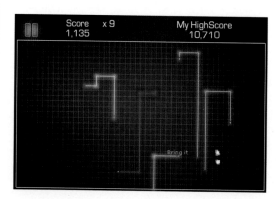

Hard Lines is chock-full of modes. The one called "Snake" works exactly as you might expect: you run around the map picking up "glowy things" (that's what the game calls them) that make your body longer, while—you know the drill—refraining from running into yourself or the walls. "Deadline" is a timed mode in which you grow as much as you can while avoiding other snakes within three minutes. "Time Attack" is a similar mode in which you have to keep grabbing points in order to live longer and extend the time on the clock. In "Gauntlet," dozens upon dozens of lines stream out from the sides of the screen endlessly, and your goal is to survive for as long as possible. "Piñata" is probably the most interesting mode of the bunch, largely because of its emphasis on killing other snakes and grabbing the delicious bits that pop out of their bodies to make yourself longer and to gain points.

The game's presentation is extremely simple due to the fact that all of the on-screen characters are lines, but it still manages to look good thanks to the *TRON*-inspired neon look that Spilt Milk Studios went with. Despite the minimalist visual design, each of the lines in *Hard Lines* has a surprising amount of character: your line and the lines around you constantly spout quips, taunts, and references to pop culture as you battle it out. Much of this is little more than random babbling, but sometimes the lines are pretty funny, particularly in single-player modes like "Snake," in which your line will launch into amusing monologues about subjects like the origin of strawberry milk.

Behind the Game

Hard Lines began out of a discussion between friends about the quality (or lack thereof) of the new *TRON* movie—Andrew Smith liked the movie, but Nicoll Hunt didn't. Their tastes in movies mightn't have aligned, but both agreed that the official *TRON* iPhone game didn't live up to its potential. "Fiddly controls, pointless objectives, and messy graphics ruined what could've been a fun little arcade game," Smith says.

Smith suggested that they could do a better job of making a *TRON*-style game based on the light-cycle segments of the movie, and with that, work began on what Smith and Hunt affectionately called Project #2. The two laid out the basics of what they wanted the game to be, including bikes with tails, collisions with walls, and AI-controlled competitors. Hunt then downloaded a free game engine, Cocos2D, which let him create a working version of the game in just four hours. The men agreed to a 50-50 split for proceeds from the game.

In the game's earliest stages, two buttons (one to turn right and one to turn left) controlled a player's line. Smith and Hunt were quite happy with this control method, but found that testers were often confused by it, since the turning was dependent on the direction their line was facing. The team then implemented a tap-based control scheme. "Tap in the top half of the screen, it'll move up," explains Smith. "Tap in the left half, it'll move left, etc."

This solution didn't work either. Players who were used to gaming on the iPhone would try to swipe at the screen and become confused by the nonresponsive controls. Smith and Hunt began to think about implementing a tutorial system. They argued over how best to handle the tutorial and weren't satisfied by any of their ideas. Suddenly it hit them: why not have the lines talk to the players? "Likely quite high on mutual congratulation, we thought it was the best idea ever, implemented it, and immediately forgot the whole point of the system," says Smith. "Rather than specifically help the player, we just made the lines say fun things."

Smith and Hunt began to pack short lines of dialogue into the game. Snarky comments, bad jokes, pop-culture references, and (of course) tips to help players with the game were stuffed in by the dozens, turning the game into something much more than a simple arcade experience. "All of a sudden [it] went from an addictive, but dry, score-chasing game to something brimming with character and incidental humor," says Smith. "This was a huge success, and something we planned on exploiting to its fullest."

The true potential of including dialogue in the game began to reveal itself to Smith. "The biggest single effect on the game is that it has an immediate appeal to more casual players, drawing them in and extending the period of play they're willing to spend on it," he notes. "If they play for the humor and the fun of these little characters, and then pay (or stay) for the score chasing, then we've really hit on something."

Recognizing the need for more player feedback, Spilt Milk Studios advertised a first-come, first-serve beta on its Twitter account. The account had around 500 followers at the time, and 30 of those signed up for the beta. Smith and Hunt built a version of the game with stat-tracking features built in and sent it out to their test audience. Feedback was largely positive with some users raving about the game on their own Twitter accounts. "It was really morale-boosting and encouraging that complete strangers with no investment in the project would so enthusiastically talk about our game all of a sudden," says Smith.

As development on *Hard Lines* began to wrap up, Smith started thinking about ways to spark more interest in the game. He liked the idea of hosting a preview event for the game and emailed all of the beta testers and journalists who he thought might be interested in it.

On the day of the big preview event, eight or nine people showed up, none of whom were journalists. "Not bad, to be honest, though a tiny piece of me wanted it to be a surprising success," admits Smith.

It could hardly be called a crowd, but Smith says it was a day full of good times, and he was able to gather a lot of helpful feedback. The big event of the day was a *Hard Lines* tournament held later in the afternoon. By then, only four of the attendees were still hanging around, but they happily participated in a best-of-three challenge. The winner of the tournament was

---

Statistics

- **Development time:** 2 months
- **Total budget:** $1,600
- **Times downloaded:** 22,000

Fun Facts

- Spilt Milk Studios came up with 44 other potential names, including gems like *Angry Lines*, before settling on *Hard Lines*.
- You can read an incredibly lengthy dev diary (over 13,000 words!) by Andrew Smith about *Hard Lines'* creation on GamesBrief.com.
- Smith says that positive reviews of his game on major websites (like SlidetoPlay.com, TouchArcade.com, and Eurogamer.com) had almost no effect on his sales.
- Other apps by Spilt Milk Studios include *ContractorCalculator* and *Crunch – The Game*.

Joe Shepard, and he was awarded a hug and a glass of champagne. "That's how we roll," explains Smith.

Despite having lots of contacts with the press, *Hard Lines* wasn't entirely successful right out of the gate. The game sold only a few hundred copies in its first week, and it took getting featured by Apple to give it the motivation it needed to make it into the top charts. The iPad version of the game now has a (surprisingly awesome) "HD EXTREME" mode that can be bought from within the app—it increases the size of the arenas by four times, and Spilt Milk Studios hopes to make a little extra cash from sales of the mode (which can be bought for $1.99).

Helsing's Fire

Platform: iPhone/iPod Touch (iPad version available separately)
Price: $.99
Developer: Ratloop
Publisher: Clickgamer
Released: July 11, 2010

What Is It?

In each level of *Helsing's Fire* you'll help Dr. Helsing and his jovial associate Rafton destroy monsters using the power of light. Players can place torches in any area to immediately

flood the level with light, but light can't pass through solid objects, so some parts of the environment will remain dark. To get around this, you'll have to use multiple torches to make sure all of the baddies are properly brightened.

You're given a limited number of potions so that you can destroy the enemies you've illuminated. For instance, if you light up a blue bad guy with a torch, you'll want to then activate one of your blue potions to take him out (or at least damage him, if he has armor). In almost every level, the goal is to take out all of the enemies without harming innocent civilians who sometimes populate levels.

The lighting system in *Helsing's Fire* is so well done that it's fun just to move torches around to see how the light plays on the environment's nooks and crannies. I wouldn't go so far as to call it realistic (because of the cartoonish style of the game), but it looks great. It's really satisfying to figure out the exact spot where a torch will light up all of the enemies of a certain color, allowing you to take them out with one well-placed potion.

The light mechanic is not just reserved for levels with stationary enemies; some of the boss-battle stages pose challenges unlike anything else in the game. These boss monsters often move around, requiring you to use your torches in ways you normally wouldn't; I often found myself looking forward to the next one just to see what Ratloop would throw at me next.

Helsing's Fire is lent an interesting personality thanks to both the strange art style and hilarious characters. Dr. Helsing and Raffton both embody a sort of comedic Sherlock Holmes vibe that makes the between-level dialogue something you'll actually look forward to reading.

Helsing's Fire is a total package as far as puzzle games go. Everything—the art, the dialogue, and the puzzles themselves—is so incredibly inventive that it makes other puzzle games look bad by comparison.

Behind the Game

It was 2009, and Lucas and Keiko Pope had recently moved to Japan from LA, both leaving behind jobs in the games industry. Lucas had worked as a programmer on *Uncharted 2*, and Keiko was a programmer at Zindagi Games, creators of Sony's *Sports Champions* franchise. The husband-and-wife team had created games together before, and shortly after their move to Japan they decided to look into the iPhone as a platform for a new project.

The few months that followed saw Lucas goofing around in Xcode, Apple's software-development program. Lucas came up with a prototype for a game about dodging traffic, but it never developed into anything. While he was working, however, he thought of an idea that would allow him to create a simple shadow-casting mechanic in a game.

From there, the game entered what Lucas calls phase one of development. He made a prototype of a game called *Castle in Shadow*, which he describes as being similar to a roguelike. "The idea was that you were a lone wizard called to aid the king in his castle as it's being overrun by monsters," says Lucas. "You approach the castle from afar, wiping out the enemy army one square at a time. Light up the color-coded enemies, then drink a potion to send a shock wave from the light source that damages like-colored monsters."

At this point, Lucas was working on the game by himself. He attended a Japanese language school for a few hours each day, while Keiko worked at a programming job she had found (which was, unfortunately, a three-hour commute from the Pope home).

Lucas continued to work on the game and slowly refined it to become less like an action-packed roguelike. Roguelikes are often about dealing with lots of randomly generated enemies at once, and that wasn't conducive to the style of gameplay that Lucas had hoped to create. "I realized that what I was creating was too shallow," he says. "The players were getting too much gold and could buy all the potions they wanted. If you missed with a potion, or used the wrong one, it was no big deal; you could always buy more."

Lucas turned the game into a slower paced puzzle game in which enemy positions were fixed and a limited number of potions were available to the player. "Bingo," says Lucas. "The game became way more fun now that you were presented with a clear win/fail condition. And solving a puzzle requires constantly moving the light around to see how the shadows cast, which reinforces the unique look and feel of the game." From a mechanical perspective, the game was beginning to resemble the *Helsing's Fire* that we know today, but its visual style had not yet been refined.

Lucas attended GDC 2010 in San Francisco and met up with a few of his old coworkers from Naughty Dog. He got lots of positive feedback about the gameplay, but nobody was very excited about the way the game looked. "You should add graphics," commented one particularly snarky ex-coworker.

Lucas became more confident about his overall idea, and Keiko left her programming job to help him work on the game. Work on the game continued, the art style improved, but Lucas began to worry about how to market the game. "Even though our original plan was to self-publish, the App Store was no longer the free-for-all utopia that it started as," says Lucas. "There was some stat floating around that 80 new games are released every day in the App Store."

This frightened the Popes, and they began searching for a publisher. One deal fell through, and subsequently they contacted Chillingo, who loved the game's concept but also offered some valuable criticism. Lucas recalls that Chillingo's people hated the first enemy in the game, a slime who "just sits there and gets killed," in Lucas' words. "He looked like s——," says Lucas. "Literally like a piece of s——." Lucas fought the feedback initially, but ultimately decided that the publisher was right. "Looking back now, I don't know how I ever settled for that slime," he says. "Thanks, Chillingo."

Upon release, *Helsing's Fire* appeared to be a success. The game was riding strong at the top of the strategy and puzzle charts, and it was number eight overall on the US Top Apps list. "And then it fell, fell, fell," says Lucas. "Slowly at first, then quickly."

Ratloop released several updates, each adding features, new content, and vital bug fixes. Updates resulted in small sales spikes, but they weren't enough to keep the game on the top charts.

Lucas claims that he and Keiko aren't done with *Helsing's Fire*. They have numerous ideas for the game, but want to create something that's inherently different from the

30-second puzzles the game is currently based on. "Maybe [we'll make it] into something more RPG-like," muses Lucas. "Or maybe we'll wrap around back to the beginning and make it more action-based."

Hook Champ

Platform: iPhone/iPod Touch
Price: $2.99
Developer: Rocketcat Games
Released: October 16, 2009

What Is It?

Hook Champ is the first in a trilogy of titles from Rocketcat Games, all of which revolve around the concept of using a grappling hook to navigate a two-dimensional, side-scrolling environment. In *Hook Champ* you'll have to grapple and swing your way through a number a dungeons using your hook, which is unleashed by a simple tap on the upper area of the screen.

Hook Champ is all about momentum. You'll want to time your jumps so that you get as much forward momentum as possible from your swings, and then use equally good judgment to decide where to place your next hook. As you progress you'll unlock improvements for all of your equipment—including rocket boots (useful for launching yourself out of deadly situations), better grappling hooks, and even guns that can be used to blast through certain types of obstacles.

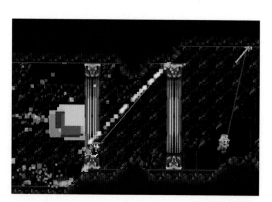

Improving your completion times for individual levels is a big part of the strategy—faster times allow you to get more coins, which in turn allows you to improve your equipment, which completes the loop by helping to improve your completion times.

Hook Champ benefits a lot from its humor, which reveals itself in the little bits of dialogue at the beginning of each level. The banter between characters and goofy unlockable costumes give the game a lighthearted vibe that feels like an extra-sarcastic *Indiana Jones* adventure, which is helpful in infusing a bit of a unique flavor into an otherwise traditional-looking pixel-art game.

Sometimes levels in *Hook Champ* kill you with obstacles that you couldn't have foreseen, but that's why the game has been designed to accomodate multiple playthroughs—to help you progress. In some ways its high-difficulty level feels like an attempt to mask its short length, but most players will appreciate the challenge and get a solid amount of replay value out of the levels.

Behind the Game

Kepa Auwae was fed up with mainstream gaming. He saw a developing trend in which mainstream games were getting steadily less innovative: everything was becoming more focused on "grinding" against enemies in repetitive battles, yet budgets continued to soar. "We saw a future where eventually all games would be designed to basically be just joyless, part-time jobs," says Auwae. "Jobs that offer 15-dollar micropayments that let you skip content so you can get right to the achievements."

Despite having never developed a game before, Auwae got together with two friends he had met while on an IRC chat channel (Jeremy Orlando, a programmer, and Brandon Rhodes, the team's artist) and formed Rocketcat Games, a team made up of people who lived in three different places (Washington, Arizona, and Japan), and who all had full-time jobs to worry about. It wasn't the strongest start, but the team had raw, cynical determination on their side.

Platformers constitute a genre that requires incredibly precise controls: players need to be able to make tiny changes in their movements at any given moment, so access to physical buttons is vital to these games' control schemes. That is obviously something the iPhone is unable to provide. Kepa Auwae of Rocketcat Games recognized this, and set about thinking of alternate ways to handle jumping in a platformer.

Auwae and his team experimented with a number of different options like flight, gravity-flipping, and explosive propulsion, but settled on a grappling hook for the superior control experience it offered. "Instead of jumping and then having to control your horizontal movement with arrow buttons and your second hand, we went for a hold-to-launch, release-to-let-go hook-mechanic," says Auwae. "This moved the 'jump' controls from tactile buttons to a mixture of visual cues and rhythm."

Development on *Hook Champ* had begun before *Canabalt* had popularized the "automatic-running" genre, so the team was determined to allow players to have some level of control over the movement. They wanted most of the game to be about swinging, but also wanted to give players the option to run slowly along the ground should they get caught in a sticky situation. "The other team members said that just having most of the game be automated, except for one or two functions, would be too boring," says Auwae. "How young and idealistic we were back then!"

Hook Champ was released in October of 2009 and became a success in its own right. Its sequel, *Super QuickHook*, was the highest-rated iOS game of 2010 according to Metacritic.com. The third game in the series, *Hook Worlds*, also received rave reviews. The three members of Rocketcat Games were able to quit their jobs and become full-time game developers, and they've already released an action-RPG called *Mage Gauntlet* that they say is the start of a new trilogy.

Throughout our interview, Auwae's cynicism (he prefers to call it "realism") about the games industry was all too apparent. He was eager to lay out his thoughts about the sales environment in the App Store, going so far as to lay out a list of three strategies that he believes makes iOS games successful.

The first strategy he suggests involves creating a low-budget, cartoonish game that emulates *Cut the Rope* in as many ways as possible. "Ideally you want the puzzles to mostly rely on blind luck but give an impression of skill," Auwae says. "Make the game 99 cents. Cross your fingers. Sorry if that sounds cynical, but imitating trends is profitable and extremely cost-effective; that's why so very many people do it."

The second strategy involves making lots of mediocre games. He calls this strategy "flooding the market," and notes that although it isn't as effective as it once was, he still sees it work on occasion. "Never forget that the App Store charts are based off popularity, not quality," he says.

The third and final option Auwae gives to aspiring developers isn't nearly as cynical as the first two. "Make the best game you can," he says. "Treat all your titles as niche games, and assume that they have some low cap of possible total sales. Due to this, price your games accordingly. Don't try to compete with 99-cent titles if you think your game is worth three dollars. If you tried, it would just mean you'd get a third of the money."

This seems to fly in the face of the advice that many other developers gave me, but it's working out relatively well for Auwae and his team. They're doing very well financially, and they've created a strong fan base that will gladly gobble up whatever innovative title they pump out next.

Statistics

- **Development time:** 8 months
- **Total budget:** $0
- **Times downloaded:** 50,000

Fun Facts

- The first game Rocketcat Games worked on was an unreleased Flash game starring the cat that now serves as its company logo.
- *Hook Champ* was originally going to have a level editor, but then someone spelled "PENIS" using gigantic letters made of lava.
- Auwae still frequents the IRC channel where he met Brandon and Jeremy nearly 20 years ago.
- Other apps by Rocketcat Games include *Mage Gauntlet* and *Hook Worlds*.

Auwae had one last piece of advice for me to share, and I think it's an appropriate note to end on. "Becoming a game developer has given me even more appreciation for games that I consider great. Great games are extremely unlikely to exist, just based on the odds they face. When you add up human error and market reasons to avoid innovation and depth, great games really shouldn't exist at all. But they do, and they continue to get made. I have no idea how, probably some combination of dumb luck and creators who are extremely creative and driven, yet also terrible businessmen."

The Incident

Platform: iPad/iPhone/iPod Touch (universal app)
Price: $1.99
Developer: Big Bucket Software
Released: August 10, 2010

What Is It?

What if random objects started falling from the sky, crashing into the ground around you and putting you into serious danger? What would you do, especially if you were left with very little room to move to escape the incoming aerial barrage?

In *The Incident*, you'll get to answer that question. As a nondescript businessman in a shirt and tie, you'll be faced with a world bent on destroying you with a relentless torrent of stuff. Everything from household furniture to Egyptian sarcophagi stream from the sky, forcing you to tilt your iDevice while tapping the screen so you can hop and run from left to right to avoid getting splattered.

Garden gnomes. Barber-shop poles. It doesn't matter what it is; it will kill you. Luckily you can take three bashes to the head before succumbing, and you'll occasionally be able to collect coins and hearts, which can give you extra lives and restore your health. There's also a white line that appears at the top of the screen to tell you where the next object will fall from (as well as the relative size of the object), allowing players to get out of the way in time.

As objects stream down from above they'll begin to pile up into heaps, which you'll have to scale in order to avoid getting lost in the piles of garbage. Eventually the heaps rise above street level, and then above the rooftops. Soon enough you'll see mountains in the background, and after enough time you'll break through the clouds and begin to leave Earth altogether. The trick is to constantly keep moving to keep your head above the churning waves of stuff below your feet. It's difficult, but players who make it to outer space will get a nice surprise.

One of the coolest features of *The Incident* is that the iPad version allows you to export the game to your TV (assuming you have the proper equipment). If you're one of those rare people with both an iPad and an iPhone (or an iPod Touch), you can also use the smaller iOS device as a wireless controller for the iPad, even when it's in TV-mode. In essence it turns your iPad into a game console for your television, and *The Incident* looks surprisingly good with this setup—the pixel art looks great even when blown up on bigger TVs.

Behind the Game

The idea for *The Incident* came to Matt Comi out of nowhere. "I turned to a colleague and asked what he thought of a simple game where random things are falling from the sky and your job is to jump and dodge them," he says. "When you die, your score is your height." The seed had been planted in Comi's mind, and he contacted his friend Neven Mrgan who agreed that the game sounded like a good time. The two men got to work, concentrating on the game as much as they could during their spare time.

Comi and Mrgan have only seen each other face-to-face on Skype or Facetime because they live on opposite sides of the globe; Comi is from Australia, while Mrgan lives in the United States. According to Comi, this didn't turn out to be much of a hindrance. "I Internet-met Neven when he linked to my TV Forecast Dashboard Widget from his blog in 2007," he explains. "Each day, there was a window of a few hours where we were both awake. We used that time to catch up on each other's prog-

> **Statistics**
>
> - **Development time:** 9 months
> - **Number of unique items in the game:** 367

ress." Comi says that the mutual reliance on each other kept them both motivated and working on the game.

When development on *The Incident* began, Comi had a decent stream of money coming in from other apps he had created, so he decided to switch to a four-day workweek. "The whole financial-crisis thing was happening so the company I worked for was only too happy to pay me less money," he says.

Whereas most games (and indeed, many of the games in this book) are initially too ambitious and have to be scaled back as the development process evolves, *The Incident* followed a different pattern. Comi's original idea for the game didn't extend much beyond hopping up on things as they fell from the sky. Comi and Mrgan found that the prototype they created from his initial idea wasn't actually very much fun. They began to brainstorm, coming up with ideas for changing backgrounds, hazards, and collectable items.

As development on *The Incident* continued, Comi became more confident that it would be a success. He and Mrgan were continually adding new things to the game, and they weren't planning on stopping until they were convinced that the game would be fun. Comi approached his boss again and asked to work only three days a week. "He wasn't too thrilled about that," he says.

Comi and his boss agreed on a compromise: Comi could use his annual leave one day a week until he ran out of days. At that point, Comi would have to negotiate a new deal. For Comi, it was a win-win. By his estimates, *The Incident* would be complete before his leave would run out, so by the time work on it was finished he'd be able to make a decision about whether or not he wanted to remain in his job.

The Incident launched to great acclaim and big sales numbers. Dozens of major blogs like Kotaku, Gizmodo, and Engadget reviewed the game, allowing it to shoot up the charts with nearly 7,000 downloads on its first day. "The first month's sales was more than my annual salary so that made my decision to leave my day job easy," says Comi.

Sales dropped off a bit after the first month, but continual updates from Comi (including one update that added iPad support and a separate release of a Mac version) have allowed him to take Big Bucket Software into full-time indie development.

Fun Facts

- There are dozens of references to *Lost* in *The Incident*, including the number of the apartment building (815) on the first level.
- *The Incident*'s soundtrack was contributed by Cabel Sasser, one of the founders of popular Mac software developer Panic, Inc.
- Other apps by Big Bucket Software include *Pocketball* and *TV Forecast*.

Infinity Blade

Platform: iPad/iPhone/iPod Touch (universal app)
Price: $5.99
Developer: ChAIR Entertainment Group
Released: December 8, 2010

What Is It?

Infinity Blade is the game you show to your friends whenever they express doubt about the validity of the iPhone as a valid games platform. The graphics are so ridiculously good that its creators couldn't wait to show the world, so they put out a free tech demo to showcase the Unreal Engine's incredible lighting and textural effects months before *Infinity Blade* was released (you can find it on the iTunes Store by searching for *Epic Citadel*).

But what is it? Games journalists love to compare it to Nintendo's classic *Punch-Out!* games, but how does that formula transition to a modern game running on Unreal Engine 3 graphics? Quite well, actually.

The game is effectively a series of battles against enemies both small and large. Swiping on the screen allows you to attack with your sword, and you can also dodge and block attacks from your enemies by tapping on-screen buttons. Each enemy

attacks with a certain pattern, and you'll need to avoid attacks and then counterattack with your own slashes at the right moment to emerge victorious. There are a lot of ways to customize and upgrade your character as you advance and win more battles, and thanks to a certain plot element (no spoilers!) the game has a lot of replay value.

It's all technically on-rails, but players have the ability to collect hidden treasures in the environment with a simple tap, which ends up working in the game's favor.

Behind the Game

Donald Mustard's first foray into the games industry was with *Advent Rising*, a science-fiction epic for the PC and Xbox. *Rising* was to be the first in a planned trilogy of games, but low sales and mixed reviews prompted the game's publisher to kill that idea.

Fast-forward three years to 2008, and Donald and his brother Geremy had opened up a new game studio, ChAIR Entertainment. After releasing one positively reviewed game (an underwater shooter called *Undertow*) for Xbox Live Arcade in 2007, ChAIR was acquired by Epic Games, creators of the *Gears of War* series and the Unreal Engine. The following year saw the release of *Shadow Complex*, an Xbox Live Arcade exclusive. *Shadow Complex* shattered sales records for the Live Arcade platform, selling nearly a quarter-million copies in its first two weeks alone.

Donald Mustard describes the moment he realized the potential of the iPhone as a gaming platform. It was January of 2010, and Donald had been playing *Mass Effect 2* on his Xbox. At the same time, he had a save going in *Sword and Poker*, an iPhone game developed by GAIA Co. "I was sitting on the couch, and I finally had some time to go play a video game," he recalls. "I felt like going to play *Mass Effect*, but then realized that I wanted to play *Sword and Poker* more. That was a big moment for me; it kinda changed the way I thought about things."

Statistics

- **Development time:** 4.5 months
- **Number of people working on *Infinity Blade*:** 12
- **Net revenue generated by *Infinity Blade*:** $12,000,000

Donald began to think about what a ChAIR-developed game for the iPhone might look like. Unbeknownst to him, Epic had already put together a small team of engineers who were working on getting the Unreal Engine working on iOS devices. Soon Epic approached ChAIR and asked Donald and Geremy if they'd be interested in creating a game that could demonstrate the power of its engine on iOS. Donald says that the team decided to suspend work on its current project almost immediately and work on *Infinity Blade* instead.

ChAIR had been brainstorming ideas for a game built around one-on-one sword fighting, but the team had been thinking about making it into something for the Kinect or the Wii. The game they had been discussing was in part a reaction to other sword-fighting games from recent years, games like *God of War* and *Heavenly Sword*, which rely on traditional controllers with buttons. "That doesn't really simulate sword fighting," says

Donald. "And we thought that's something that a touch screen could do better than a controller could."

Although Donald says that development of the game went pretty smoothly, there were some bumps in the road (most notable was the fact that several babies were born over the course of development—even Donald and his wife Laura were expecting a child). The studio also decided to move its office to a new location while work on *Infinity Blade* was in progress. It was a lot to cope with all at once, but ChAIR was able to get the game running and looking great in time to show it off at a special event that Apple held on September 1, 2010.

Donald and Epic President Mike Capps went on stage with Steve Jobs to demonstrate *Infinity Blade*, which was code named *Project Sword* at the time. "I don't think anyone was really prepared for how powerful these devices really are," Donald says. "I had executives from Apple looking at it saying 'Wow. This changes everything.'"

The first version of *Infinity Blade* only took about four and a half months to create, but it went on to become a huge success for ChAIR. The game has made the small team at ChAIR millions of dollars, even bringing in more money than the chart-smashing hit that was *Shadow Complex*.

ChAIR fully intends to make *Infinity Blade* into a franchise. Donald says there are many things in the first version that were placed specifically to support further expansion. "We spent a lot of time making sure that the few lines of dialogue in the game, and even the castle that you see, has a really strong foundational story around it," he says. "It's a story that we just haven't told yet."

> ### Fun Facts
>
> - Donald Mustard met his wife, Laura, while working on *Advent Rising*. She's a video game publicist.
> - There are numerous references to *Shadow Complex* hidden in *Infinity Blade*. Look around in the God King's high-tech labs to see a few.
> - Other apps by ChAIR include *Infinity Blade: Awakening* and *Infinity Blade II*.

Jet Car Stunts

Platform: iPhone/iPod Touch
Price: $1.99
Developer: True Axis
Released: November 13, 2009

What Is It?

In *Jet Car Stunts*, you're placed inside the cockpit of a rocket on wheels and tasked with conquering a series of obstacle courses set high in the sky. Although it's primarily a time-trial challenge, the game is also about pulling off various high-flying jumps using the jet engine on the back of your car. Turning is accomplished by tilting your iPhone to the left or right, and acceleration and brake/reverse have their own on-screen buttons. There is also a button to fire your rocket, and another to activate an air brake (which is useful for slowing down while in flight to avoid overshooting platforms).

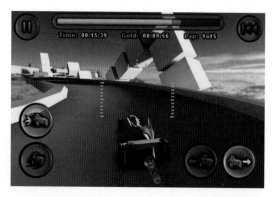

Many of the levels in *Jet Car Stunts* are designed to be exploited. If you can figure out a way to beat the system and hop to an otherwise out-of-reach area of the track, you're usually free to do so, so long as you're not skipping any checkpoints. This allows you to get creative sometimes and hit jumps at a weird angle so you can fly to a separate part of the level, which can be really satisfying (in the same way that running above all of World 1-2 in *Super Mario Bros.* just feels so right). Your jet fuel is limited and only refills after checkpoints, so there's motivation to conserve your fuel occasionally instead of rocketing through every level without ever letting off the juice.

Jet Car Stunts has fantastic track design. Levels are supposed to be hard, and they are extremely challenging, particularly as the game progresses. Thanks to the incredible shading engine that the game uses, those tracks also look pretty fantastic, even on the oldest iOS devices.

Behind the Game

The story behind *Jet Car Stunts* stretches all the way back to 1999, when Luke Ryan was hired by Torus Games to work on the third *Carmageddon* game. *Carmageddon 3* wasn't a particularly good game (I'll leave it to you to go search out some reviews online), but it was an incredibly valuable experience for Ryan, who was still relatively new to the games industry.

Ryan's assignment at the time was to work on implementing a car power called "Afterburner" into the game. When activated, Afterburner acted like an incredibly powerful boost ability; players' cars would rocket forward with their front wheels off the ground. "You could go really fast, but you had no control," says Ryan. "Except you could let go of the Afterburner button at any time to regain control and manage the fuel."

> **Statistics**
> - **Development time:** 6 months
> - **Total budget:** "Mostly sweat"

The feature had existed in the second *Carmageddon* game, but it was Ryan's task to update and improve it. After tinkering with the feature for a bit, he decided to make the power-up act like a rocket attachment. "You could fly across the entire map with it if you found the right jump," says Ryan. "It was over-the-top."

Ryan's watershed moment with the feature was when the team's level builder created an enormous level set in a post-apocalyptic New York. "You would do a massive jump off a broken freeway, over the ocean, onto the top of a half-submerged skyscraper," recalls Ryan. "From there you had to keep your speed up to be able to keep up a string of big jumps across building tops until you returned to dry land."

The level was eventually cut from the game for a variety of reasons, but Ryan played the course over and over again, tweaking his Afterburner feature as he went. "For years after I would wonder how to make a game out of just doing ridiculously big jumps and stunts, and using rocket power," he says.

Years later, Ryan was still involved in the games industry, doing a variety of things like working for Firemint (before it got big on iOS with *Flight Control*) and developing his own physics engine, the True Axis Physics SDK. Ryan got together with Andy Coates, who was adamant about developing for the iPhone. Ryan says he had been avoiding the platform, but Coates was eventually able to convince him to look into it.

Coates pointed out that there was a big hole in the market for stunt-based racing games on the iPhone, and all of Ryan's old ideas came flooding back. With a little inspiration from classic games like *Track Mania* and *Stunt Car Racer*, Ryan and Coates had a real gem of an idea on their hands. "I was convinced we could execute this game really well and do the best driving physics on the iPhone," Ryan says.

Ryan designed all of the levels in *Jet Car Stunts* himself, a liberating process for a guy who had always been employed as a programmer. He made the game brutally difficult on purpose, but also designed it in such a way that players could seek out and find shortcuts all over the map.

After six months of work True Axis released *Jet Car Stunts* to the masses, and it was a success. Critics loved it, and it wound up on more than a few best of 2009 lists. Ryan wasn't willing to talk exact sales numbers, but says that he and Coates are continually surprised by the game's long sales tail. "People continue to buy and love our game," he says. "I hope we can keep people happy with our next projects as well."

Karoshi

Platform: iPad/iPhone/iPod Touch (universal app)
Price: $.99
Developer: Jesse Venbrux
Publisher: YoYo Games
Released: February 7, 2011

What Is It?

There's one rule that almost every video game forces players to adhere to: don't die. It's something so obvious that games almost never spell it out explicitly. You should try to avoid getting shot, and obviously you should avoid falling into bottomless pits. Dying is bad. Death equals losing.

Karoshi is a twisted little game that turns this idea on its head. The game stars an overworked Japanese businessman named Mr. Karoshi, and his only wish is to kill himself. As the player, your goal in each level is to find a quick and easy way to assist Mr. Karoshi in his suicide. This can be done in many different ways: early on, you'll be able to finish Mr. Karoshi off by simply having him hop into a spike pit; in other levels, you'll have to figure out how to activate a switch to cause a chain reaction that ends with Mr. Karoshi getting crushed by some falling object.

It's a dark game with a morbid sense of humor, but the puzzles are often interesting, thanks to the fact that players have to approach them in exactly the opposite way they would approach puzzles in any other platformer. Instead of facing numerous ways to die (as in most games), there's only one way to die, and you'll usually have to work for a bit to figure out how to get to it.

Things get especially interesting whenever Mr. Karoshi's boss and wife are added into the mix. Whenever Mr. Karoshi touches his boss, he gets sad. As a result the world becomes more dreary, and Mr. Karoshi loses his ability to jump as high as he could before. On top of this, things that were once pleasant become deadly—for example, a field of flowers will become a pit of deadly spikes, which Mr. Karoshi can then use to quickly end his pain. Conversely, whenever the boss is killed, Mr. Karoshi will become happy, allowing him to jump higher than before.

Here's the really crazy part: touching Mrs. Karoshi will make Mr. Karoshi happy, and he'll become sad if she's killed—so some levels actually require the player to kill Mrs. Karoshi so that the world will become a sad, dangerous place and Mr. Karoshi can kill himself. Like I said before, this is a ridiculously dark game, and I'd urge parents to keep kids away from it. But for older gamers who aren't offended by its themes, *Karoshi* is a fantastic title that works by consistently toying with players' expectations.

Behind the Game

In Japan, *kar shi* is a word that refers to an almost uniquely Japanese phenomenon in which younger members of the workforce suddenly die from being overworked. It's such a serious epidemic that the Japanese Ministry of Labor began to publish statistics counting *kar shi* deaths in the late 1980s, after several prominent Japanese business executives succumbed to death attributed to work-related stress. "The first *Karoshi* game was originally made as not much more than a joke," says Jesse Venbrux, the series' creator. Venbrux had read about Adult Swim's popular Flash game *5 Minutes to Kill (Yourself)* and later played Michael "Kayin" O'Reilly's incredibly difficult platformer, *I Wanna Be The Guy*. "In [*I Wanna Be The Guy*] I found the deaths to be kind of satisfactory in terms of audio and video, and by combining these different concepts the idea for *Karoshi* was born in my head," says Venbrux.

Venbrux created *Karoshi* as a free-to-download Windows game, like his other freeware creations: *You Probably Won't Make It* and *They Need To Be Fed*. To his surprise, *Karoshi* quickly became his most popular game. Naturally, he made a sequel. And then another, and another. All told, Venbrux has created five *Karoshi* titles for the PC and Flash platforms, making it his biggest and most popular work ever.

Venbrux was approached by YoYo Games, who wanted to publish a commercial version of a *Karoshi* game for the PSP.

> ### Statistics
> • **Development time:** 3 months

Venbrux could have simply ported one of his previous releases, but instead he decided to come up with fresh ideas and make an entirely unique sixth entry in the series. To achieve this, he dreamed up the game's relationship mechanic, which was built around the two new characters—Mrs. Karoshi and the boss. "Their relationships in the story affect the gameplay and thus the puzzles," he explains. "The inspiration for this idea came from watching Japanese drama TV shows, which usually provide a relationship chart online."

Venbrux had figured out the mechanic that would make the sixth *Karoshi* game stand out but was surprised when a last-minute change of plans was handed down from his publisher. "The game was already about done when YoYo Games decided it would be good to focus on mobile first," Venbrux says. The game was now destined for the iPhone. This was an unfortunate change for Venbrux, who had designed the game's puzzles without thinking about ways to utilize the iPhone's touch screen or gyroscope. He says that if he ever gets the chance to make another *Karoshi* game, he wants to design it to take advantage of device-specific features.

> **Fun Facts**
>
> - You can find and play the first five games in the *Karoshi* series for free at http://www.venbrux.com/karoshi.php.
> - *Karoshi* is also available on Android, the PSP, and the PS3.
> - *Fallout 3* lead producer Gavin Carter has written extensively about his love for the *Karoshi* series and its inventive puzzles.
> - Other apps by Jesse Venbrux include *They Need to Be Fed*.

Although YoYo games is tight-lipped about *Karoshi*'s download numbers, Venbrux says he has been making a nice profit from sales of the game each month. That's quite a change for a developer who's so acclimated to creating free games. For Venbrux, the biggest joy comes from seeing people play his games. "What I love most is seeing people make the mistakes I want them to make," he says. "When I design these levels I imagine someone playing it and doing as I hope, and it gives me great satisfaction to see my predictions coming true."

In a somewhat ironic twist, Venbrux now works for Q-Games (creators of the *PixelJunk* series), which is a Japanese company.

Labyrinth 2

Platform: iPhone/iPod Touch (iPad version available separately)
Price: $4.99
Developer: Illusion Labs
Released: December 1, 2009

What Is It?

It's an incredibly simple idea—allow players to tilt their devices to roll a ball into a hole. A lesser game developer would have filled a few dozen levels with some mazes and simple obstacles and called it good, but Illusion Labs held nothing back for *Labyrinth 2*. Gorgeous

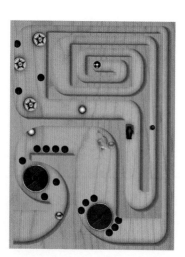

three-dimensional graphics, multiplayer modes, a more fully-featured level creation/sharing system, new game elements like multiple balls and magnets, and iPad-only levels make *Labyrinth 2* the ultimate ball-rolling game.

Seriously, I have no idea what you'd have to do to make *Labyrinth 3*. The game already offers unlimited content thanks to the fact that players have created hundreds of thousands of levels, so the only way to make a better *Labyrinth* game would be to come up with even more puzzle elements and tack on some extra modes (lengthy, hazard-filled racetracks with online multiplayer? I'd play it).

It's not just that there's a lot of stuff to do in *Labyrinth 2*—what *is* there is *so* good. The ball physics feel just right, it's fantastic visually (especially if you're playing on an iPad 2), and there's enough puzzle variety to erase the word "repetitive" from your vocabulary. *Labyrinth 2* is the perfect example of a well-designed iOS game.

Behind the Game

The first *Labyrinth* game was also the very first iPhone game ever created. Sure, there were around 500 apps available at the launch of the App Store, but *Labyrinth* was available for purchase before the App Store ever existed. Carl Loodberg and Andreas Alptun had been working on the game before developer tools for the device even existed, and they sold it using PayPal. When the App Store launched, they simply moved it over to the store, officially forming Illusion Labs. Around that time, Loodberg and Alptun brought two more people on board; one was Marcus Andersson, whom I spoke to at length about the process of making *Labyrinth 2*.

> ### Statistics
> - **Development time:** 9 months
> - **Total budget:** $300,000
> - **Times downloaded:** 500,000

After releasing *Touchgrind*, the team had begun thinking about their next project. "We had tons of ideas but we wanted our next product to be extremely intuitive and groundbreaking," says Andersson. "We had set the bar very high for how groundbreaking our new game would be and none of our ideas felt 100% right. So we decided to do a sequel to *Labyrinth* instead of launching a completely new idea."

For Illusion Labs, *Labyrinth 2* was all about more, more, more. They wanted to expand the online level editor, build more obstacle types into the game, add in a multiplayer mode, and improve the visual style (specifically the three-dimensional elements). The team even decided to completely ditch the original game's code in favor of creating a new base so the game could run as smoothly as possible.

Illusion Labs didn't really run into problems while developing the game, in part due to its willingness to expand the team size. Eventually the team grew to five software developers, one art director, and one part-time three-dimensional-graphics designer. Andersson says that the hardest part of development was the level-creation system, which demanded both a clean interface and complexity to facilitate interesting levels. "We had to tone down the original complexity of the logic system to make the level creation simpler," he explains. "I think we got a pretty intuitive UI [user interface] in the end, but there were a lot of discussions and designing to get a UI that was easy to understand and at the same time had a lot of different features."

> ### Fun Facts
> - *Labyrinth* is five dollars and always has been. "We at Illusion Labs don't believe in sales and doing tricks with the price," says Andersson.
> - Illusion Labs created a *Touchgrind* game for the Mac OS X that's available exclusively in the Mac App Store. It uses the MacBook multitouch trackpad in some interesting ways.
> - Other apps by Illusion Labs include *Sway* and *Foosball HD*.

Both *Labyrinth 2* and its iPad-only HD version (released at the same time as the iPad itself) were big hits. The game has generated millions for Illusion Labs, who have since expanded in size and created a number of original iOS games (including the best foosball game on the iPad).

Land-a Panda

Platform: iPhone/iPod Touch (iPad version available separately)
Price: $.99
Developer: Big Pixel Studios
Released: March 9, 2011

What Is It?

It's impossible to look at *Land-a Panda* without thinking of the barrel levels in Nintendo's *Donkey Kong Country* series. Essentially, *Land-a Panda* takes the concept behind that mechanic and expands it into an entire game. In each level, you take a panda (whose name is Yang Guang) and try to help him reach his girlfriend, a cute little panda named Tien Tien. In the game, you have no control over the panda himself; you're simply launching him from barrel to barrel by tapping on the screen. There are sliding barrels, rotating barrels, and automatic-firing barrels, among others, so a lot of the game becomes about timing—for instance, waiting for two barrels to line up so you can launch Yang Guang safely through the air and into another barrel.

For reasons the game's fiction doesn't bother to explain, the entirety of *Land-a Panda*'s action takes place high in the sky. That means that missing a barrel will certainly send Yang Guang to his doom, but there are other ways to fail as well, particularly as the game progresses; flying enemies and traps can pose a big threat and force you to think of creative ways to get around obstacles while collecting coins and working your way towards Tien Tien.

Ultimately, *Land-a Panda* is another game that offers bite-sized, very lighthearted puzzle solving. It's probably not going to give your brain a cramp because it's meant to be a bit of a snack. If you want a meal you should look to something meatier like *Infinity Blade* or *Osmos*, but *Land-a Panda* is designed for people who want a fun, skill-based puzzle game that they can pick up and put down on the go. If you fit that demographic, by all means commence panda-launching.

Behind the Game

Big Pixel Studios is a bit more experienced than your typical indie developer. The company often does work-for-hire projects to help fund the development of its original games. It's a tactic that Big Pixel CEO Paul Virapen describes as a safety measure. "Even if the worst happens and a game completely bombs in the App Store, we should still be able to pay our bills and (hopefully) eat," he says.

Whenever Big Pixel begins work on a new original game, it has a simple, efficient process. "A member of the team has an initial idea, and we all sit down and discuss the possibilities of it," says Virapen. "From there a brief one-page concept document is produced, which can be used as the basis for a developer to knock up a quick demo."

The "quick demo" for *Land-a Panda* only took a few days to create. At that stage, it was little more than cannons launching a circle (the team still hadn't decided what sort of character to use) back and forth. According to Virapen, if the demo isn't fun, it's not unusual for development of a game to cease.

The early prototype for *Land-a Panda* seemed appealing to the Big Pixel team, so they set to work fleshing out the game. The team allocated a strict maximum of three months to finish. They had learned much from the experience of releasing several other original games and wanted to keep the project as short and low-risk as possible. From here, the team had to decide on a character. "Initially we were playing around with a few different cat- and dog-based characters, but none of them felt quite right," says Virapen.

> ### Statistics
> - **Development time:** 3 months
> - **Total budget:** $56,000
> - **Times downloaded:** 150,000

When the idea of using pandas as the main characters surfaced, everything clicked. It's a cute character, and it even created a (semi) logical explanation as to why the panda would want to get from one side of the screen to the other—making babies for the sake of pandas everywhere. "I'm sure most people are aware that the giant panda is an endangered species, and they have some trouble breeding, so it just seemed like a nice story to try and save the panda population by getting these two pandas together," says Virapen. The fact that the female panda is actually a gold digger is something that was added later. "It was a nice way to add some human-based characteristics to the panda characters," Virapen explains.

Land-a Panda has been a major sales success, and Virapen gives a majority of the credit to the fact that Apple featured it as Game of the Week in most of the European App Stores. "As most iOS developers know, getting a good feature in the App Store is worth more than all other possible marketing activities combined," he states. Since launch, Big Pixel has expanded the number of levels in the game (there were 80 at launch) by 50%. It was always a value proposition, but now it's a must-have.

Fun Facts

- Big Pixel created a surprisingly good *Thor* Flash game for Marvel. Find it by Googling *Thor: Bring the Thunder!*.
- There's an extremely odd Flash game on the front page of Big Pixel's website: http://bigpixelstudios.co.uk/. Collect all the coins for a big surprise!
- Virapen says that players who collect at least half the coins in *Land-a Panda* and complete it will get to see a bit of a twist in the game's story.
- Other apps by Big Pixel Studios include *Piyo Blocks 2* and *Meow Meow Happy Fight*.

Minigore

Platform: iPhone/iPod Touch (iPad version available separately)
Price: $.99
Developer: Mountain Sheep
Publisher: Chillingo
Released: July 30, 2009

What Is It?

Despite having almost no story and relatively little content, *Minigore* was one of the first great dual stick-shooters in the App Store. The game's setup is simple: you're in a forested arena, and little black monsters called furries come at you from all angles. You'll also have to deal with bigger monsters that split into large groups of furries once you shred them with your machine gun. As the game progresses, you'll be confronted with more and faster furries, until you're inevitably swarmed and succumb to the hordes.

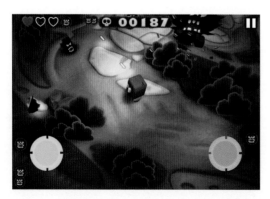

Minigore has been improved immensely over time via updates. At first *Minigore* involved nothing more than you with a machine gun versus all of the insane critters that wanted to kill you. Now there are weapon drops, tons of playable characters, and multiple arenas to play in besides the basic forest level.

Minigore does use a virtual stick-control scheme, but it does it in an unobtrusive, effective way. In fact, it was probably the first game I ever played that made me realize that virtual controls can be done well. Two years after its release, it's still one of the best implementations of virtual controls in the App Store.

Minigore's not really that deep when it comes down to it—there's no leveling system, and there's no single-player campaign. It's just a good, arcade-style shooter that you play over and over again to earn a higher score (and earn more points to unlock new characters).

Behind the Game

In the summer of 2008, Mountain Sheep had just finished work on its first game—a PSP title called *Super Hind*. That hadn't gone so well. The game's production budget had exceeded several hundred thousand dollars and failed to make much back. Ten people had worked on the game, and almost all of them had to be let go shortly after *Super Hind*'s release.

For *Minigore*, Mountain Sheep had to really tighten its belt. The team had been sliced down to just two members: Timo Vihola and his brother, Kimmo Vihola. "It was a make or break it situation," Timo says.

The two brothers hadn't given up, and were looking to create a new action game, most likely for the PlayStation Network. Vihola says that the company had been working on prototypes for as many as 15 different game ideas when he purchased an iPhone and started downloading games for it. "I suddenly realized—it's not just a phone or a music player, it's a damn fine handheld gaming system!" Vihola says. The idea for *Minigore* was born soon after, and the team put everything else they had been planning aside to begin work on the game immediately.

A few months into the development of *Minigore*, Chillingo published another dual-stick shooter called *iDracula*. Vihola calls it "the first great example of an iOS dual-stick shooter," and says that the quality of it bolstered Mountain Sheep's confidence that it too could create a solid game using similar mechanics.

What didn't look as promising were the technical hurdles that *Minigore* still had to overcome. The team was using engine technology from their work on the PSP, and that didn't translate quite as well to the iPhone. "The PSP is great with polygons and bad with textures. The iPhone 3G, as it turned out, was exactly the opposite," explains Vihola.

iDracula ran beautifully because it's a two-dimensional game; *Minigore* was to be almost entirely three-dimensional. This was its biggest problem, and it was an issue that Mountain Sheep almost didn't overcome. "One month before release,

> ### Statistics
> - **Development time:** 6 months
> - **Total budget:** $55,000
> - **Times downloaded:** 3,000,000

> ### Fun Facts
> - All voice work in the game is done by Egoraptor, best known for his work on the *Metal Gear Awesome* series of comedy videos on Newgrounds.com.
> - *Minigore*'s sound effects guy, Tapani Liukkonen, also created sounds for the award-winning horror game *Amnesia: Dark Descent*.
> - Search for the secret spot marked by an X, and stand still on it for a bit. You'll be in for a surprise.

the game was running at 5 FPS [frames per second] with only a few enemies on screen," says Vihola. "It was a scary moment." The Viholas made some drastic cuts to the polygon count on all of the characters and changed the way the lighting worked, but managed to get it running smoothly just in time for the release. The work paid off—*Minigore* remained in the top 100 action games chart for the next two years.

Notably, the Viholas kept the game interesting by updating it regularly to include new, unlockable characters from other games. Enviro-Bear from *Enviro-Bear 2010*, Jake from *Hook Champ*, and Lizzie from Illusion Labs' *Sway* all become playable after killing a certain number of enemies in the game. These updates were integral to keeping *Minigore* high in the charts for as long as it's been there, and Vihola says the team continues to make good money off the game. "We have a real office now with six full-time people working on *Minigore*," he says.

Mountain Sheep is back.

Monkey Island
Special Edition 1 & 2

Platform: iPhone/iPod Touch (iPad version available separately)
Price: $2.99
Developer: LucasArts
Released: July 6, 2010

What Is It?

The original *Monkey Island* and the sequels that followed are renowned for being some of the early greats in the point-and-click adventure genre. The titles are humorous—goofy stories centered around Guybrush Threepwood, who wants nothing more than to become a pirate. Guybrush's character changes drastically between the first and second games, but the gameplay remains the same: traverse from one location to another while taking part in story events, chatting it up with characters, and solving puzzles using items you've collected and stashed away in your inventory.

The remakes of *The Secret of Monkey Island* and *Monkey Island 2: LeChuck's Revenge* are incredible, both in terms of fan service and suitability for the iPad platform. The game has new voice work, a completely remastered soundtrack, and new high-definition graphics that you can turn on or off at any

point. The second game even has full audio commentary from the game's original writers (Ron Gilbert, Dave Grossman, and Tim Schafer), which can be activated whenever you enter and leave certain areas. Perhaps most importantly, the updated graphics and voice-overs stay true to the original game while offering an overall experience that looks and feels like a new game.

If anything could possibly turn you on to point-and-click adventures, these remakes are the games that will do it. They may have been some of the earliest games in the genre, but they set a high bar that few games have reached. These types of games don't get made any more (with a few rare exceptions: check out the excellent iPad version of *Machinarium*), and as such are valuable pieces of gaming history that are worth experiencing in this modern form.

Behind the Game

Craig Derrick says that from the day he began work at LucasArts, he knew he wanted to make a *Monkey Island* game. He came into the company with high hopes, but quickly had those hopes shut down. "It became very clear that the golden years of classic adventure games were behind us and that we were forging ahead in a new direction," Derrick says. He was disappointed at first, but says he held out hope that he might eventually convince his superiors to take another look at the aging franchise he so dearly loved.

Derrick had been brought to LucasArts to build and lead a team dedicated to the development of novel ideas for characters and game worlds that could be used in new titles. In mid-2007, Derrick's team (internally referred to as Team 3) reviewed a big batch of their ideas and pitched the best ones to George Lucas. Lucas really liked one of the ideas, and Team 3 set to work readying an early build of the game.

About a year later, a change in management at LucasArts left Team 3 with nothing to work on. The new president of LucasArts (Howard Roffman) approached Derrick and asked him if he had any ideas for what his team could do next. Derrick saw his opportunity and took it. He mentioned an idea for a new *Monkey Island* game, and Roffman liked it. After putting together a comprehensive business plan for the game, Derrick was given permission to do what he'd always wanted—create a *Monkey Island* game.

> ### Statistics
>
> - Number of floppy disks the first *Monkey Island* game came with: 8
> - Number of floppy disks *Monkey Island 2* came with: 11
> - Number of companies that produced floppy disks in 2011: 0

Derrick says that the biggest challenge he and his team faced while making the first *Monkey Island Special Edition* game was convincing others of the idea. "At LucasArts the management had decided years ago to move away from adventure games and to no longer revisit classic franchises such as *Monkey Island* or *Maniac Mansion*," says Derrick. "And here I was pitching an idea to re-imagine a nearly 20-year-old classic PC adventure game from 1990 for a platform that hadn't yet established itself as a viable market. I definitely got some stares and folks second-guessing the viability of the plan, but fortunately our president at the time believed in the idea and gave the team a shot."

The first special edition *Monkey Island* game was a huge success, so Derrick had a much easier time getting a remake of the second game in the series approved. Unfortunately, the vast majority of team members who had worked on the first game were busy on a new project, so the team was augmented with staff from around the world, with its core based in Singapore.

Monkey Island Special Edition 1 & 2 have been made available on a variety of platforms (Xbox Live Arcade, PlayStation Network, PC, and iOS), but Derrick says that the games have been the most successful by far on iOS. He believes there are a few reasons for this. "First and foremost the iPhone and iPad are perfectly suited to play adventure games, as the touch screen is a natural input for point-and-click styled games," Derrick says. "The quality of the art comes alive on the screen and the casual-oriented, puzzle-solving gameplay and portable nature of the devices give people the opportunity to play the game in short bursts while still feeling a sense of progression."

> **Fun Facts**
>
> - The new version of *Monkey Island* includes references to LucasArts games that came out after the original game (like *Grim Fandango*).
> - At first, Derrick considered remaking the games in a style reminiscent of a three-dimensional pop-up storybook.
> - Derrick wanted to get in-game commentary from Gilber, Schafer, and Grossman for the first *Monkey Island Special Edition*, but scheduling conflicts prevented it.

Derrick also gives a lot of credit to the App Store itself, which he says allows developers to communicate with consumers in a personal way that isn't possible on other platforms. "There's an instant link to those folks who love or hate the game that we as developers can use to instantly respond to."

Derrick tells me that LucasArts doesn't reveal data like sales numbers, but does say that both games have "exceeded expectations," both critically and commercially.

Mos Speedrun

Platform: iPad/iPhone/iPod Touch (universal app)
Price: $1.99
Developer: Physmo
Released: April 6, 2011

What Is It?

Speedrunning is the process of memorizing a game's level layouts and strategies, and then practicing to complete them in the fastest time possible. It's a trend that has been growing in popularity in recent years, especially amongst hardcore gamers who record their runs and post them to YouTube.

As you might guess by the name, *Mos Speedrun* totally embraces the art of the speedrun. Speedrunning isn't all that the game is about, however—there are several goals to

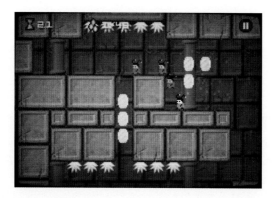

pursue in each. Of course, one of them is to make it to the end of a level successfully, which will earn you one medal. Completing a level isn't usually too difficult; the real challenge is beating the "par" time that's set for each level in the game, which will earn you a second medal. This requires non-stop, full-blast sprinting, which in turn requires an intimate knowledge of the level itself. There's also a third medal that can be found through careful exploration.

The beauty of this setup is that you're never trying to get all of the medals at once. You can do one run-through of a level just to finish it and familiarize yourself with the place, another to find the hidden object, and then several more to practice for the speedrunning medal.

One of the coolest things about *Mos Speedrun* is that after you've died once, you'll run alongside ghostlike recordings of your past attempts the next time you try the level—so if you fail six times, six ghosts will accompany you on your seventh try. It's the most accurate way imaginable to keep track of your progress, because you're literally seeing your previous attempts play out right in front of your eyes.

Behind the Game

Mos Speedrun's main character began as a doodle that Physmo lead designer Nick Donnelly drew in his free time. Donnelly would occasionally post his drawings on B3ta.com, a British message board. Years after Donnelly first drew the character, he and a college friend (programmer Tony McBride) began discussing the possibility of creating an iPhone game together. "I had always wanted to use that character, so we decided to knock up a quick prototype of a platform game with simple 8-bit graphics, and the game just kind of grew from there," Donnelly says.

Early on in the process of creating *Mos Speedrun*, Donnelly and McBride decided to make the game about speedrunning. This greatly influenced the design of their levels, and they built the game from the ground up to provide a challenge for players attempting to quickly finish levels.

> **Statistics**
>
> • **Development time:** 3 months (nights and weekends)

Donnelly says that he and McBride each played every level in the game dozens of times, makings notes about things that needed to be changed to make everything flow more smoothly. Of particular interest to the team was the process of removing obstacles that could cause sudden deaths—that is, anything that a player did not have a chance to avoid. "That is one of the biggest problems with fast platformers like *Sonic*," says Donnelly. "There are too many deaths from things you have no chance to react to."

About a month into developing the game, the two-man Physmo team realized that their game could be completed in almost no time at all. The entire game was built around the act of running quickly through levels, and players not interested in shaving seconds off their time could finish it in a matter of minutes. Since Physmo didn't have the resources to create hundreds of high-quality levels, they needed to alter the design philosophy of the game to produce a meatier experience. "We already had the idea of giving the player badges for completing certain objectives throughout the levels, so we changed that concept to make the badges the 'currency' to progress through the game," says Donnelly. "Because progress was metered out like this, it encouraged the player to play each level a number of times in ways that spanned a number of different play styles."

Throughout the three-month process of creating *Mos Speedrun*, Donnelly and McBride worked from their own homes, collaborating through services like DropBox and Google Docs. Donnelly calls the services "perfectly suited to developing games," saying that he could update levels and graphics on his side, and McBride would immediately see his changes. "It's a much better way of working than when we worked on shareware PC games in the 90s, passing 3.5-inch floppy disks around," Donnelly says.

Once *Mos Speedrun* was finished, Physmo submitted it to the App Store and waited for what Donnelly calls a "traumatizing" two weeks. He had heard scary anecdotes from other developers who waited weeks before learning that their games had been rejected, so he was careful to make sure that *Mos Speedrun* was up to Apple's standards. Despite this, *Mos Speedrun* has failed to move many units. "Sales have not been amazing," Donnelly admits. "I think the 8-bit look can put off the more casual audience, and I think that's where the bulk of buyers are. There are a lot of people who just want an easy game as a distraction, and perhaps *Mos* doesn't meet that criteria."

Nimble Strong
Bartender in Training

Platform: iPhone/iPod Touch
Price: $4.99
Developer: Nimble Strong LLC
Released: July 10, 2010

What Is It?

So here's the story: you're a total screw-up. You've lost both your wife and your best friend, and you have no job. Somehow you manage to land your sorry self a position as a bartender at a local pub. The only problem is, you have no idea how to mix drinks—ANY drinks. Fortunately, outside knowledge of cocktail mixing isn't required because your patrons will happily teach you how to make them.

During the game your customers will saunter up, tell their stories (which are usually pretty interesting, surprisingly enough), and order drinks. There are over 70 drinks in the game, and the ingredients are all at your disposal. In order to make the requested drink you'll have to know the actual recipe, and that's where your patrons come in handy. The rest of your challenge is pouring the correct amount of each ingredient into a glass, which you do by holding anywhere on the screen. The goal is to pour just the right amount in one try, and that can sometimes be pretty difficult. *Nimble Strong: Bartender in Training* is educational and entertaining since it's essentially a bartending class wrapped up in a fun, *Phoenix Wright*-style puzzle game.

Behind the Game

Adam Ghahramani had just launched his big new site (theOtaku.com), and he was exhausted. Ghahramani decided to allow himself a one-month vacation in Vancouver, where he spent time exploring the sights and thinking about what he should do next.

Ghahramani had heard that gaming legend Will Wright (creator of *The Sims*, *Sim City*, and *Spore*) was giving a lecture at a local university, so he wangled his way in by getting a press pass. Wright, who is known for his eloquence, delivered a powerful speech that Ghahramani called inspiring. "I left it amped up with the confidence that maybe my web experience and wealth of game industry/gaming expertise could translate into actually making a game," he says.

As he walked back, Ghahramani thought about what sort of game he'd like to make. He knew that he wanted it to be for the iPhone because the development cost would be low, he'd have control over the distribution, and the App Store was beginning to take off. He also knew that he wanted to do something in an anime/Japanese style. That wouldn't have come as a surprise to anyone—Ghahramani's recently launched theOtaku.com later grew into one of the web's most popular sites for Japanese anime.

Ghahramani had already been thinking a lot about educational games like *Cooking Mama* and *Wii Fit*. He was inspired by those games' ability to entertain while teaching, but says that the games are too dumbed-down to be counted as truly valuable educational tools. "All these thoughts were circling in my head," says Ghahramani. "Suddenly, I was struck by inspiration when I saw a sign outside a building advertising a bartending class for a few hundred dollars. The spark of an idea set in and it became a possibility."

Ghahramani came up with other game ideas, but says that an educational bartending game was the idea he kept coming back to. The more he thought about it, the more he liked it. He decided that the best way to make the game interesting and educational would be to add in story elements. "I wanted to make a darker game, something that retained the quirkiness of a Japanese-style game but with the dark neo-noir feeling of a more Western title," Ghahramani says.

Ghahramani returned from his vacation to his home in New York City and decided to put off finding a full-time job to focus on his game idea. His first order of business was to learn more about the bartending industry, which he says he knew very little about. "Of all my friends, I was one of the least frequent drinkers," admits Ghahramani. "So it was a bit odd to make a game about cocktail culture."

Statistics

- **Development time:** 1.5 years
- **Total budget:** $30,000
- **Sales revenue:** $15,000

Ghahramani described the four-step research method that he used to quickly familiarize himself with bartending:

1. He signed up for a $300 bartending course.
2. He bought multiple books on the topic from Amazon.com. These included both technical books from mixologists like Gary Regan, and autobiographical/historical books "to get a feel for the culture."
3. He signed up for a couple of advanced-education classes taught by local spirits enthusiasts/mixologists.
4. He "obsessively" went to all the top bars in New York City.

In his very first bartending class Ghahramani realized that making drinks was inherently suited to video gameplay, thanks to the sense of timing that bartenders have to rely on to pour each drink. "A typical shot takes three seconds to pour with a standard free pour," explains Ghahramani. "But bartenders have no progress bars or anything like that; they need to build a sense of what three seconds is intuitively. As a game this was interesting because we can have 'perfect' pours that are exactly three seconds, 'good' pours that are a little less or above, and 'worse' pours that are much less or well above. I realized that the combined mechanism of timing and remembering recipes would make for a glorious gameplay dynamic." This was important, because it provided a way for the game to be fun, not just educational. "I was super excited," Ghahramani says.

Ghahramani was further interested to learn that many drinks are closely related, and can often be divided into separate families. "Swapping one ingredient for another would often quickly make another drink altogether," he says. This, Ghahramani says, would serve as the basis for the game's educational progression. Players could start by learning one drink, and then easily pick up on others in the same family by swapping out just a few ingredients.

Since the bartending game was to incorporate storytelling in a major way, Ghahramani began reading up on playwriting. He completed his first draft and showed it to Don Gatterdam, whom he describes as a friend and mentor. Gatterdam didn't hold back his criticism. "The mixology content is inauthentic, the dialogue sucks, and nothing in the story reminds me of a real bar," he told Ghahramani. Humbled, Ghahramani scrapped his first draft.

> **Fun Facts**
> - Nimble Strong's silence is an homage to the classic, silent video-game hero (like in *Zelda* or *Chrono Trigger*).
> - The gay couple in the game (Steve and Willy) are based on the characters from Apple's "I'm a Mac" commercials, but named after Steve Jobs and Bill Gates.
> - Many of the characters in *Nimble* are based on people who Ghahramani knows in real life.

Around this time, Ghahramani was introduced by a friend to Jefferey Lindenmuth, a well-established journalist who has written about spirits for outlets like *Wine & Spirits Magazine* and *Men's Health*. Lindenmuth agreed to help out with the project, even going so far as to put Ghahramani's second draft through a significant round of edits. "In the end the script balanced my quirky JRPG/manga/video game sensibilities with his deep knowledge of cocktail culture," says Ghahramani.

Ghahramani had made it this far, but he still didn't have a developer to program the game for him. He posted ads, attended meet-ups, and asked friends for connections, but had no luck finding someone with the programming prowess to take his idea and turn it into something real.

Some weeks after Ghahramani had stopped posting ads, he got a call from Joshua DeBonis, a professor of game design at the Parsons school in NYC. DeBonis was also fascinated with educational games. "We clicked instantly," Ghahramani recalls. Development on the game commenced, and Ghahramani dipped into his personal savings to fund it. He managed to raise a little extra money from friends, but as the game neared completion, he was broke and in debt.

A little over a month before *Nimble Strong* was released, a Korean game developer released an iPhone game about bartending. It had anime-style art, quirky characters, and it only cost 99 cents. Ghahramani had planned to release his game for $4.99. This was devastating for Ghahramani. He had already been stressed out about the fact that *Nimble Strong* didn't run very well on older iPod Touch models, but this was an unbelievable coincidence. "While this game was nowhere near the quality of *Nimble*—it lacked the education, the gameplay wasn't very fun, and it didn't have much of a soul—it did come to market first and had very good graphics," he says.

The game that Ghahramani is referring to is *Bar Oasis*, developed by Corners Studio. I picked it up and played it for a bit to make my own judgments about his quality, and I have to say that he's right. The interface is sloppy, the writing is unbearable, and the tutorial dragged on FOREVER, but it does have very nice art. Its flaws didn't matter to the biggest iPhone game-review sites, though, which lauded *Bar Oasis* for its originality. 148Apps.com praised it for being new and "refreshing," and TouchArcade.com called it "unique." Ghahramani knew that it would be incredibly difficult to convince these sites to review a second game in the same genre so soon after they had already covered *Bar Oasis*, and he says he became depressed, "complete with nightmares." He also knew that he couldn't compete with the 99-cent price tag.

Ghahramani sums up the day that *Nimble Strong* launched: "The first day of *Nimble's* launch was one of the worst days of my life," he says. "I posted about the game on a message board and it got SHREDDED. People mocked its price, saying they would never download a game that expensive. They said it was a cheap clone of the other Korean game. The first few sites we asked to review it didn't because they'd already reviewed the Korean game. First-day sales were pretty bad."

Everything changed when Justin McElroy from Joystiq.com picked up *Nimble Strong* and gave it a glowing 4.5/5 star review. When Ghahramani read it, he was overwhelmed with emotion. He calls it "one of my life's favorite moments." McElroy introduced the review by saying "finally video games have a purpose," and lauded it for being one of the first games to teach him a real-world skill.

McElroy's review brought the game into the limelight, and soon The Unofficial Apple Weblog (TUAW.com) posted its own review of the game, calling it "quite a gem." *Nimble Strong*'s sales surged, and the game got mentioned in the *New York Times*, GamePro (I actually wrote that one), and Reddit.

Nimble Strong never became profitable (Ghahramani estimates that he's made back about 50% of what he put into it), but it did lead Ghahramani to get an excellent job in the beverage industry—he's now associate director of mobile for *Wine Spectator* magazine, where he helps drive the company's mobile/tablet product strategy. He was integral to the launch of *Wine Spectator*'s VintageChart+ app, which has enjoyed very positive reviews. The game currently has more four-star reviews than any other app I've seen on the App Store. Who knew that wine aficionados could also be snobby about review scores?

Ghahramani says that he would love to do an Android port of the game, but money is still an issue. "My dream would be to make a Kinect port," he says.

No, Human

Platform: iPad/iPhone/iPod Touch (universal app)
Price: $2.99
Developer: vol-2
Released: August 24, 2010

What Is It?

There's really no way to ease you into this, so I'll just come out and say it: In *No, Human*, you play as the universe. Yup. THE UNIVERSE. Disrespectful humans have been attempting to colonize you lately, and as we know, the universe wants no part of that. Fortunately the silly little spaceships and buildings that humans have created are hilariously vulnerable to meteors, and as the universe, you happen to possess quite a few of those.

Puzzles require that you lob meteors into human constructions by slinging them

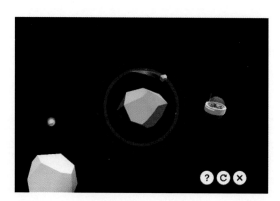

around planets. You'll have to deal with all sorts of weird obstacles like high-gravity asteroids and glass-like ice asteroids, but the majority of the game is about carefully placing shots that direct the meteors straight into human structures, hopefully causing lots of damage along the way.

The story and puzzles in *No, Human* are great, but it's the game's presentational aspects that really set it apart. It sports a weird, low-polygon-count art style that looks really great, and whenever the game zooms in and goes into slow motion to show you the seeds of your destruction at the end of each level, the blocky textures actually look nice in their own unique way. The game's soundtrack is a beautiful, piano-driven score that works as an amusing juxtaposition to the game's dark humor.

Behind the Game

Since he was a child, Rolf Fleischmann has always dreamed of creating a game by himself. He didn't have any specific ideas, but he was determined to come up with something, so in early 2010 he took some time off from work in an effort to pursue that dream.

Fleischmann found himself in a local park, sitting in front of a local art museum. Fleischmann, with his good sense of humor and cynical distaste for modern art, thought to himself, hey, they get away with being bold! I can do that! "That's when I decided to let the player play the universe, whose only distraction from being universal is to troll humanity," Fleischmann says. "Just like modern art does!"

> **Statistics**
> - **Development time:** 4 months
> - **Total budget:** $3,000
> - **Times downloaded:** 17,000

According to Fleischmann he knew from the beginning that the game would have to take place in outer space, so he decided to design the mechanics of the game around its elements (endless voids, meteors, space trash, etc.). His description of his thought process in creating the rock-flinging mechanic is particularly funny. "Now, since I couldn't ask the universe how it would get rid of unwanted guests, I took my best guess and went with throwing rocks," Fleischmann says. "You can't fail with throwing rocks. Everyone can do it."

The process of developing *No, Human* was a learning experience for Fleischmann, because he had no prior experience with programming. It sounds crazy to quit your job so that you can create a game when you have no idea how to actually make it work, but Fleischmann embraced the challenge. "I like learning by doing, so it wasn't much of a problem after all," he says nonchalantly.

Fleischmann had saved up money for the ten years prior to his decision, and he lived off of that while working on the game. He couldn't afford to pay someone to write the code, so he taught himself how to use the Unity 3D engine, which he says made learning programming relatively easy.

> **Fun Facts**
> - Fleischmann planned an arcade mode for the game, but it was cut because he couldn't figure out a way to make it fun.
> - *No, Human*'s 1.1 update added an entirely new storyline to the game.
> - Failing a single level seven times in *No, Human* has an interesting result . . . .

Against his better judgment, Fleischmann decided to release the first version of *No, Human* without a soundtrack. "It was clearly a beginner's mistake," he says. "But at the time I was disappointed that I couldn't get the type of music I wanted—slow, melancholic cello-type music."

After receiving dozens of emails complaining about the lack of a score, Fleischmann relented and got in touch with a friend (Sebastian Elser) who played piano. His friend agreed to record some tracks similar to the style that Fleischmann had originally wanted, and the music was added in retroactively via the game's first update (which also added new levels).

Fleischmann says that one of his biggest regrets is that he went into the project alone. "About three months in on the project, it became pretty clear to me that working on games all alone is not that much fun. Having someone to talk to over a game idea or a design for a level is something I still miss today." In his trademark humorous style, Fleischmann blames his inability to find a willing partner on the small size of the nation of Switzerland.

No, Human never sold more than 20,000 copies, but Fleischmann considers it to be a success. He was excited by the positive coverage his game received from professional review sites and outlets, and says that he made enough money from sales of the game to fund the development of another title. "Nice for a single developer's first game I guess," he says. I can practically *hear* him shrugging.

Osmos

Platform: iPhone/iPod Touch (iPad version available separately)
Price: $2.99
Developer: Hemisphere Games
Released: August 4, 2010

What Is It?

In *Osmos* you control a mote: a small blue orb that looks like the goo from a lava lamp. In each level, your mote floats around in a two-dimensional, outer-space area with other motes of varying colors. Your mote is always blue, but the color of the motes around you changes depending on your size—motes that are larger than you are red, and motes that are smaller than you are blue. The blue motes can be absorbed, but bumping into the red motes will result in you getting absorbed yourself. Your goal is to become the largest mote, and you'll have to choose your targets wisely to do so.

Movement in *Osmos* is simple. Tapping anywhere on the screen causes your mote to expel a bit of its mass in the direction you tapped, propelling your mote in the opposite direction. There's a balance between expelling enough mass to build up sufficient momentum to catch smaller motes, and expelling

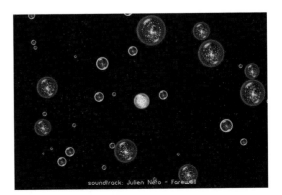

soundtrack: Julien Neto - Farewell

so much that you become too small to be competitive. It's a nice, complex set of mechanics that makes for a satisfying overall experience, which is only improved by the game's wonderful zen-like soundtrack.

Osmos doesn't fit into any traditional genre. You can call it an "arcade absorb-'em-up," but there's nothing out there like it. This is something entirely new, and it deserves your support. After all, if this is an example of what Hemisphere Games is capable of, I'm excited to see what's next.

Behind the Game

Osmos began when Eddy Boxerman took a class on spacecraft dynamics while in college. At the time Boxerman was pursuing a degree in mechanical engineering, and what he learned in the class stuck with him.

Years later, Boxerman had long since graduated and established himself in the real world. He worked as a programmer specializing in physics and animation for a company called Xtra Normal, and even did some work for Ubisoft. One night he was doing the dishes when an idea for a game suddenly came to him "all in one shot," as he puts it. "I like cloth simulation and fluid and stuff like that," Boxerman says. "I always thought it would be kinda cool to make a game where you're just this blobby thing floating around and absorbing other things. Sort of like a lava lamp."

The spacecraft-dynamics course Boxerman had taken in college came back to him, and he thought of an idea that combined his lava-lamp concept with his more scientific side. He wasted no time turning his game idea into reality. "I just had to sit down at that point and start prototyping it," he says.

Within a few days, Boxerman says he had a prototype with all of the basic mechanics. Players could zoom in and out, absorb smaller motes, and even warp time, just like in the final version of *Osmos*. Then, he spent weeks working on the sound for the game. "I'm not really a musician," he says. "I play guitar, but I got really into the vibe of the game. I was listening to a lot of ambient electronica at the time and it just worked so well for the game. I got really into that aspect." The focus on sound design for *Osmos* became an obsession for Boxerman, who says that he got to a point where he was listening to hundreds of tracks to figure out which track fit which level perfectly.

Statistics

- **Development time (for iOS):** 7 months
- **Number of times Boxerman has reduced the difficulty level in *Osmos*:** 30–40
- **Percentage of players who give up on *Osmos* after each successive level:** 5%

An important focus during *Osmos*'s development was making the game easy enough for an average player. Boxerman became incredibly good at the game, and after playing it for months, lost perspective on how other players would perform when picking it up for the first time. When Boxerman began letting random online gamers play the game in its beta stage, the feedback was unanimous—"it's too hard."

Boxerman recognized that the beta testers were right, and set about making small tweaks to make the game easier. "Sometimes when a professor has been teaching a course for too long, he can't even explain things anymore because he can't remember what it was like to not know the subject," he says.

The levels that proved to be the most trouble for the game's testers were the "orbital" levels, in which hundreds of motes rapidly orbit a star in the middle of the stage. Boxerman's understanding of spacecraft dynamics allows him to complete these levels with ease, but according to early reports he gathered, about 95% of players were unable to figure them out. Boxerman did lots of stats analysis during *Osmos*'s beta stage. He says that his records show that one (unnamed) tester played and failed a single level in *Osmos* over 130 times before finally giving up.

The analysis Boxerman was doing allowed him to make very specific notes about the way players were interacting with *Osmos*. When I asked him for advice on how to play the game better, he responded by noting that each level type requires a different play style, and that different players prefer to use unique but equally valid approaches. "Some people play really slowly, almost as if they're deep-sea divers," he says. "They click, and then they just drift, and they absorb something, and they click again and drift some more. You also get some people who are super aggressive, but in doing so they're blowing a ton of mass."

> **Fun Facts**
>
> - Boxerman put up a video walkthrough on YouTube to help players with the super-difficult orbital levels.
> - Despite being significantly cheaper than its PC counterpart, the iOS version of *Osmos* accounts for over 80% of the revenue earned from sales.
> - Boxerman's previous employer, Xtra Normal, provides a service that allows people to create animated scenes by typing text. Visit xtranormal.com to see for yourself.

While Boxerman was gathering data, he was also keeping close tabs on player feedback. His favorite observation method was through Twitter. He could do a search for "*Osmos*" and see what people around the world were saying about his game. "It's really the most honest data that you can collect, because Twitter users aren't your friends," Boxerman says. "You have Joe Blow who's like, 'I just played this game and failed a level 20 times, so I rage quit and it sucks.' In ways it's even more honest than App-Store reviews."

Boxerman kept listening to feedback and decreasing the game's difficulty level, but the complaints just kept coming in. "I probably made those levels easier ten times during development, and another ten times during the beta," he says with a laugh. "It's not about how hard I think the level should be. It's about what creates the best player experience," he says.

Boxerman worked on the game off and on for the better part of a year, but got more serious about it when he began thinking about submitting the game to the 2008 Independent Games Festival. He recruited the help of a few longtime friends, and set to work using their talents to improve the game's visual style. Unfortunately, *Osmos* didn't win any nominations at the IGF. Boxerman was a bit discouraged, and so work on the game continued slowly.

A full year later, another IGF deadline was looming, and Boxerman was determined to get some buzz going about his game. He recruited the help of some more friends, most notably Dave Burke, who had experience working on games in the *Gears of War* and *Unreal Tournament* franchises. Burke helped Boxerman cram to get *Osmos* into shape for the 2009 IGF, and then the two men waited and hoped. This time, *Osmos* was a massive hit with the judges. It scored four nominations, and even won an award—the Direct2Drive Visions Award.

After *Osmos*'s stellar performance at the IGF, Boxerman began to see the game differently. It went from being a simple hobby-type project to something deserving of much more time and energy. Boxerman quit his job and set up an office in his mother-in-law's sewing room. In August of 2009, the PC version was released. The iOS version followed a year later, and has outperformed the PC version's sales by a factor of ten. Apple then gave *Osmos* a healthy boost in sales when it named the game its iPad Game of the Week, and another when it awarded the game the title of iPad Game of the Year. Later that same year, *Osmos* was also awarded a prestigious Apple design award. Now, Boxerman says he and his small company have the luxury of time to work on whatever they want. "Another game is on the way," he promises.

Pizza Boy

Platform: iPhone/iPod Touch
Price: $1.99
Developer: ACNE Play
Released: September 7, 2010

What Is It?

Life isn't always easy for pizza delivery boys. Sometimes you get stuck in traffic, customers occasionally forget to tip, and every once in a while a giant bird steals your pizza, forcing you to embark on a quest for pepperoni and justice. *Pizza Boy* is a side-scrolling platformer that shares much in common with the early *Mario* games. Hopping on enemies kills them, and there are collectible items scattered everywhere—all pretty standard fare for platformers.

What makes *Pizza Boy* far better than your average iOS platformer is how wonderfully polished it is. The game runs smoothly, and even better than the gorgeous pixel art is the retro soundtrack with its fat chiptune beats and generally cheery tone.

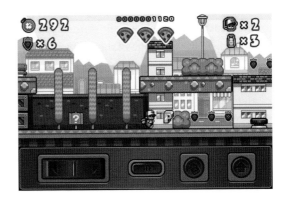

The gameplay itself isn't all just *Mario*-inspired, either. Each level has the letters P-I-Z-Z-A hidden throughout (sound familiar, *Tony Hawk Pro Skater* fans?), and it can be a pretty interesting challenge to try to grab them all—especially on timed levels where the stage constantly prods you forward. If you're a parent looking for a game that will instill healthy eating habits and good manners in your kids, *Pizza Boy* is probably not your best option; the pizza boy eats copious amounts of gooey, cheesy pizza to restore his health, and enjoys murdering wild animals by hurling soda bottles at them.

If you're a former Super Nintendo–lover who could do with a good blast of nostalgic platforming, try this game out.

Behind the Game

ACNE Productions is in no way a small company. It began as a design and communications company (ACNE is supposedly an acronym for Associated Computer Nerds Enterprise), but the ACNE Group is now a collection of Swedish companies that has its hands in all manner of businesses, including fashion, web design, advertising, and even feature films.

Lucas Duroj landed a summer job creating Flash-based websites for ACNE, but he didn't plan on sticking with the company forever—he wanted to attend Playground Squad, one of Sweden's most respected game-design schools. Duroj told several ACNE employees about his plans to attend Playground Squad. He mentioned that his dream was to start a small game-development company focused on creating original games that he himself would love to play. The CEO of ACNE Productions apparently heard about this, and approached Duroj with an idea. "Well, why don't you do that here?" he asked Duroj.

With that, the newest member of the ACNE Group—ACNE Play—was born. Duroj, who planned on working as a programmer, asked his friend Kaj Inazawa to join him, and Inazawa agreed.

> ### Statistics
>
> - **Development time:** 6 months
> - **Total budget:** $62,000
> - **Times downloaded:** 79,000

I spoke to ACNE Play's production manager, Annica Strand, who admits that ACNE Play's story isn't like that of most first-time game developers. "Many of the stories you hear of by indie developers will be stories of financial struggles, noodle dinners, postponed deadlines, and basement offices," says Strand. "This is not one of those."

Duroj and Inazawa were allowed access to ACNE Production's capital to help fund their projects, so at no point were they hurting for money. Money wasn't the only way the two received help from ACNE; Mikael Ali Larsson (an artist at ACNE Production) contributed art to *Pizza Boy*, and one of ACNE's founding fathers, Tomas Skoging, also lent a personal hand to certain aspects of the development process.

Pizza Boy was actually the second game created by the newly formed ACNE gaming division. The first was *Comet*, a colorful but simple arcade game. "It was made in many ways as a demo, a way for us to test our wings," explains Strand. "It did not sell particularly well, but now we had a core engine to build upon."

Pizza Boy's development went off without a hitch. The team focused on mechanics first when building the game, and all of the pizza-related story elements were added in later to create a comprehensive theme (that explains the game's milk-bottle lobbing mechanic).

Upon completion of the game, ACNE Play began to think up ways to handle marketing. Since most of the company's ties were to fashion magazines, it decided to try its luck and sent mail announcing that ACNE was "getting into the pizza business" to some of the biggest Swedish fashion publications. "Quite a few thought it was funny and wrote about the game," says Strand. "I don't think we could pull that one off again, though; it was a one-time trick."

According to Strand, *Pizza Boy* ended up selling almost 80,000 copies to date, which means the game has now paid for itself almost twice, making ACNE Play into yet another of the ACNE family's profitable groups. Strand says that ACNE Play's next game, *My Little Hero*, will have a significantly higher budget than its previous two games.

> ### Fun Facts
>
> - ACNE lead designer Jonny Johansoon has stated in interviews that "ACNE" stands for "Ambition to Create Novel Expressions."
> - Yes, the word "acne" is synonymous with the unpleasant skin condition in Sweden, too.
> - Other apps by ACNE Play include *Comet*.

Plants vs. Zombies

Platform: iPhone/iPod Touch (iPad version available separately)
Price: $2.99
Developer: PopCap
Released: February 14, 2010

What Is It?

Planting bean-shooting shrubs to defend yourself from a zombie invasion is pretty ridiculous, but even ignoring that, *Plants vs. Zombies* is an unconventional game. Most notably, it's a fresh take on the tower-defense genre, which has become quite stale thanks to the countless releases over the years that have added nothing to the concepts introduced in some of the first tower-defense games.

    PvZ turns tower defenses into a single-screen game built around five bowling alley–style lanes filled with shuffling zombies. You have the ability to plant a variety of plants using sun power, which can occasionally be collected as it falls from the sky, but which is also generated by the sunflowers you plant. Everything about *Plants vs. Zombies* is weird and over-the-top in the best way possible. The zombies in particular are more amusing than they are

threatening, thanks to their often-unfortunate choices in attire (traffic cones make bad helmets, but zombies don't seem to care). A likely favorite is Crazy Dave, an insane hobo who sells players new items and plants out of the back of his car in between levels.

The PC release of *Plants vs. Zombies* was fantastic, but the iOS version is even better. It has the right pacing to work as a mobile game, and the touch interface could not suit it any better.

Behind the Game

Before creating *Plants vs. Zombies*, George Fan made a name for himself at PopCap by single-handedly creating *Insaniquarium*, a game in which players are tasked with taking care of a virtual fish tank that occasionally gets attacked by fish-devouring aliens. During this time, Fan was also working days as a programmer for Blizzard, and that proved to be a miserable experience. Upon completion of *Insaniquarium* he elected to take a full-time position with PopCap, where he'd gotten the chance to create a new game.

> ### Statistics
> - **Development time:** 3+ years
> - **Times downloaded (across all platforms):** 9,000,000

Fan had been playing a lot of tower-defense mods for Blizzard's *Warcraft III* (the now-popular genre was created first by modders of *Warcraft*). "I had to ask myself what it was about them that I liked so much," he says. "I came to the conclusion that they reminded me of that feeling you get when you'd hole up in your self-made pillow forts as a kid. As a game designer, I love tapping into childhood experiences because those are some of the purest examples of fun you can find."

Fan liked tower-defense games conceptually, but was disappointed by the lack of character in the mods he was playing. After all, it's a bit hard to fit character into a game about towers. Fan began thinking of a way to inject more personality into a tower-defense game, and the idea of replacing the towers with plants stuck. "Plants were something that people expect to remain stationary yet I felt that I could inject a lot of character into," he explains.

Fan began working on a prototype for a tower-defense game about plants doing battle against aliens (he reused the aliens from *Insaniquarium*, presumably to save time developing new assets). "I guess the aliens had given up their seafood diets and now wanted to munch on plants or something," Fan jokes. The alien element of Fan's game (which he had tentatively been calling *Weedlings*) didn't last long before he fell in love with the idea of including zombies in the game. Zombies fit for a number of reasons—they're slow and they move in packs, making them excellent for a tower-defense game. Fan added in the zombies and changed the game to utilize the five-lane structure that players see today. *Plants vs. Zombies* was born.

Fan's development team at PopCap was small—only four people worked on the game full time. One of the team members, Laura Shigihara (now Fan's fiancée), was in charge of music and sound design. Fan had a funny anecdote from the game's development period about her. "Laura was going through the list of sounds needed for the game and saw that we needed a sound effect for when butter lands on a zombie's head," Fan says. "She went to the fridge and found a stick of butter and made a bowl of oatmeal and recorded the sound of throwing the stick of butter into the oatmeal."

According to Fan, Shigihara was unsatisfied with the sound the oatmeal produced. She gave Fan a look that he says he'll never forget. "Can I borrow your head?" she asked. "So the next five minutes was spent with me kneeling under the microphone and Laura repeatedly slapping butter on my head," Fan recalls. "Let me tell you, getting butter slapped on your head is one of the weirdest sensations ever. We both couldn't stop laughing, and I actually had to cover my mouth so my laughter wouldn't get recorded."

After talking to Fan, it becomes apparent that the development of *Plants vs. Zombies* was filled with a lot of pleasant experiences. "What might've been unique about the development of *Plants vs. Zombies* was just how painless it was," he says. "We had a remarkable amount of freedom and time to make the game we wanted to."

Fan gives much of the credit to his fellow team members, Tod Semple (programming), Rich Werner (art), and, of course, his butter-flinging fiancée, Laura Shigihara. "I'd be hard pressed to name a programmer/artist/musician I'd rather work with at this point, and I think that totally shows as I've chosen the exact same team to work on my current game project," he says.

After its release *Plants vs. Zombies* became a success on every platform it was released on, but on the iPhone and iPad (where it's considerably cheaper than on the PC), it's been a phenomenon. "Of all the platforms *Plants vs. Zombies* has been released on, iOS has been the biggest-selling one by far," says Fan.

Fun Facts

- You'll have to play through the game twice to completely fill out the zombie almanac (and see every zombie type).
- Fan names the Disney-produced *Swiss Family Robinson* movie as one of his major inspirations for the game.
- Fan is a big fan of *Magic: The Gathering*, and at one point considered adding "deck-building" elements to *Plants vs. Zombies*.
- Other apps by PopCap include *Bejeweled 2 + Blitz* and *Bookworm*.

Pocket God

Platform: iPhone/iPod Touch (iPad version available separately)
Price: $.99
Developer: Bolt Creative
Released: January 9, 2009

What Is It?

Pocket God is one of those incredibly popular early iPhone games that almost everyone seems to know about. In its earliest stages, it was really more of a toy than a game. As the god of a few cartoon pygmies on a small island, your job consisted of little more than torturing the pygmies in various ways. You could throw them into water to watch them drown, electrocute them with lightning, and feed them to sharks, but it was really a some-what shallow app. Then the updates started rolling out. Bolt Creative has dropped dozens of updates since the game's initial release, slowly morphing *Pocket God* from a mere toy into the digital equivalent of a theme park. Just finding all of the hidden minigames and ways to interact with your pygmies can take hours, making it a pretty incredible value considering that Bolt Creative still only charges 99 cents for the game.

Whether you're a kid who can be entertained for hours by poking at interactive toys or an adult who fondly remembers the days of *Interactive Buddy*, *Pocket God* is like a Swiss Army knife, packed with trinkets that will amuse everyone.

Behind the Game

David Castelnuovo's involvement in the games industry stretches all the way back to 1992, when he worked for Visual Concepts as the lead (and, in fact, only) programmer on the Super Nintendo/Sega Genesis game *Clayfighter*. Castelnuovo says it was a fulfilling experience—he loved having to "just figure it out along the way."

In 2001, Castelnuovo formed Bolt Creative, which started as a developer of software and games based on Adobe's Flash technology. He mostly did contract work for clients, but he wasn't entirely happy with this setup—"I had always wanted to get back into working on real hardware as opposed to using browser-based technology," he admits. The iPhone and its App Store came along, and Castelnuovo saw an opportunity to get back into the type of small-team software development he had enjoyed while working on *Clayfighter* in the early 1990s.

> ### Statistics
>
> - **Development time:** 1 week (and continual development after that)
> - **Times downloaded:** 4,500,000

Castelnuovo wasn't prepared to quit his job, where he was billing over 80 hours per week. Nonetheless, he was convinced he could do more. "I knew I had to make room for iPhone development," he says.

Castelnuovo recalls setting up "sprint" projects—dedicating a day or a few hours to creating an entire application for the iPhone—as a way to train and familiarize himself with the hardware. The first application he created in this way was a simple (and not very well received) image-warping application called FWARP! "I gave myself a budget of ten hours to learn iOS, build the app, and submit it to the App Store," says Castelnuovo. He priced the app at 99 cents and released it onto the App Store, where it sold 100–300 units per day for quite some time after its release.

Castelnuovo experimented with another app (which sold even less well), and decided he had now enough experience to create something more interesting. He met over lunch with his longtime friend Allan Dye to discuss potential ideas for the iPhone. "In order for it to work, and not end up starting something we couldn't finish, I made it clear that we had to finish our next project within a week," says Castelnuovo. Castelnuovo's employer was closed during the week between Christmas and New Year in 2008, and he wanted to use that short window of time to create something cohesive.

At the time, an iPhone app called *Koi Pond* had become very successful. The app wasn't very complex—interactivity was limited to running your hand through the on-screen water and scaring the Koi fish in the little pond. You could also feed the fish, but that was about it.

Castelnuovo suggested creating a similar game that focused on small human characters. An island setting lent itself to this scenario naturally, and Dye drew some cartoon pygmies on a napkin who wound up being pretty close to the ones in the final version of *Pocket God*. "I thought it would be funny to throw them in the water and watch them drown," says Castelnuovo. That emphasis on dark humor set the tone for the app, and the two men agreed to attempt to create the game in a single week.

Their plan for a one-week development cycle was successful, and *Pocket God* was approved on January 9, 2009. The app began selling quickly—about 500 units per day. There was a lot of feedback from users, too, and not all of it was positive. Players complained that there wasn't enough to do in the game, and posters on popular iPhone message boards suggested that it was unlikely that Bolt Creative would support a simple game like *Pocket God* with future updates.

They were very, very wrong. Fourteen weeks later, Castelnuovo and Dye had released 14 free updates for *Pocket God*, and each one contained a considerable amount of new content

> **Fun Facts**
> - The first issue of the *Pocket God* comic book sold over 150,000 copies.
> - In 2003, Bolt Creative and Sony collaborated to create an online Flash version of *Wheel of Fortune*.
> - Other apps by Bolt Creative include *The Jackie Button* and *Pocket God: Journey to Uranus*.
> - There's a hidden (but playable) version of the classic arcade game *Joust* in *Pocket God: Journey to Uranus*.

along with bug fixes. "Our audience really responded and a lot of them started rooting for our success," Castelnuovo says proudly. After nearly three months of continued support and updates, *Pocket God* reached the number one slot on the App Store sales charts in the United States. Apple hadn't promoted it, and no news site had covered it—its success had been entirely through word of mouth.

Pocket God held onto its number-one position for nearly a month and has never fallen below a top-50 ranking in the years since, in part because Bolt Creative never relented updating the game. It's nearing the release of its 50th content update as of the time of this writing, and it doesn't plan on slowing down. "I wouldn't be surprised if we hit 100 [updates]," says Castelnuovo.

Along with the long-term success of the original *Pocket God* app, Bolt Creative has since expanded on its IP with another *Pocket God* game (subtitled *Journey to Uranus*) and a full-fledged comic book series, which Castelnuovo claims regularly outsells the entire combined catalogs of Marvel and DC's comic book apps.

All of this growth is even more impressive when you consider that Bolt Creative is still just as small as when it began. "I do all the programming, Allan Dye does all the art," says Castelnuovo. "We have other contractors who work on some of the offshoots, but Allan and I are very involved in all our projects, and the flagship *Pocket God* game is kept up-to-date by just the two of us."

Castelnuovo says *Pocket God* is the first project he's worked on that reminds him of his days as a lone programmer working on *Clayfighter*. Time will tell if he can hang onto that ideal as the *Pocket God* empire continues to expand.

Pocket Legends

Platform: iPad/iPhone/iPod Touch (universal app)
Price: Free
Developer: Spacetime Studios
Released: April 8, 2010

What Is It?

Pocket Legends has often, perhaps unfairly, drawn comparisons to *World of Warcraft*. Unlike Gameloft's *Order & Chaos Online*, *Pocket Legends* is actually not structured at all like *WoW*, thanks largely to the fact that Spacetime designed it from the ground up for mobile devices. It does take a few lessons from Blizzard's titanically popular massively multiplayer online game, but for the most part the game is designed to be enjoyed in small bites. Because of this fact, *Pocket Legends* manages to outclass every mobile MMO that has come before it.

In *Pocket Legends*, players choose one of three classes: bears, eagles, or elves. Bears are the close-range, melee class; eagles are, of course, bow-wielding rangers; and elves are magic users. It's a very cartoonish, kid-friendly game, and all of the characters have big heads, which makes the violence look like something out of a *Tom & Jerry*

episode rather than the hectic, fantastic battles in most modern MMOs. Much of *Pocket Legends* is instanced (that's MMO-speak for "there's a limit to how many people you can take on missions with you"), presumably to avoid crashing issues that would result from having hundreds of woodland creatures populating an area all at once.

Pocket Legends is a free-to-play game, but Spacetime Studios isn't shy about trying to monetize it. There are a lot of ways for you to spend money to get ahead in the game, but if you want to play without dropping any coin, you can absolutely get away with that. Even if you never spend a dime you'll get to enjoy Spacetime's near-continual post-launch support, which has kept the game world thriving and the game's community sticking around.

From a purely objective standpoint, I can confidently say that *Pocket Legends* is absolutely the best MMO on iOS. It's been great since the day it launched (simultaneously with the first iPad), and its only close competitor is *Star Legends*, another Spacetime game.

Behind the Game

Spacetime Studios has always been an MMO developer. The company was formed in 2005 by four veterans of the games industry, each of whom had extensive experience working on MMOs like *Ultima Online*, *Wing Commander*, and *Star Wars Galaxies*. By mid-2006, Spacetime had a contract with NCSoft to publish its first MMO, an outer-space sci-fi epic called *Blackstar*. Unfortunately, that contract was canceled less than two years later by NCSoft, which had recently suffered big financial hits due to the underperformance of other MMOs like *Tabula Rasa* and *Auto Assault*.

With no publisher and an unfinished game on its hands, Spacetime deteriorated. The studio had once employed more than 40 team members, but over time that number was cut to just six—the four founding members and two other employees. Luckily, the studio had been paid a reasonably-sized termination fee by NCSoft, so they had some time to consider new options.

> ### Statistics
> - **Development time:** 6 months
> - **Average time players spend in a single session:** 25 minutes
> - **Times downloaded:** 3,000,000

Spacetime was also able to retain ownership of the software and tools it had created for developing MMOs, which meant that creating a game might not be too difficult if the team could come up with an idea. At first the team continued trying to find a publisher for *Blackstar*, but that didn't go well. Spacetime Studios chief creative officer (and co-founder) Jake Rogers explains: "As we were traveling around the world meeting with publishers, it became clear that even the largest of them were starting to grow weary of making such expensive bets," he says. "There were only a handful of successful MMOs out there, and only one (*World of Warcraft*) that was considered a model for success."

The team had the technology to build an MMO, but they weren't doing much with it. They had resorted to doing contract work for other developers, but that wasn't satisfying for Spacetime—it was a studio that had been created with big ambitions in mind. "We were making a living doing work for hire, but we were not changing the world the way that we had originally thought we would," says Rogers.

The Spacetime members did a lot of traveling while looking for publishers, and often spent time poking at apps on their iPhones during downtime. "I have vivid memories of the four of us in airports and car-rental lobbies, our faces buried in our phones," says Rogers. "We liked finding and showing them to each other, but we became increasingly aware that there weren't many multiplayer games available. Even the available multiplayer games were typically asynchronous, or turn-based, games."

In the middle of 2009, Spacetime began to ask itself the obvious question—why don't we make an MMO for phones? The devices were already connected to the Internet, and possessed the power to display three-dimensional graphics. Better yet, owners of smartphones were already used to buying things like ringtones and songs from their devices, so they'd be more likely to accept the "microtransaction" model. "No one had done it before, but that didn't mean it couldn't be done," Rogers says.

Spacetime wasn't ready to put its logo on apps, so it created a secondary company called Clockrocket Games, which it used to release several experimental games for free. Cheap, throwaway titles like *Shotgun Granny* and *Zombie Weatherman* allowed Spacetime to familiarize itself with the App Store and the iPhone without risking damage to its brand. Near the end of 2009, Spacetime finally began to feel comfortable with the iPhone, and it began developing what would become *Pocket Legends*.

Work on *Pocket Legends* was largely characterized by optimizing both its engine and art to get the game working properly. Quests had to be shortened to 5–10 minutes, characters had to be designed simply so that dozens could appear on screen at once without causing a major slowdown, and common MMO-design principles were thrown out the window. Even for a team of experienced MMO developers, the work was a real challenge. "I think we all drew a lot from our experience making this kind of game in the past, but looking back, that experience only took us so far," says Rogers. "We ended up changing a lot of our fundamental assumptions about what an MMO should be, so along the way our experience was just as often a curse as it was a blessing."

It was difficult, but Spacetime was able to adapt. *Pocket Legends* was released as a universal app alongside the first iPad in early April 2010, and has since become a massive success. The free-to-download game has over three million downloads on iOS alone, with 10% of those players eventually purchasing in-game items using real money. Over one million additional players downloaded the game on Android, where it was also made available.

Rogers says that *Pocket Legends* is continually growing, and Spacetime has supported the game with over 200 updates and countless more in-game patches (averaging 1.7

Fun Facts

- Spacetime Studios released preproduction gameplay footage of the never-released *Blackstar*. You can still find it on YouTube.

- The Clockrocket website makes no mention of the company's connection to Spacetime Studios. Check the "about" page on clockrocket.com for a laugh.

- Other apps by Spacetime Studios include *Spacetime Community* and *Star Legends: The Blackstar Chronicles.*

patches per day as of the time of this writing). The studio has also released a second mobile MMO based on the *Blackstar* universe—*Star Legends: The Blackstar Chronicles.*

Poto and Cabenga

Platform: iPhone/iPod Touch
Price: $.99
Developer: Honeyslug
Released: February 17, 2011

What Is It?

Poto and Cabenga gets a whole lot of gameplay out of some incredibly simple controls. At first glance it looks like yet another *Canabalt*-style endless-running game, and in many respects it is. The twist? You're tasked with simultaneously controlling two characters in completely separate locations.

Poto is a girl who gets eaten by a huge bird at the start of the game, and Cabenga is her trusty steed (who may or may not actually be a cow). The screen is split horizontally across the middle, with Poto on the top and Cabenga on the bottom. Here's where it gets interesting: all of your interaction with both characters revolves around whether or not you're touching the screen.

Touching your device will cause Poto to jump and Cabenga to run faster, and lifting your finger will cause the opposite to happen—Cabenga will jump and Poto will

speed up. Both characters are constantly barraged with aerial and ground-based hazards, and you'll have to time your taps so that each character can sprint under and hop over their respective threats. The feeling is a bit like trying to rub your belly and pat your head at the same time, and when it finally clicks for you, you'll feel like you've conquered your own brain.

Behind the Game

Like several other games in this book, *Poto and Cabenga* was created specifically in response to a challenge: in this case, the Gamma IV One-Button Games challenge. Under the rules of the Gamma IV contest, six winners would be chosen and their games would be displayed at a big party during the Game Developers Conference in San Francisco. Ricky Haggett of Honeyslug knew he wanted to create a game for the event, so he and Richard Hogg, a longtime friend, began kicking ideas around. "Early on there was an idea to do something with rhythm," says Haggett.

One of those ideas was a game in which players controlled a guy with a massive gong leading a line of people down a street. Hogg had his own ideas involving a "bouncing fellow" (which Haggett hinted might appear in a future Honeyslug title). Soon the two men began thinking about ways to implement one-touch controls into a platforming game in which the single button controlled jumping. "Dick then said something that became the seed of the basic idea," says Haggett. "He was talking about *Rhythm Tengoku/Paradise*, about how much he liked the feeling of the games where you take your stylus off the screen to make something happen." This sparked an idea in Haggett's mind for a platform game in which players control two characters at once: one that jumps when players press a button, and one that jumps when the button is released. "I thought about that all day," says Hagget. "Then on the bus home I started thinking about possibilities for holding the button (and not holding it), because those are the four things you can do with a single button (press it, release it, hold it down, and not hold it down)."

> ### Statistics
> - **Development time for the Flash version:** 2 weeks
> - **Development time for the iPhone version:** 1 month

The following weekend, Haggett and Hogg began work on a prototype. Since it was just a prototype, they decided to save time by using graphics from *Super Mario World* instead of creating their own characters. "No scrolling, just a top screen and a bottom screen, Mario and Luigi jumping over Koopas," says Haggett.

Haggett describes spending "a lot of time" stressing over the physics of jumping in the game. "It was a tricky problem, because in some ways, nice floaty, controllable jumps felt good, but in other ways they made the game too difficult," he says. "I eventually settled on a really square-wave jump, where there are basically two heights: on the floor, or in the air, and the characters move very quickly between them."

After Haggett had perfected his jumping mechanism, it took only another week and a half to finish the game and send it off to Gamma IV. He got his brother Rob and another friend (Dave Trehearn) to contribute to the game's music, while Kwok Fung Lam did the game's animation. *Poto and Cabenga* was accepted by Gamma, and Haggett and crew had a great time in San Francisco.

On the show floor at GDC, the Honeyslug crew was stationed directly across from Steve Wiebe, who was once again trying to break the world record for *Donkey Kong*, the 1981 Nintendo arcade game (check out *The King of Kong*; it's a wonderful documentary that'll tell you more about Wiebe's story). "It was a combination of amazing to watch, and kind of sad," comments Haggett.

Poto and Cabenga was a big success at the show, although Haggett recalls a variety of reactions to the game from show goers. "One guy walked right up, picked up the controller and aced the entire game, losing only a couple of lives," he says. "Others did less well—my favorite was the guy who threw the controller down in disgust at the moment Poto gets eaten by the Wyrm."

After the show, Honeyslug decided to put the game up for free on its website, where over a million people played the game. The response was so strong that it decided to hire someone (Trevor Wilkin) to do an iOS port of the game. Haggett says that *Poto and Cabenga* hasn't made Honeyslug rich, but the game has been covered by plenty of blogs and received lots of critical praise, which is good enough for now for these indie developers.

Fun Facts

- Honeyslug has developed tons of games, including *Balloon Headed Boy*, which is free for download in the App Store.
- Poto and Cabenga are named after a pair of America twins who spoke in a language only they understood until the age of 8. Google it!
- You can still play *Poto and Cabenga* online for free at www.potoandcabenga. com.
- Other apps by Honeyslug include *Ric Rococo: International Art Thief* and *Kahoots.*

The Raging Dead

Platform: iPhone/iPod Touch
Price: $.99
Developer: GhostBird Software
Released: January 14, 2010

What Is It?

In *The Raging Dead*, you have a bird's eye view of a zombie apocalypse as it overtakes a city. In the game, zombies are represented by red dots, and humans are represented by blue dots. At the start of each level you'll be faced with several city blocks with hundreds of uninfected humans and just a few scattered zombies, but those few can quickly multiply by catching the blue dots and converting them into more zombies.

As the player, you can take out zombies and save humans using either bombs or machine guns. There are a few tricks to this. For one, your weapons have limited accuracy and relatively slow reload speeds, so you'll have to make every shot count—at least until you can upgrade and get access to bigger, badder, faster weapons. Also, replaying levels allows you to get better upgrades for your weapons, which is beneficial, because some later levels are much easier if you

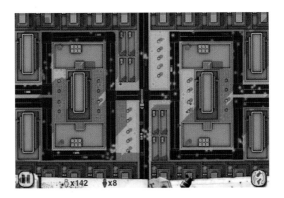

have the right tool for the job. For instance, while the machine gun is good for targeting a few problematic zombies who have wandered off on their own, the bomb is much better for taking out lots of zombies in one hit—but it can also cause damage to the city, which will count against your end-level score. Other factors that will impact your score include the number of humans you saved and the amount of time it took you to complete the level.

Although *The Raging Dead*'s graphics are simple, the human dots have a surprising sense of self-preservation. They'll sometimes group together while fleeing from zombies, and this can be both a good and bad thing. If all of the blue dots in a level have clustered together for safety, you'll have a much easier time of spotting incoming threats and eliminating them. On the other hand, if just one red zombie makes it through your barrage of bullets and explosives and bites a human, your sea of frightened blue humans will quickly devolve into a thrashing mass of crimson undead.

The Raging Dead's average iTunes review score is pretty low thanks to some users who aren't happy with the game's admittedly simple visuals. Frankly, those people are missing the point. I love *The Raging Dead* for its originality, and I love it for the fact that it's not just another zombie-based dual-stick shooter. It's a zombie game with an original twist, and it's a shame that more people haven't embraced it.

Behind the Game

Few developers I've ever spoken to have sounded more downcast than Travis Houlette, programmer and designer of *The Raging Dead*. Even games that don't sell many copies like *Nimble Strong* (pp. 151–155) have their shining moments when fans or critics reward game developers with praise, but *The Raging Dead* never had its day—there was no silver lining for GhostBird Software.

That part of the story is yet to come, though. The story behind *The Raging Dead* began in the summer of 2009, when Travis Houlette and his friends began working on an idea they had for a zombie simulation game. They'd been inspired by Valve's zombie apocalypse masterpiece *Left 4 Dead*, and wanted to create a game that focused on the spread of a zombie virus through a human population.

Their idea also borrowed heavily from a demo of a zombie apocalypse game they had found online (you can play that demo at hardcorepawn.com/zombie3/). The demo in question features thousands of randomly moving pixels. Green pixels represent zombies, pink pixels were humans, and green pixels spread by converting the pink humans into zombies. In the demo, players have an aerial perspective, and their goal is to wipe out all the green pixels by clicking frantically to drop bombs that killed any zombies (or humans) in their path. Houlette liked the idea but believed he and his team could create a fully fleshed-out game by focusing on enhanced human/zombie AI, an interactive cityscape, and a variety of upgradable weapons.

From the start, *The Raging Dead* was a rough project to work on. Houlette and the others maintained day jobs while working on the game, dedicating hours of their spare time to create it. "Development was extremely exhausting," says Houlette. "I'd come home from my day job making games and work on *The Raging Dead* until I couldn't keep my eyes open."

The Raging Dead's difficulties began with its AI, which Houlette describes as being the hardest problem the team had to tackle. "Unlike the zombie demo whose humans/zombies would simply randomly gyrate around, we wanted beings that would move and react like you would expect zombies and scared humans to move," Houlette explains. "This meant zombies that could see prey and begin chase, and humans who could spot a threat and attempt to escape. This also meant humans would need to be able to navigate though a city environment, i.e., run down alleys and around cars, trees, and other obstacles."

GhostBird also programmed in more subtle behaviors like the tendency for frightened humans to run with crowds. Whenever applying this complex AI to hundreds of on-screen beings (represented by single pixels), older iOS devices did not fare well. GhostBird's solution was to cap the number of on-screen entities at 600. Even with that relatively large number, the team was able to get the game to run smoothly at 30 FPS, a feat that Houlette is proud of.

Houlette had his more intelligent AI and his interactive environments (buildings get destroyed as levels progress, and players earn points by minimizing city damage), but it was the upgradable weapons that ended up being *The Raging Dead*'s weak point. The GhostBird team wanted to maintain the frantic nature of the demo they'd seen, but *The Raging Dead* has fewer on-screen characters that are more widely spaced than the humans and zombies in the web demo. The team's solution was to make the initial weapons slow, with long reload times. "This meant players would need to pick their shots and not just tap indiscriminately," says Houlette.

Unfortunately, the game's upgrade system allows players to continually improve their weapons until they become giant death machines requiring almost no reload time. GhostBird Software was dissatisfied with the result, but the team had been working on the game for six months, so they released it. "Ultimately the game did not end up exactly how we imagined," admits Houlette. "It was probably released too soon and would have benefited from more content, alternative game modes, and more gameplay tuning. The gameplay was just not as fun as it should have been. There's many reasons for this and I could probably tear my own game apart better than anyone else, but when it comes down to it, just watching the mayhem spread was often more enjoyable than actually playing the game."

> **Statistics**
> - **Development time:** 6 months
> - **Paid copies downloaded (in the first 3 months):** 3,000
> - **Pirated copies downloaded (in the first 3 months):** 10,000

> **Fun Facts**
> - GhostBird is largely profitable now as a creator of photography-focused apps in the App Store.
> - Other apps by GhostBird include *Dotopop* and *PhotoForge2*.

In the end, says Houlette, GhostBird recognized that spending more time on the game wouldn't be practical. The game was released but was effectively dead on arrival, selling only 3,000 units in the first three months. In total, it never made more than $4,000. Reviews were tepid, but lots of people pirated it. GhostBird made the game free for two days, and nearly 50,000 people downloaded it during that time. "In total, including pirates, about 75,000 people have played the game," Houlette says. "Though I have yet to meet someone in real life who has even heard of it."

I'm going to take a moment here to say that I think Houlette is being far too harsh on his creation. He's right that the game could've benefitted from some extra modes, and the end-game could be better balanced—by the last level it's more about how quickly you can spot and tap zombies than anything else—but there's value to be had in *The Raging Dead*. GhostBird did such an excellent job on the artificial intelligence that you can feel the humanity in the fleeing human-pixel people. They'll run down an alley, unaware of the pack of zombies awaiting them on the other side, and you'll find yourself actually feeling sorry for them as they struggle to escape the hordes.

I'm not saying that *The Raging Dead* is a perfect game, but there are parts that are unmistakably brilliant. I only wish others would see that brilliance.

Robosockets
Link Me Up

Platform: iPad/iPhone/iPod Touch (universal app)
Price: $.99
Developer: Tatem Games
Released: February 21, 2011

What Is It?

If you glance at a screenshot of *Robosockets*, it doesn't look like much more than another riff on the "falling blocks" genre of puzzle games. Luckily for you, that's not the case.

In *Robosockets*, all of the puzzle pieces are little living robots with various numbers of sockets that extend from their four sides. Some bots are completely covered in sockets, whereas others only have one or two. These sockets are useful for connecting one robot to another, which is important for your survival, because connecting more than five robots will cause all of them to blow up, clearing the play area and allowing you to continue matching the various bots that fall from the sky.

Much of *Robosockets'* strategy has to do with laying down bots in a way that will leave you with the most options. The game does tell players what type of bot will be coming next (a feature added six months after the game first hit the App Store), so you'll be able to examine the piles of robot parts at the bottom of the play area and use that information to quickly connect as many robots as possible, while trying to not let any get stuck with nowhere to go.

At first the game will seem a bit simple, but as you make your way through the single-player campaign you'll slowly be introduced to new power-ups and strategies that really open the game up and make it into something that can be fun to fool around with for a long time. A lot of these power-ups (like the bomb or the pusher-bot) allow you to push robots out of their otherwise locked-in positions, so that you can break up bad situations and potentially salvage a game you're losing.

Like the games that it draws inspiration from, *Robosockets* is the type of game that can offer hours of fun. It's just up to you to try it first.

Behind the Game

Tatem Games' roots go back to 1995, when Ukranian game studio Action Forms was founded. Tatem Games is a smaller company within Action Forms, focusing largely on mobile gaming.

Tatem had an early hit on the App Store with *Racer*, a simple traffic-avoidance game that got solid early reviews and lots of sales. The success of *Racer* convinced the company to pour more resources into the iOS platform, and it expanded from three employees to seven in anticipation of the increased development it would be doing.

Robosockets producer Ivan Pogodichey says the idea for the game came to him while he was taking a shower in the early fall of 2009. His idea was simple: what if you replaced the Terominoes in *Tetris* with the pipes from *Pipe Mania*? "It seemed so obvious a combination that the main concern was whether such a game already existed," says Pogodichey. The team scoured the App Store and Flash-game web portals for similar games, but they couldn't find anything that used the game's mechanics. Pogodichey presented the game idea to the rest of his staff, and prototyping began that day.

> ### Statistics
> • **Development time:** 1.5 years
> • **Percentage of people who upgrade from the free version of *Robosockets* to the paid version:** 5%

Originally the game was to have a circus theme, but the low-resolution screen of the iPhones and iPod Touches on the market at that time wouldn't have supported the detailed art style the team hoped for. Tatem Games didn't want to take the easy route and slap a doodle theme on its game, so it discarded the circus theme and went back to the drawing board. Before long it came up with a prototype that resembled a completed game, albeit one without a decent art style. "We joked that the game could be released as it was, but we had ambitions to create something outstanding," says Pogodichey.

Without any clear direction, the game that would later become *Robosockets* languished, and the team moved on to other projects. Sales of *Racer* had slowed, so they ported an old

Action Forms PC game, *Carnivores: Dinosaur Hunter*, to the App Store as a way to test the hardware capabilities of the second-generation iPhone and make some money.

Carnivores sold well, and the team was flush with cash and ready to move on to another project. They took another look at their incomplete puzzle game, and almost immediately the idea to outfit the game with a robot theme struck them. The only problem was finding an artist. Tatem Games PR rep Nadia Sydorenko elaborates: "When you ask an independent developer about financial constraints, the answer is always the same," says Sydorenko. "We hardly had a game design document, but the budget was plain: the less money we spend, the better."

Tatem Games ended up hosting a contest on a freelance website and chose an artist who impressed it with concept drawings of robots designed in a 1960s style. Although the artist spoke Russian like the rest of the Tatem Games team, there were a number of communication difficulties throughout the process. Pogodichey describes the artist's strange attitude toward modern-day chat clients like Skype or Instant Messenger. "I had to revive my long-forgotten ICQ client for the sole purpose of contacting the artist," Pogodichey says. "Despite having worked with him for over a year, we never heard each other."

Robosockets' release date was delayed numerous times, eventually getting pushed all the way back to early 2011. The game's soundtrack didn't receive attention until the very last moment, when Pogodichey was on vacation in Thailand. He actually sat down with his iPad, and using recording software, tapped out the beats that would become *Robosockets'* score. Sydorenko says that Pogodichey would take boat rides from one island to another, composing and recording as he went.

At release, *Robosockets* failed to make a huge splash. The game was covered on many major sites and did well at first, but sales soon slowed to a crawl. The Tatem Games team recognizes that they should have completed and released the game earlier, but although *Robosockets* hasn't been a huge success, it does do something unique, and it does it well.

> ### Fun Facts
>
> - Tatem Games intended to use ngmo-co's Plus+ social system with its game, but found that it was too glitchy. It went with Game Center instead.
> - The first release of *Robosockets* had some balancing issues—most players found it impossible to get past level 13.

Rolando

Platform: iPhone/iPod Touch
Price: $.99
Developer: HandCircus
Publisher: ngmoco
Released: December 18, 2008

What Is It?

Rolando was the first game to offer proof of the potential that iPhone games have. Whereas many of the first iPhone releases were titles that felt crammed onto the device, it's obvious that *Rolando*'s developer looked at the device and asked himself, what if I made a game that would only be possible *here*? Apparently, HandCircus discovered the answer to that question.

Rolando has you trying to get little round creatures (called, appropriately enough, Rolandos), to the exit of 36 levels. In many respects, it would be fair to call it a side-scrolling strategy game, because you'll almost always be in control of an entire group of little Rolandos. Touching and dragging selects more than one character at once, and tilting will make the currently selected characters roll. It's a simple set of commands, but the game adds lots of elements on top of that to make *Rolando* a rich and varied experience throughout.

The environment is filled with platforms and objects that you can interact with by touching the screen, and some Rolandos even have special abilities that help them navigate the environment. You might pull down an elevator for one group of Rolandos, then use a "sticky" Rolando to cling to the level's walls and activate a switch to help the rest of the group progress. In some levels there are even gigantic royal characters, most notably the King of Rolandoland, who can't move on his own and has to be pushed by a group of smaller Rolandos.

Rolando is designed to utilize its touch-screen platform brilliantly. For instance, you normally pan the camera around levels by using two-finger swipes, but the game has been designed so that all the Rolandos in a level appear on the edges of the screen as little bubbles that point towards their locations. If you tap on one of the bubbles, the camera automatically zooms over and centers on that Rolando's location. It's little touches like these that keep the game accessible without sacrificing any of its complexity.

Even when compared to the newer hits on the App Store, *Rolando* holds up as a fantastic game. It's representative of a design philosophy that any iOS developer could learn from.

Behind the Game

Before *Rolando*, Simon Oliver was a sort of digital-media jack-of-all-trades. As a freelancer he created websites, Flash games, and educational software. He even worked for the Science Museum and the Natural History Museum in London. Oliver wasn't entirely dissatisfied with his career, but his real aim was to break into the games industry. Realizing that he'd need to possess more relevant skills to get a position in the industry, Oliver began learning all he could about game design and teaching himself a few programming languages. He spent the next year working on various game prototypes that he hoped to use for a portfolio.

Unfortunately for Oliver, his lack of experience in the industry became an obstacle. Whenever he applied for a position, he'd ace the interviews but then inevitably lose the position to another applicant with more experience. Oliver was competing with veteran game developers, and it didn't go well for him.

During this time the indie games scene was really beginning to grow. Many developers were producing successful titles without using a publisher, and Oliver was inspired. "That demonstrated what a small team with a great idea is capable of," says Oliver. "Not just critical acclaim, but also commercial success due to the new

Statistics

- **Development time:** 9 months
- **Original price of *Rolando*:** $9.99
- **Times downloaded:** 200,000+

opportunities provided by digital distribution." The success of *World of Goo* and other indie titles inspired Oliver to forgo the traditional games industry and strike out on his own. He had a lot of ideas, but his first step would be to choose a development platform.

Around this time the iPhone was released. Oliver was impressed by what he'd seen of it, so he lined up on launch day, bought one, and promptly hacked it so he could tinker around with it and create his own programs (the hacking community released an unofficial software development kit, or SDK, for the iPhone soon after it was released). Keep in mind that this was 2007, and Apple had yet to launch the App Store. Oliver says that working with the hacked iPhone was a huge challenge, but within a few days he had created a basic game (similar to a Flash game called *Roadies* that he had created years earlier) and had it running beautifully on his new toy.

In March of 2008, Apple announced the impending launch of both an official iPhone SDK and the App Store, the combination of which would allow developers to create and sell their own apps. "I realized that this was the platform I'd been waiting for," says Oliver."

The day the SDK was released, Oliver threw himself into creating prototypes for games on the device. He had no idea what would and wouldn't work on the device, and there was no way to communicate with other developers working on software to share information—the App Store still hadn't been opened at that point, and those using Apple's SDK had to sign a nondisclosure agreement stating they wouldn't talk about the projects they were working on. Oliver was on his own, but he was making progress. "It became apparent that some genres and mechanics just didn't work due to the setup," he says. "Ports just weren't going to cut it—the only way to create a game for the iPhone was to design purely around it. On-screen buttons were (and continue to be) a massive failure, so traditional input schemes had to be thrown away."

With this new design philosophy in mind, Oliver finally created a prototype that he was happy with, a simple game starring ball-shaped characters. "The original idea was much more RTS [real-time strategy]-like, much less platformer-focused," Oliver says. "The idea was that you would pan around issuing instructions and the characters would follow them, so you'd have them rolling all around independently."

According to Oliver, this idea didn't work too well. Once the player had to manage more than a few characters at once, things inevitably descended into chaos. It was too hard to pan around the small screen quickly enough, making the game impossible to control. Oliver experimented with locking the game's camera onto the actively selected characters, and everything changed. "You could still control independent characters (which became Rolandos) but had the level of control and visibility that you needed," Oliver says. "That was probably the moment I realized we had a solid enough kernel for the game, and it was worth growing into something more substantial."

At that point, Oliver was still doing some freelance work part time, making *Rolando* a project for nights and weekends. But as the game progressed and developed into something promising, he decided to take a few days off work each week. At the same time, he

Fun Facts

- *Rolando*'s characters are largely inspired by the Zeroids from the 1980s British sci-fi show *Terrahawks*.
- ngmoco used to use (and maybe they still do) a small statue of Freddie Mercury to press a button to make their games go live.

kicked off a search for an artist who could give the game some personality. It didn't take long for Oliver to find Mikko Walamies, a talented illustrator with a quirky, charming art style. Oliver sent Walamies some screenshots and level layouts from his prototype and asked if he'd like to get involved. Walamies quickly agreed, and the HandCircus team was born.

The following months saw Oliver and Walamies dedicating themselves to the game, but it wasn't ready for release in time for the App Store launch in June of 2008. Oliver wanted to build some hype around his game's eventual release, however, so HandCircus put out a teaser trailer for the game about a week before the App Store opened. The trailer was a huge hit—numerous press outlets picked up on the game, and the trailer quickly surpassed 100,000 views.

A few days later Oliver received an email from Alan Yu, one of the founders of ngmoco. The company was interested in becoming *Rolando*'s publisher. At first this prospect didn't excite Oliver. "My first response was, why do I need a publisher? This is the iPhone, it's digital distribution!" says Oliver. "But we had some really good conversations, and it became apparent that a partnership was going to be really beneficial to both of us. There were some parts of the business that I know next to nothing about (marketing, PR, QA, localization), and these guys were seriously smart."

Oliver flew out to San Francisco to meet the ngmoco team, and the meeting went well. "It just clicked," he says. "It felt like the right move, and we began working together." ngmoco provided HandCircus with a number of valuable resources—a soundboard, some licensing work that got the game its soundtrack, and even programmer Andrew Hynek—that Oliver says were invaluable.

For the last month of *Rolando*'s development Oliver was holed up in a hotel in San Francisco, working alongside ngmoco and participating in press events that included an Apple event that *Rolando* was featured at. "I remember the day/night it was released, frantically watching the reviews come in," says Oliver. "It was a very strange feeling—I had no idea how it was going to be received."

Oliver shouldn't have worried. The first published review of the game came from Tracy Erickson of PocketGamer.co.uk, who gave the game a perfect 10/10 score and called it "the year's best iPhone game." A 9.6 score from IGN.com soon followed, and *Rolando* climbed the App Store sales charts, eventually landing in the top ten. HandCircus had created the first great iPhone game.

A Short Game About Jumping

Platform: iPhone/iPod Touch
Price: $.99
Developer: Snarp
Released: June 10, 2010

What Is It?

A Short Game About Jumping is not the best-looking game to be mentioned in this book. It's also obscenely difficult, and I can't decide whether the out-of-place early-20th-century swing music soundtrack is charming or just strange, but *A Short Game About Jumping* (let's call it *ASGAJ* from here on out, shall we?) is easily one of the most enjoyable "one-touch" games in the App Store.

ASGAJ stars an odd-looking blue fellow with remarkably bad hair. The ugly critter au-

tomatically runs from left to right, and players can only interact by touching the screen to make him jump. Each level is short, as the title suggests, but will likely take a few tries to complete due to the brutally precise timing required to successfully make some of the jumps.

The game benefits from a pretty great sense of humor. Players are spoken to in text form by some sort of omniscient being (presumably the game's designer himself), and there are more than a few one-liners in the game that made me laugh. What makes *ASGAJ* a worthwhile game is that it's just so incredibly rewarding to clear all the obstacles in a level. You'll scrape by spike pits and have to deal with changing gravity, and when you actually make it to the finish line you'll feel like you've really achieved something.

Behind the Game

It was the spring of 2010, and Swiss psychologist Markus Ruh had recently created Snarp, a one-man software development company focusing on "psychological software, learning tools, and interactive films." If that sounds completely nondescript to you, you're not alone—even Ruh wasn't sure what he wanted to do with the Snarp name at first. "That is the main reason that my company is called Snarp," states Ruh. "With this sort of name, it's easy to change the type of products completely. It doesn't matter if I write computer programs or guard sheep, the name always fits." When Ruh told me this during our email interview, he concluded his statement with a happy-face emoticon.

> **Statistics**
>
> • **Development time:** 5 weeks (updates included)
> • **Total budget:** $0
> • **Times downloaded:** 200–300

Flexibility was important for Ruh in part because of his varied educational background—he's studied programming, psychology, film science, and criminology. Although he still wasn't entirely sure how he wanted his company to be represented, Ruh decided he would need some sort of product to show to potential customers, so he set to work creating *A Short Game About Jumping*, which he then released as a Flash game.

Ruh is quite candid about his shortcomings as a game developer and his reasons for implementing some of the stranger elements in the game. He recounts the creation of the game's main character this way: "I didn't really have time to design anything when making the Flash version, so I drew a circle with two feet and hair using MyPaint and animated it by warping the image a bit." He cheerily admits that the character looks "a bit crappy if you look at him closely," but says that he was happy with the result.

> **Fun Facts**
>
> • The sky in the background of each level is a photo Ruh took from the balcony of his flat.
> • Despite only selling 300 copies, *ASGAJ* still has fans: http://goo.gl/T5caF.
> • You can play *ASGAJ* for free online at http://jump.snarp.ch/.
> • Other apps by Snarp include *Mimir Art of Memory* and *Mimir Mental Math*.

Next came the music. As noted above, the soundtrack in *ASGAJ* is one of its most curious features. According to Ruh, this is because he's just not all that great at composing music, so he turned to other sources. "I temporarily added public domain music from 1910," he says. "The chosen music was perfect for the atmosphere of the game, and everything else I tried later would have ruined the game." Ruh says that at one point he had recorded some music himself using a didgeridoo, "but the game's atmosphere became very dark."

The Flash version of *ASGAJ* was created over the course of only three days, but it took Ruh an additional three weeks to port the game to the iPhone. Upon release there the game essentially flopped, selling only a few hundred copies despite receiving relatively long-term support from Ruh in the form of free levels added via updates.

So let's take a step back and examine this. Why is *ASGAJ* worth your hard-earned dollar? Its creator is completely honest about the shortcuts he took to get the game running, and it's hardly notable as far as iOS titles go. All signs say that the game is little more than shovelware, so why is it worth anyone's time, especially when you compare the finished product with the rest of the games in this book—glossy, polished titles that represent months of labor and striving?

Because, despite the weird music, bad art, and unforgiving difficulty, *A Short Game About Jumping* is, well, fun.

Shot Shot Shoot

Platform: iPad only
Price: $1.99
Developer: Erik Svedäng
Released: August 4, 2010

What Is It?

Shot Shot Shoot is a two-player competitive game that's exclusive to the iPad. In it, you attempt to take out your opponent's five bases with missiles while simultaneously using those missiles to defend yourself. You can attack by tapping anywhere on the screen, and missiles will scatter from your fingertips just as quickly as you can poke the screen. Spamming isn't always the best strategy, though, and smart players will keep close tabs on their ammo supplies to ensure they don't end up shooting blanks while a more patient opponent strikes back with a few well-placed strikes.

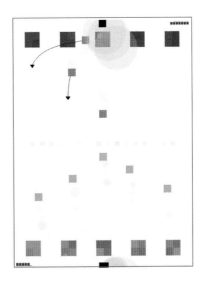

Most games in *Shot Shot Shoot* don't last longer than 30 seconds. It's an unbelievably fast-paced game, and because of this it can take quite some time to learn the best strategies. The game does have multiple computer opponents of varying skills for you to play, but the real fun in *Shot Shot*

Shoot is had whenever two people sit down in front of an iPad and play together, learning as they go.

Shot Shot Shoot is not a game that you'll be good at immediately. You're going to have to put in a little time to understand the game's underlying strategy, and the best way to do that is to grab a friend and learn the game together. Once you've done that, gameplay will slowly evolve into a battle of wits, with each player deploying his or her missile arsenal patiently and intelligently to whittle down the opposition's defenses.

This might seem like a weird observation, but *Shot Shot Shoot* has one of the best interfaces I've ever seen. The graphics are extremely minimalist, but in a very clean, appealing way. All of the menu options are big and pretty, but unobtrusive, and the game's design is focused on providing gameplay that's easy to see.

Shot Shot Shoot is not the most intense game in the App Store in terms of graphics, but it's an excellent title that demonstrates some of the unique capabilities possessed by tablets.

Behind the Game

Nearly ten years ago, Erik Svedäng created a little game called *Canon* using a simple game development program called Klik n' Play. It was a one-on-one competitive game; each player had control over four turrets, each governed by a keyboard key that you used to fire at your opponent. "It was obvious that the design lacked something," says Svedäng. "It was way too symmetrical and did not lead to that many strategic choices. Even so, it was a pretty fun game for me and my pals when we were 14–15 years old."

Years later, when he was a student in the Game Design program at the University of Skövde in Sweden, Svedäng was asked to participate in an event in which he would lead a team made up of students from the school to create a game during a conference. They would be given about two-and-a-half days, and Svedäng was to lead the design of the game.

> **Statistics**
> - **Development time (iPad version):** 2 months
> - **Total budget:** $0
> - **Times downloaded:** 15,000

Svedäng struggled to come up with something, and after a bit remembered the Klik n' Play game he had created as a kid. He began thinking of ways to improve his old design. "Like most good ideas, it came to me almost instantaneously," Svedäng recalls. "I realized the game would be a lot more interesting if the shots could be controlled instead of just launched straight at the opponent."

Svedäng created a prototype of his newly refined game idea that day, and as he fooled around with it he began to see how to develop the game's underlying strategy. He designed the game so that players can choose to launch either a barrage of simultaneous shots or fewer, precisely controlled ones. He also added in the game's "shared speed" mechanic—the more shots you have in the air at once, the slower they'll move.

When the event came and Svedäng's team coded the actual game, it turned out to be a lot of fun. The prototype got quite a bit of play on the show floor, but after that the game lived in a folder on Svedäng's computer where it was effectively forgotten.

A few years later Svedäng was living with his girlfriend in New York, and the first iPad was about to be released. He had been in touch with a lot of game designers from NYC, and he'd been thinking about a way to create a solid multiplayer game for the iPad. "I'm a big board-game player and was super excited about the possibilities of such a big touch screen that could be placed in the middle of the table and that you could gather around with several people," says Svedäng. Once again, he remembered his old prototype. "At this point I had to redesign a few things, both because of the iPad's form factor, and because I had improved as a game designer and didn't like some of my old decisions," says Svedäng.

Svedäng reworked several elements of the game's design—like ammo placement and the controls—and took it to a bar frequented by game developers. They responded enthusiastically, and Svedäng felt motivated to pour even more work into the game.

One of the things that Svedäng is most proud of is the game's slick, minimalist art style. He's especially happy with the big, rotating "start" button that appears before and after each game. "It's so big that you almost HAVE to press it when it appears," he brags. "That makes it very likely that you will play a rematch."

Svedäng released *Shot Shot Shoot* to little fanfare, but changing the price to 99 cents got him featured in the American App Store, and for a while the game was on the top-ten iPad games chart. The game has received mixed reviews from customers who couldn't deal with its difficulty (it really is a hard game), but it was later nominated as Best Mobile Game at the 2010 Independent Games Festival awards.

> **Fun Facts**
> - Svedäng tried adding multitouch for each player, but found that players ended up accidentally sliding their iPads all around the table.
> - Svedäng later released *TRI-TRI-TRI-OBELISK*, a re-skin of *Shot Shot Shoot* with new features.
> - *Blueberry Garden* was Svedäng's final thesis project, and it's available for the Mac and PC on Steam.
> - Other apps by Erik Svedäng include *Kometan*.

Silverfish

Platform: iPhone/iPod Touch
Price: $1.99
Developer: Chaotic Box
Released: November 9, 2010

What Is It?

Ever since the release of *Geometry Wars: Retro Evolved* and its sequel for the Xbox Live Arcade platform, dual-stick shooters have taken off in a big way. Screenshots of *Silverfish* might lead one to believe that it's just another clone, but not so—*Silverfish* has neither dual sticks nor shooting.

The first thing you'll notice when popping into one of *Silverfish*'s various modes is that movement is restricted to up, down, left, and right. This is a big departure from a lot of

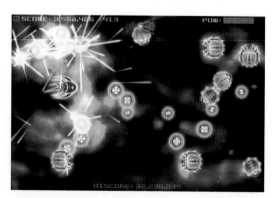

similar games in the genre, but it allows players to control the game really well on a touch device (just swipe in the direction you want to move) and ensures that games will play out far differently than the action in a game like *Tilt to Live* (more on that in a minute).

As you navigate your glowing space fish (I think that's what it is) around a small arena, both enemies and bombs periodically appear. You'll want to navigate around and between groups of enemies, and detonate bombs when large numbers are nearby—this will increase your score but creates a near-constant sense of tension, because good players will try to keep packs of baddies right on their tails in an effort to lead more of them into a bomb's explosive range. More risks equals more rewards, and that's the sort of stuff that great arcade games are made of.

Behind the Game

When Frank Condello began work on *Silverfish* in December of 2008, he wanted to create something new and exciting that drew from the classic games he liked. He describes the initial design document for the game as "basically *Pac-Man* minus the maze and versus the bugs from *Galaga*," but also cites more modern games like *Geometry Wars* and *A7Xpg* (which is a free-to-download game for Windows) as inspiration. "In many ways *Silverfish* is a sponge, soaking up bits of games I've enjoyed over the years," says Condello. "I can't claim there are many original mechanics in the game, but it was my hope to put things together in a way that was fresh and introduce a few twists."

> **Statistics**
>
> • **Development time:** 2 years (off and on)
> • **Times downloaded:** 10,000
> • **Copies needed to be sold in order to break even:** 20,000

Condello's Chaotic Box is a one-man studio, and he likes it that way. "I don't think I could do any one thing month after month, so tackling a game on my own lets me take a break from myself," he muses. "When I'm sick of programming I can work on art or audio/music (and vice versa). Not the most efficient way to make a game, but it helps maintain my sanity."

Early on in *Silverfish*'s development, Condello was inspired by an Xbox Live Arcade/PlayStation Network game he encountered called *Powerup Forever*. It used an innovative fluid simulation for its background, and Condello wanted his game to use something similar. This became a primary focus for him, and it made development far longer. "I was entirely unprepared for complexities this would introduce," says Condello. "Work quickly went from designing game mechanics to tweaking and optimizing the fluid simulation. I felt I had to nail the fluid sim before I could move on, and became somewhat obsessed with that task."

At the time, the powerful iPhone 3GS had not yet been released, so Condello was developing with weaker, first generation iPhone hardware in mind. It took months for him to get his fluid simulation working, and he realized he would need to begin focusing on client work to make money. "To cut my losses I cleaned up the fluid testbed in June 2009 and released it as a free entertainment app called *Flux* (later renamed to *flOOid*)," says Condello.

Soon after work on the fluid simulation ended, Condello began to become increasingly bored with doing client work. He decided that he needed a quick project to release on the App Store. He had an idea for another game (called *Pollywog*) and worked on it in between his contracted projects. Five months later it was released—and promptly flopped.

Condello calls *Pollywog's* failure "demoralizing," but since he had already created the shell of his "*Pac-Man* minus walls" game, he returned to it with the intent to rework it and release it as a full game. He had trashed a lot of his earlier design decisions and came up with nearly a dozen unique power-ups and weapons for the game. It was now January of 2010, and he spent the majority of the month working on his newly renovated project.

Condello had begun to make progress on the game when another iOS game called *Tilt to Live* was announced (see pp. 227–229 for more). His prototype and *Tilt to Live* handled movement differently, but many of its power-ups were similar to the ones Condello had come up with for his game. Condello panicked—he didn't want to create a game that would be called a rip-off—and once again canceled his project.

By the end of May, Condello was starving for something new to work on. In the intervening months he had created numerous prototypes for other games, but felt that none of them had much potential. Desperate, he opened up his old project once again and decided that it still had potential. "I scrapped all the power-ups/fluff from the second redux and started from scratch yet again," he says. "Over the next three months I designed dozens of enemies and game modes, reworked the fluid simulation for newer hardware, and came up with a half dozen treatments for the graphics before settling on the final look."

It had been almost two years since the first version of the game had been created, but Condello finally released *Silverfish* in the App Store near the end of 2010. Critical reception was solid, but some fans criticized the game for perceived similarities between it and—you guessed it—*Tilt to Live*. "Despite my conscious effort to differentiate *Silverfish* from *Tilt to Live*, I was surprised—and a little horrified—at how many people instantly labeled it a rip-off," Condello says.

So some buyers were unhappy, despite the fact that in reality, Chaotic Box's *Silverfish* and One Man Left's *Tilt to Live* don't play similarly at all. To make matters worse, the game's sales never picked up—Condello says he only sold 9,000 units in the game's first six months. But *Silverfish* wasn't all bad news for Condello, and he recognizes the silver lining in the cloud of poor sales. "Seeing *Silverfish* earn a 5/5 score on GamePro, and 8.5/10 (plus Editor's Choice) on IGN were definite highlights, and a sure sign that I must've done something right, even if the game wasn't a financial success."

Fun Facts

- *Silverfish's* main theme is a combination of the songs *Subdivisions* and *Tom Sawyer* by Rush. Condello describes himself as a "Rush freak."
- *Silverfish's* "Reaper" and "Haste" modes are tributes to *Pac-Man*—there's even a "wakka" sound when you eat enemies.
- Other apps by Chaotic Box include *Match Panic* and *Pinch n Pop*.
- *Match Panic* is one of the first titles to support the iCade.

Sissy's Magical Ponycorn Adventure

Platform: iPad only
Price: $2.99
Developer: Untold Entertainment
Released: July 12, 2011

What Is It?

Sissy's Magical Ponycorn Adventure is a point-and-click adventure designed by a 5-year-old girl named Cassie. Cassie did all of the art and many of the voices for the game, so the end result is a ridiculously adorable, strange, crayon-filled adventure. From a design standpoint, *SMPA* is fine (thanks in no small part to the role that Cassie's father played in coding the game and making it all come together in a comprehensive experience), but its real value is that it allows you the chance to look inside the mind of a 5-year-old, and the experience is pretty hilarious.

The game opens up with a bit of exposition from Cassie, who excitedly explains that she "friggin' loves ponycorns," (ponycorns are, of course, a combination of unicorns and ponies). The puzzles are all built around solving simple logic puzzles in order to get access to ponycorns, which Cassie then puts in jars. One of my favorite examples

involves a giant, anthropomorphic lemon, which you have to defeat with a thrown coconut. Upon vanquishing the lemon, Cassie shouts "that's what you get for being evil! AND a lemon!"

SMPA was originally designed as a Flash game, so the game doesn't really fit the iPad's native resolution; I suppose nobody could coax Cassie to redraw the game's visuals in 4:3 aspect ratio. Despite that, the game is totally worth the three dollars just for the novelty factor. It's short, but you'd have to be completely heartless to play through the game without cracking a smile. Here's hoping this is the start of a promising career in the games industry for Cassie.

Behind the Game

Ryan Creighton is a game designer, husband, and father of two little girls, and he admits that he's always wanted a son. "I grew up without a father, and I really wanted to have that father/son experience," he says. "But God sent us a second little girl." Creighton's desire for a son has only been magnified in recent years, as he deals with the monotony of what he calls "manufactured little-girl culture." He forbade his relatives to give his girls Disney Princess–branded stuff (they ignored this rule), and attempted to raise them to appreciate traditionally "boyish" things like comic books, to no avail. "My daughter said to me the other day, 'Daddy, I don't like *Star Wars*,'" he says with apparent chagrin.

Like many other independent developers, Creighton's studio, Untold Entertainment, often does service work for clients as a way to make money to fund original game development. One of the places that Untold Entertainment creates games is at TOJam, the annual Toronto independent game jam. At TOJam, participating game developers are given three days to create a complete, working game. Creighton was preparing to go to the event when he began to feel guilty about spending an entire weekend away from his family. On a whim, he decided to bring his oldest daughter, 5-year-old Cassie.

Statistics

- **Development time (of iPad version):** 1 week
- **Money donated to Cassie's education fund:** $3,000
- **Times downloaded on BlackBerry Playbook:** 12

TOJam organizers expressed concern about having such a young child at the event, and Creighton understood their point. "Cassie's a little firecracker of mischievous energy, and I'm hardly father of the year," he says. "They were worried she'd bounce around, make a lot of noise, and distract the other jammers . . . and frankly, so was I."

Creighton convinced the organizers that Cassie could behave, and then had a talk with her about the importance of the jam. He introduced her to many of the indie developers who would be attending, and told her that she'd be an ambassador for little girls everywhere. "Any little girl who wanted to come to TOJam ever afterward will be judged by your behavior," he told her. Cassie solemnly swore she'd behave.

Creighton spent the first day of the event creating a platform-puzzle game that utilized childlike artwork, but he wasn't happy with the results he was getting. In the final hours of the first day, he decided to instead create a point-and-click adventure game.

At the start of the next day, Creighton had a brilliant idea. He asked Cassie if she'd like to provide artwork for the game he was creating, and she agreed. He armed her with a giant box of crayons, some paper, and a sack full of My Little Ponies for referential purposes, and the father-daughter team set to work. Cassie's interest in the game surprised Creighton, who figured she'd get distracted by the sights and sounds at the event. "I had expected her to last one hour, tops, but she was having a ton of fun," he says proudly. "All told, Cassie put in an astonishing six hours of coloring for our game!" Even after a lengthy day at the event, Cassie wasn't bored. "When she heard that some of the jammers stay there overnight, she begged me to let her crash under our computer table," Creighton says. "But I was already worried someone would call child services on us, so I brought her home."

That night, Creighton and Cassie recorded their dialogue for the game. Creighton tucked his daughters into bed and returned to TOJam to pull an all-nighter in the name of assembling his daughter's work into a complete game. "In the end, the only artwork in the game that I drew is the blue circle that appears when you click/touch something, and some of the mouth charts for the characters [the way the characters' mouths animate]," Creighton brags. "Amazingly, the rest of the artwork in the game is drawn by Cassie."

The other TOJammers loved Cassie's work, and Creighton left the event with a near-complete game. He spent a few days the following week fixing some minor bugs and prepared to release it as a free-to-play online game. "The night before we released it, I had a conversation with my wife," says Creighton. "She said, 'I think this could go viral.' I agreed. Neither of us had any idea what that meant."

Creighton put the game online at www.ponycorns.com and wrote a blog post with the title "Five-Year-Old Girl Creates Video Game." He also tweeted the link to his 1,700 followers. Within hours, *Sissy's Magical Ponycorn Adventure* began getting featured on nearly every major gaming news site on the web. Within just a few days, it had gotten coverage on Kotaku, BoingBoing, Gamasutra, G4TV, Giant Bomb, The Escapist, *Wired*, and *Time*, just to name a few. "Within the week, mainstream media came calling, and we were interviewed by every major Toronto newspaper and appeared on local, provincial, and eventually live national TV," says Creighton. "Cassie had her picture on the front page of the commuter paper. It was a thrill!"

Creighton scrambled to monetize the free game. He created an online store filled with *Ponycorn*-branded T-shirts, buttons, and plush toys based on Cassie's drawings. He also added a PayPal "Donate" button to the site so players could donate to a special fund set aside for Cassie's education. To encourage people to donate, he kept updating a blurb next to the donate button that detailed (with great humor) all the things Cassie could buy at college with the funds. This included things like "ninja training."

Given the attention, Creighton decided to take the time to port the game to the BlackBerry Playbook, and then to the iPad. Since he didn't actually own an iPad, he borrowed one from a fellow indie developer (*Flew the Coop* creator Jason Kaplan). Later he scored a testing unit from Apple.

Despite getting front-page coverage from major sites like PocketGamer, Gamezebo, and Giant Bomb, neither version of the game sold well enough to be considered a success. The Playbook version was a complete waste of time for Creighton (check the stats blurb on the previous page for a good laugh), and the iPad version only made it to number 177 on the App Store's iPad charts. "Total profits from the iPad version are just about to cover the cost of our testing device," Creighton says. "I actually count it as a coup that we've been able to sell any copies of a game that's freely available online."

Creighton says he and Cassie have no plans for a sequel, but says that the experience has inspired the next thing he's working on. "Throughout our adventure, I've had numerous parents write me to say they'd really like to do something similar—to make a video game with their kids," says Creighton. "Our next initiative will be a website that does just that. We'll enable and empower parents—even nontechnical ones—to sit down on a Saturday afternoon and share the fantastic experience of game creation with their little ones."

Creighton's new website is in the planning stages as of the time of this writing, but expect to see it online at GamesByKids.com soon.

Solipskier

Platform: iPad/iPhone/iPod Touch (universal app)
Price: $.99
Developer: Mikengreg
Released: August 12, 2010

What Is It?

In *Solipskier*, you have no direct control over the game's main character; instead, you drag on the screen with your finger to create slopes of varying heights for the character to glide across. *Solipskier* probably grabs most people's attention because of its strange aesthetic. The main character has a rainbow cape that flows behind him, and it's one of the only colored things in the world—everything else is some variant of gray.

Your main goal in *Solipskier* is to gain points by slaloming between sets of gates. The game will tell you when a set is about to appear, and your job is to create a smooth, gentle slope that allows the character to ski towards the gates without losing too much speed. You don't want to create a sharp slope, which will cause the skier to slow down, but sometimes it's a good idea to create a sheer cliff to launch the skier far above certain hazards.

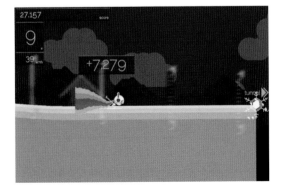

There are also gates that will kill you if you touch them, and those become more common as the game progresses. In order to avoid these consistently, you'll have to make vertical course adjustments quickly as the skier gains speed.

Solipskier is designed to be a game that you pick up and play for a short amount of time, hopefully honing your skills and learning a little bit more about controlling the skier each time. It's a unique mechanic, so you're certainly not going to understand all of the aspects of the game at first, but over time you'll improve.

Behind the Game

Mikengreg is a two-man team (Mike Boxleiter and Greg Wohlwend) that has solidified itself as a top-notch Flash game developer. The duo had already established a credible reputation by creating popular titles like *Fig. 8* and *EON*, but *Solipskier* was easily their most successful project to date.

The idea for *Solipskier* arose when Boxleiter and Wholwend were talking about the concept of parallax scrolling, which is a technique used in two-dimensional games to give an illusion of depth to the otherwise flat world (essentially, the background moves at a slower pace than the foreground). The two wanted to build a game around the concept, and they knew they wanted the game to be about speed. "Eventually Mike blurted out with wide eyes that it could be a game where you paint the terrain to determine the speed of the character," says Wholwend. "We were both thinking snow, maybe a snowmobile. Then we went into our rooms and started working."

That night, Boxleiter (who does all of the programming for Mikengreg) got straight to work on a prototype for the game. He had experience working on similar design concepts for Flash games, so it only took him a few hours to create a prototype starring a simple red ball.

The team tried out lots of interesting ideas while working on the game, and many of them got scrapped. One mock-up of the game had background elements like trees and buildings falling from the sky and creating the world as you drew. Boxleiter says they implemented that feature in one build of the game, but wound up axing it because it turned out to be really distracting. "It's one of those ideas that seems really cool in your head but doesn't work in practice," he says.

Statistics

- **Development time:** 5 months (original development plus port)
- **Times downloaded:** 100,000
- **Revenue generated:** $120,000

In *Solipskier*, there is no main menu. There's a blank screen, and then the moment you touch the screen (or, in the original Flash version, click your mouse), you'll begin to create snow and the game will start. The reason for this is that both Wholwend and Boxleiter hate tutorials in games. "They're played out," they explain. "We tested this with our friends and found most of them simply didn't understand what to do and clicked once, which resulted in their falling to their deaths instantly," says Boxleiter. "This seems like a harsh first impression of the game, but the time between failure and restarting is so short that we felt it was the best way to teach the concepts of clicking and dragging the mouse."

Wholwend and Boxleiter completed *Solipskier* in only two months, but they wanted to release the Flash version and iOS version simultaneously to maximize launch-day buzz, so they hired Joe Bergeron to do a port of the game. Flash-gaming megasite Kongregate had bought sponsorship rights to *Solipskier* for a pretty penny, but Mikengreg wouldn't be paid until it actually released the Flash version to Kongregate. Since the team had to hold out while the iOS version was in the works, they began work on another Flash game, *Liferaft: Zero*.

It took Bergeron about three months to complete the porting process (he had a full-time job to worry about), but towards the end Mikengreg got word from Apple that it had a good shot at getting featured if it waited two weeks to release the iOS version. Bills had begun to pile up at this point, so the duo decided to sell off *Liferaft: Zero* early to get together enough cash to support themselves in the remaining time.

> **Fun Facts**
>
> - Only about 1 out of 200 runs in *Solipskier* will end with a score higher than 100 million.
> - If you get going fast enough in *Solipskier,* the skier's headphones will fly off. This actually stops the game's music from playing.
> - Mike and Greg owned neither an iPhone nor an iPad before the iOS port was released.

The move paid off. *Solipskier* was featured by Apple in the App Store, and the game ended up selling nearly 100,000 copies in its first year. Wholwend and Boxleiter give most of the credit to Bergeron. "Joe is awesome," says Wholwend. "He worked nights and weekends and pretty much put it on the line for us."

Mikengreg's most recent project (as of this writing) is a multiplayer shooter called *4fourths*. Check out the trailer on their website.

Soosiz

Platform: iPhone/iPod Touch (iPad version available separately)
Price: $1.99
Developer: Touch Foo
Released: October 9, 2009

What Is It?

Soosiz was one of the first great side-scrolling platformers on the iPhone. The game plays like a two-dimensional version of *Super Mario Galaxy*. Levels are composed of tiny planets, each with its own distinct gravitational field and challenges to overcome. Progressing through the dizzying, spinning levels often requires players to search for switches that open up the path to the level exit, all while navigating a gauntlet of colorful enemies (most of which can be dispatched with a well-placed hop on the noggin).

Soosiz does a lot of things right. It implements a virtual button-control scheme that works surprisingly well, and the game runs beautifully on even the most out-of-date iOS devices. It would be excellent even if it offered nothing beyond its standard levels, but the two-man Touch Foo team wasn't content with delivering a shallow experience. There are timed coin levels that complement the main adventure levels, and each of the game's seven worlds concludes with a monumental boss battle that wouldn't be out of place in a classic Nintendo title.

Despite its age, no other iOS title can compare to the Nintendo-esque traditional platforming in *Soosiz*. The game's art, level design, and control scheme elevate it above its peers and make it one of the first games I would recommend to iPad and iPhone owners. The aesthetic is simple, and the main character looks like a green-haired spawn of Bart Simpson and Ms. Pac-Man, but *Soosiz* possesses visual charm that you don't often get from an iPhone game.

Behind the Game

Ville Mäkynen was a student at the University of Jyväskylä in Finland when he purchased an iPod Touch, his first-ever Apple product. Mäkynen had bought the iPod to use as an MP3 player, but he quickly became impressed with its power. Before buying the iPod he had been unaware of the existence of the App Store, despite the fact that it had been active for nearly six months (this was around December of 2008). "I downloaded some apps from the App Store and soon started wondering about who had made them and how they had got them on the store," says Mäkynen. "Being a programmer, I was very interested in the idea of making some apps myself."

Mäkynen began thinking more and more about the potential of creating his own games for the App Store, and his excitement grew. He had about ten years of programming experience under his belt and he had created some small games on his PC in his spare time, so he was confident that he'd be up to the task of creating a marketable iOS title.

There was only one problem: iOS developers need a Mac to create titles for the App Store, and Mäkynen was a poor college student. Buying a Mac would have been a substantial investment, so Mäkynen looked into whether he could use a PC to develop iOS titles instead, but found that he'd be making things harder on himself if he went that route. He had become more and more interested in the idea of developing a game to sell on the App Store, so he decided to take a chance and buy a Mac. Now all he needed was an idea for a game.

Mäkynen had actually created a PC-version of *Soosiz* already, for a 2006 game-design competition. At the time it starred a wizard who hopped around on floating sausages, and it had ended up winning first prize. The mechanics in the updated iOS version are nearly identical to the ones in the original version of *Soosiz,* so Mäkynen is amused whenever people compare his game to *Super Mario Galaxy,* which was released in late 2007. "When I first saw *Super Mario Galaxy* later that year, the thought on my mind was, oh, they used the same idea," says Mäkynen.

> **Statistics**
>
> - **Development time:** 9 months
> - **Percentage of profits contributed by the iPad version:** 25%
> - **Times downloaded:** 1,000,000+ (counting the free version)

Around Christmas of 2008, Mäkynen was sitting at a table with his brother Tuomas while playing with an early prototype of *Soosiz* for iOS (he had replaced the wizards and sausages with placeholder pixel graphics). He jokingly asked his brother if he'd be interested in drawing a main character for his game, and Tuomas actually did decide to get involved, joining the now two-man team as an artist. By March 2009, the brothers were working on the game together full time.

When Mäkynen went through the App Store looking for games similar to his own, he noticed that controls seemed to be a pervasive issue for developers. "While some of them were quite good looking, almost all of the games were jerky or didn't have good controls," he says. "I knew I could do better."

Mäkynen experimented with a variety of control schemes, but eventually found that nothing worked nearly as well as virtual buttons. He acknowledges that virtual buttons in iOS games are often criticized, but maintains that for the type of game he was making, they couldn't be beat. It helped that he came up with some clever ways to make the controls work better—for example, the touchable areas of his buttons are significantly bigger than the drawings on the screen would indicate.

> ### Fun Facts
>
> - "Soosiz" sounds like the Finnish word for "sausage," a reference to the original PC version of the game.
> - Soosiz's current app icon was designed by Werner Schmolmüller, a fan who created it for free.
> - On one level there's a secret route that takes players to a moon with a Finnish flag on it.

Months earlier, Tuomas's wife had become pregnant with their second child. She was due to give birth in July, and the brothers knew that it'd be difficult for Tuomas to dedicate time to the game after that. By July they only had a few levels left to design, so Tuomas was able to suspend full-time work on the game. Ville spent a few more months polishing the game and getting it ready for release, and finally submitted it for approval.

Soosiz got a bit of prerelease hype thanks to a YouTube trailer that Ville had put together, but his biggest break came a couple of weeks after the game became available, when Apple used its biggest banner slot to promote *Soosiz* in several countries. Over 100,000 paid downloads later, the Mäkynen brothers say they're working on their next game.

Space Miner
Space Ore Bust

Platform: iPhone/iPod Touch (iPad version available separately)
Price: $2.99
Developer: Venan Entertainment
Released: February 5, 2010

What Is It?

Space Miner presents itself as a sort of new-age version of *Asteroids* with RPG elements added in; there's some truth to that, but the game actually contains a lot more depth than you'd expect. For one thing it has a fantastic story, in which you are an outer-space prospector attempting to help your uncle Jeb out of his massive debt. The dialogue is snappy, funny, and well written.

You're handed a little clunker of a ship, which you use to to collect ore in the depths of space; you then sell the ore to pay off pieces of your uncle's debt. You'll constantly be unlocking upgrades for the ship as you go—like more powerful guns, bigger ore-collection tools, and better reload speeds—so you'll feel rewarded from the start. The game does use a virtual stick-control scheme, but manages to play very well despite that. It is a bit of an annoyance, and

I often rag on developers for neglecting to design with iDevices' strengths in mind, but *Space Miner* works really well.

You're pretty much guaranteed to be smiling every moment you're playing *Space Miner*, whether you're zipping around outer space collecting ore and fighting aliens or laughing at the ridiculous things Uncle Jeb says in between missions. It's not so much of a dual-stick shooter as it is a genuine adventure.

Behind the Game

It was May of 2009 when Venan Entertainment decided to take a risk and began work on its first self-published title. The small company traditionally develops titles for other publishers (examples include *Monopoly* for the iPhone and iPod Touch, and a few other iOS ports of EA titles, like *NBA Live*), and it had precious little experience working on its own original titles.

Venan Entertainment cofounder and *Space Miner* creative director Brandon Curiel describes the moment his company decided to embark on the path that eventually would lead to the creation of *Space Miner*: "It was very mysterious what exactly was happening on the App Store since there weren't any numbers posted about how games were doing financially," says Curiel. "That changed when Firemint published a blog and some graphs about how *Flight Control* went ballistic after it launched. [The graphs] had shown single months of revenue on that game that outgrossed any of our contracts we had ever done. If that wasn't a kick in the pants, then nothing is."

> ### Statistics
>
> • **Development time:** 9 months
> • **Total budget:** $250,000
> • **Times downloaded:** 97,000

Venan held a company-wide meeting to come up with some good game ideas, and decided to build a prototype around a mechanic they called "pivot." Curiel describes the pivot mechanic as being a way for players to physically move their iDevices around to get different views into a game world. In a sense, the iPhone or iPod would act as a window into the world of a game. Other companies have since tried similar ideas (Nintendo's *Face Raiders* on the Nintendo 3DS is a prime example), but Venan had a bit of trouble getting the technology to work in a way that would be enjoyable.

The team first set about making a clone of *Asteroids* (the 1979 arcade game) using their pivot technology. "We had a good bit of 3D technology from our previous titles, so getting a fairly nice-looking version of *Asteroids* wasn't too hard for us," says Curiel. "So we got the pieces together, sat down, and played it. And hated it." According to Curiel, turning the devices around while playing the game was a big pain, and even led to players accidentally dropping their hardware. "Don't even get into what happens if the device is plugged in or if someone is wearing headphones," he says. "It was ugly."

Venan abandoned the pivot idea but decided that its three-dimensional *Asteroids*-style game could be a lot of fun, so it set about finding a new control scheme for the game that

▪️◻️▪️▪️

would work. The team tried nearly everything, from methods using the iPhone accelerometer to various touch methods. Finally, Venan settled (somewhat begrudgingly) on virtual stick controls, which simulated the joysticks players might find on modern-day console-game controllers. "It was literally the last thing I wanted to use, but at the end of the day, even I had to admit it worked the best," Curiel says.

The controls were better, but Curiel still wasn't happy with the game. He admits that he never even liked *Asteroids*, but he and the rest of the Venan team chose to build around that mechanic because it seemed like something the team could do quickly. "I knew that other people liked *Asteroids*, but when push came to shove, just releasing an *Asteroids* clone did not sit well with me," says Curiel. "It [*Asteroids*] was primarily a game that came out of a series of very strict hardware limitations of its era, and unless we were making it exactly like the old game to play up on the nostalgia factor (which we weren't), we were automatically limiting ourselves out of the gate to a pretty mundane experience."

The company held another meeting to discuss what to do with their *Asteroids*-style shell, and it was then that *Space Miner* truly began to take shape. Curiel says that the game's design came naturally after the team began to answer some basic questions to provide a story context for the game. "Why are we shooting up asteroids?" team members asked themselves. "Well, to get some ore out of them," came the answer.

The logical follow-up question was "What is the ore for?" This led the team to create a rich backstory in which space-age characters were embarking on a kind of California Gold Rush for asteroid ore. The team then dreamed up one of the game's main characters, Jebediah Alouicious Gritstone, an old prospector who needed help in order to save his mining business. "I'd say about 90% of the tone and direction for the game was set in that meeting," laughs Curiel.

The bulk of the game's design had been completed, but Venan's next challenge would come whenever it found itself unable to dedicate the necessary resources to creating the game. For the first few months of *Space Miner*'s development only one programmer was working on the game, and both the design and art teams spent most of their time doing client work. The game wasn't fully staffed until September.

> **Fun Facts**
> - *Space Miner*'s sound design was done by Robert Euvino of Night Owl Productions.
> - Venan created the only version of Electronic Arts' *NBA Elite 11* that was released (although it was later pulled from the App Store).
> - Other apps by Venan include *Ninjatown: Trees of Doom* and *Space Miner Blast*.

Curiel recalls that as time went on, the game shrunk in scope. The team had originally planned to include a virtual stock market in the *Space Miner* world, as well as mobile battle stations and different types of enemies. "In the end, I think all those changes made the game better and a much tighter experience, so those aren't things I look back on with regret," he says.

Despite having what Curiel describes as "horrible, horrible marketing," *Space Miner* hit the top-20 games list in the App Store shortly after launch. The game fell off the charts fairly quickly after a couple of months or so, but not before it had sold nearly 100,000 units—not bad for a small studio with precious little experience creating original games. "In the end, *Space Miner* was a great experience for our studio," Curiel says. "It has helped in establishing our reputation such that our future products will get press attention, and it has been a great résumé piece for our contract work."

Spider
The Secret of Bryce Manor

Platform: iPhone/iPod Touch (iPad version available separately)
Price: $2.99
Developer: Tiger Style
Released: August 10, 2009

What Is It?

In *Spider: The Secret of Bryce Manor*, you play as a spider exploring a mansion that has been abandoned by its previous owners. In each level you create webs using a limited amount of silk to catch delicous insects (which are great for replenishing your supply of string). After eating enough insects, you'll be allowed to progress to the next part of the mansion. The game has a really gorgeous art style, and it's made all the more fun to look at thanks to the fact that many of the objects in the manor have a tale behind them. The game's story isn't spelled out explicitly, but as you explore you'll learn things about the Bryce family simply by being observant.

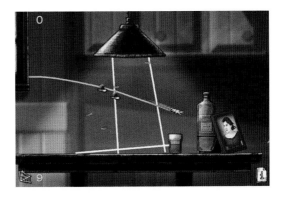

Spider's buttonless controls are a bit hard to wrap your mind around at first, but only because they're so unlike anything you've seen before. Tapping anywhere on the screen will make the spider scurry in the direction of the tap, and swiping causes the spider to leap. Creating webs is as simple as tapping on the spider to anchor it, and then swiping to jump, leaving behind a line of string which—when combined with other strings to create a geometric shape—will form a complete web that will trap insects unfortunate enough to get caught.

There are also a few minigames that become available as you progress, one of which has been released as a stand-alone, free-to-download title called *Spider: Hornet Smash*, so even after playing through the game's main story mode, there's still a lot of fun to be had with it.

Behind the Game

David Kalina and Randy Smith had spent the last few years of their life working on games that would never be released, and they were tired. After working on *Thief: Deadly Shadows* (the last game ever produced by Ion Storm before it shut down), Kalina and Smith had gone their separate ways—Kalina ended up at Midway working on a game with the working title *Criminal*, while Smith worked on *LMNO*, a would-be EA-published game created in conjunction with Steven Spielberg.

Criminal died after being in development for nearly four years (90 people were laid off), and *LMNO* also got cancelled before the gaming public got a chance to get their hands on it. Kalina and Smith were without jobs, but they had both collected some nice severance pay. "I spent several months traveling and soul-searching, not wanting to sign up for another megaproject that would eat five years of my life," says Kalina.

One day, while in Argentina, Kalina received an email from Smith, who had a pitch. Smith was looking into creating a company to develop iPhone games, and he wanted to know if Kalina would be interested in coming on board. "Just like that, I knew exactly what my next move was going to be," recalls Kalina.

Smith gathered together a group of his friends for a brainstorming session, and one of them, Jon Whitmore, contributed this two-sentence pitch: "You are a spider, and you spin your web with your finger on the screen. You have to eat the flies." Smith took the idea and expanded it into a complete design document. Kalina was immensely impressed by Smith's design doc, so he began typing up some code for the game. Work on *Spider* had officially begun, and Tiger Style was born.

Kalina and Smith were able to supply their newly created game studio with the funding it needed by drawing from their savings accounts. They cut costs by only hiring artists who would work for royalties from sales. Since Tiger Style was a brand new

---

Statistics

- **Development time:** 8 months
- **Percentage of players who find the secret hinted at in *Spider*'s subtitle:** 1%
- **Times downloaded:** 300,000

Fun Facts

- You can download a free minigame based on *Spider*'s engine from Tiger Style's official iTunes page; it's called *Hornet Smash*.
- Tiger Style's next game will be an "action-gardening adventure" set on Mars.
- Kalina didn't meet over half of the Tiger Style team prior to IGF 2009, where *Spider* won the Best Mobile Game award.

studio, finding people was somewhat difficult, but the duo didn't give up and managed to put together a stellar art team that delivered most of what was needed within a matter of months. Kalina calls it "the smoothest development cycle I have ever been a part of."

The development of *Spider* wasn't the only thing that went well. The game was showered with numerous Game of the Year awards, and went on to sell over 300,000 copies on the iPhone and iPad. Apple even added it to its iPhone Hall of Fame. As you might imagine, this was all quite a change for Kalina and Smith. The two men had gone from dealing with canceled games and studio shutdowns to successfully creating and shipping one of the most critically acclaimed games of 2009.

Tiger Style is now financially sound and working on its next title. Kalina is finally getting to do what he loves, and he has no regrets about the path he took to get where he is now. "In retrospect," he muses, "it was worth the years of suffering on difficult projects for the salaries and severance that allowed us to make Tiger Style a reality."

Super Stickman Golf

Platform: iPad/iPhone/iPod Touch (universal app)
Price: $.99
Developer: Noodlecake Games
Released: December 9, 2010

What Is It?

Super Stickman Golf is technically a golf game, but the gameplay itself is completely unlike any other golf game you've ever played—in fact, it has a lot more in common with physics puzzlers like Donut Games' *Cave Bowling* than anything else. The game takes place from a side-view perspective, and all of the courses are completely surreal, with fantastic elements like floating islands, underground mazes, and even moon levels that mix things up and make the challenges far more interesting than bland old realistic golf courses.

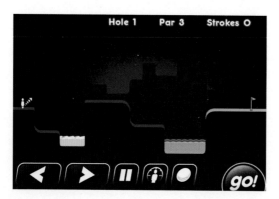

Like in real golf, your goal in *SSG* is to minimize the number of strokes it takes to get your golf ball into the hole. You have control over the angle you hit the ball and the amount of power behind each swing. Other than that, the game bears little resemblance to golf—its power-ups and crazy levels give it its own unique flavor.

All of the levels in *SSG* are designed to encourage risk-taking. There's almost always at least one "easy" and one dangerous path to the hole, the latter of which is usually designed to allow you to make it to the hole with considerably fewer shots than the former. For example, there might be a tiny hole in a wall that separates you from the flag. The default path through the level might take five shots to get to the hole, but shooting the ball through that pesky hole may get you there in only two or three. Just remember that if you miss, you've wasted a shot and likely doomed yourself to a poor score.

Like everything else in the game, *SSG*'s multiplayer mode isn't what you'd expect from a game with "golf" in the title. Instead of taking turns with other players (whom you can find using Wi-Fi, Bluetooth, or Game Center), the multiplayer is a fast-paced race to the finish. Because of the emphasis on speed, it plays a lot differently from the game's single-player mode, but it's extremely fun.

Behind the Game

Jordan Schidlowsky is partly responsible for the creation of one of the best golf video games of the last ten years, and he's remarkably candid about his motivations for entering the game-design business. "I wasn't really big into video games," he says. "We wanted to go into the best market for making money." I've interviewed literally hundreds of game developers, and not once have I heard anyone admit that money was the primary motivator for becoming a game designer. Schidlowsky's honesty is refreshing.

For Schidlowsky and Ty Bader (the other founding member of Noodlecake Games), the first *Stick Golf* game was little more than a prototype— something they could release onto the App Store to test the waters and see if it had the potential to be profitable. "We looked at mobile, and all the money was in games," Schidlowsky says. "I don't know what the exact percentage is, but like 80% of mobile downloads are games. It was clear that games were the right choice."

> **Statistics**
> - **Development time:** 4 months
> - **Times downloaded (free):** 1,500,000
> - **Times downloaded (paid):** 150,000

Schidlowsky took that information and began learning all he could about game design. He familiarized himself with Cocos2D (a popular, free-to-use iOS game engine), and in fewer than two months Noodlecake had completed and submitted *Stick Golf*, a simple two-dimensional golf game with just a few levels and some rudimentary graphics.

The response was tremendous. *Stick Golf*'s sales weren't phenomenal, but they were certainly acceptable, and the game benefitted from positive reviews from numerous major outlets. At this point, Schidlowsky and Bader sat down and began planning a "real" mobile game. They had created a great shell of a game; now all that was necessary was refinement. As Schidlowsky so eloquently puts it, "More polish, better graphics."

Polish and new art weren't the only things that Noodlecake wanted to do with a sequel. The team added power-ups, new and better levels, and Game Center support. *Super Stick Golf* was an improvement over the original in nearly every way, and it burst onto the top-20 sales charts upon release.

Unfortunately, Noodlecake had decided to release its game about a week before Christmas. This seemed like a good idea at first (more people will have iPhones to buy our game, right?), but turned out to be a serious miscalculation. Four days after *Super Stick Golf* hit the market, EA held a massive Christmas sale on all of its games. Every EA game in the App Store was reduced to 99 cents, and the megapublisher dominated the sales charts for the duration of the holiday season. "It just destroyed everyone's ranking," Schidlowsky says. *Super Stick Golf* disappeared from the top sales charts just as quickly as it had arrived, but Noodlecake wasn't prepared to give up just because of a sales hiccup. The duo was making just enough money to live on, so both men decided to quit their jobs and work at Noodlecake full time.

The next big thing for Noodlecake was a massive update for *Super Stick Golf* that added in online and local multiplayer modes through Game Center. It was a big undertaking, especially for a team with only one programmer. "*Super Stick Golf* 1.0 took about four months to make," says Schidlowsky. "But it probably took me two-and-a-half months to get the multiplayer working."

The hard work paid off. With the release of the multiplayer update, things turned around for *Super Stick Golf*. The game got tons of buzz from fans, and download numbers soared. The game was even a hit during E3 (Electronic Entertainment Expo) 2011, according to Schidlowsky. "There were a lot of judges at E3 who wound up download-ing the game," Schidlowsky says proudly. "The judges get bussed around to the different game studios the week before E3, and I heard through the grapevine that a bunch of these judges had downloaded *Super Stickman Golf* and were having these massive multiplayer battles on the bus. That was pretty cool, to hear that."

You may have noticed that in the previous quote, Schidlowsky referred to his game as *Super Stickman Golf*. There's a reason for that, and it has to do with a legal scuffle between Noodle-cake and a company called Stick Sports.

As you might gather from their name, Stick Sports is a Flash game developer that spe-cializes in (you guessed it) sports games. It's created games like *Stick Tennis*, *Stick Baseball*, and *Stick Cricket*, but it hasn't (yet) created a golf game. If it was to do so, you can imagine what it might be called.

As it turns out, Stick Sports had been interested in getting into App Store develop-ment, and it came across Noodlecake's *Stick Golf* and *Super Stick Golf* games. In short, it wasn't too happy about what it saw as a violation of its trademark, so it asked Noodlecake to change the name of its games. Schidlowsky and Bader didn't want to deal with the ex-pense or the time commitment of a court battle, so they changed "stick" to "stickman" in both of their games titles.

Schidlowsky doesn't seem too bothered by this turn of events. "I've had a lot of people tell me that every legal decision is an economic decision as well," he says. "So just because you're right doesn't mean you should fight it. Legally, I think we could've fought it, and that's the advice I got from a few people, but it just would have cost more money in the end than what it would have been worth." Schidlowsky admits that he thought *Super Stick Golf* was "a cooler name," but says the name change didn't actually cost Noodlecake much in terms of brand recognition.

Noodlecake had to redesign the logos for both games when it renamed them, and the result is nothing short of hilarious. Almost as if defying the people who forced it to slap the word "man" on its game titles, Noodlecake literally forced the word into its existing logo. "Man" is actually sideways—stuffed right into the space between the words "Stick" and "Golf." When I point out the possible symbolism behind their new logo, Schidlowsky laughs. "It doesn't make any difference to us, so we put 'man' in the middle of our game's name," he says. "We changed the name and we've done really good with that name, too. I think it was the right decision for us."

> ### Fun Facts
>
> - Schidlowsky suggests that players having trouble with "The Dungeon" course should scroll down while playing the sixth hole to find a helpful secret.
> - A company called Traction Games released a game called *Stick Skater* on the App Store in April of 2010. It has since been renamed *Stickman Skater*.
> - The music for *Super Stickman Golf* was done by Whitaker Blackall, who was also behind the soundtrack for *Tilt to Live*.

You could say it's surprising that *Super Stickman Golf* is as fantastic as it is; when the primary motivation for an artistic creation is money, the result is often a rushed, low-quality product. Most of the developers interviewed for this book professed a lifelong desire to make games, so how did a nongamer like Schidlowsky come along and help create something so incredibly fun?

From Schidlowsky's perspective, the answer is simple. "It's like any business," he says. "If you want to build a product, build a good product. That gives you more opportunities for success."

Superbrothers
Sword and Sworcery EP

Platform: iPad/iPhone/iPod Touch (universal app)
Price: $4.99
Developer: CAPY/Superbrothers/Jim Guthrie
Released: March 23, 2011

What Is It?

From the very first moment you boot up *Superbrothers: Sword and Sworcery EP*, you'll know this is a game unlike anything you've ever played before. Right off the bat you'll be struck by the game's visuals: all the characters are incredibly lanky, with limbs that are only a single pixel thick. It's almost as if graphic-design principles from the Atari era have been brought into our modern, high-definition times. Surprisingly, the result is gorgeous.

The game itself is a sort of point-and-click adventure that takes more than a few story

cues from the *Zelda* series. You play as the Scythian, a female warrior sent on a quest to find three golden triangles. Players tap on the screen to move, and use the iPad's accelerometer to manage their inventories and keep track of their quests.

For the most part, *S&SEP* is a very slow-paced game in which you're supposed to just calmly soak in the story, sound, and visuals while solving puzzles. On rare occasions, though, the story will put you in a combat situation. This scenario requires you to turn your iDevice to its portrait position, and thrusts you into a real-time battle in which you'll have to use timing and on-screen buttons to block attacks and defeat foes.

The story includes a cast of mostly ridiculous characters—there's Logfella the axman, Dogfella (Logfella's faithful canine companion), and Girl, a shepherd. Occasionally you'll be able to read these characters' thoughts in a giant magical book called *The Megatome*, which can be useful for figuring out what to do or where to go next. The dialogue in the game is humorous, and makes you feel like the characters don't take themselves very seriously. It's a unique element of the game's design, and is yet another thing that makes the game stand out in the crowded App Store marketplace.

Behind the Game

Sword and Sworcery's story began in 2009, at a party thrown by 1UP.com during the Game Developers Conference. While waiting in a hallway for a friend, Kris Piotrowski and Nathan Vella noticed a "tall blonde dude" handing out postcards with his artwork on it. "We grabbed one and, immediately recognizing the lanky Superbrothers-style pixel art, starting yelling 'WE HAVE TO MAKE A GAME TOGETHER' at Craig D. Adams' face until he said yes," claims Piotrowski. "That's pretty much how the project started."

Six months later, the newly-formed Sworcery team set out to make what they called "a strange, musical, Twitterable, pixel-adventure game." Superbrothers (an art and design company where Craig Adams works as creative director) was to lead the game's art and design, and Canadian singer-songwriter Jim Guthrie was on board to create an experimental soundtrack. Piotrowski and Vella's company, CAPY, was tasked with providing additional design, project support, and technical muscle. "We started off with a very loose concept, more like an idea for a high-level goal," says Piotrowski. "We wanted to create 'a record you could hang out in'—a magical, relaxing, inviting little world that you could go for a walk in, poke and prod, and listen to Jim's music set to Craig's beautiful artwork."

> **Statistics**
> - **Development time:** 1.5 years
> - **Total budget:** $196,000
> - **Times downloaded:** 250,000

Piotrowski and Adams had a considerable batch of ideas that they hoped to squeeze into the game. Among many other things, they wanted to somehow fit in a combat mechanic inspired by Nintendo's classic *Punch-Out!* series and an environment that changed according to moon phases in the real world. Not surprisingly, it was a considerable challenge to fit all of their ideas into one game. "We spent most of our time trying out crazy ideas and coming up with even crazier ideas to fix our earlier crazy ideas," Piotrowski says.

One of the earliest builds of *Sword and Sworcery* was a short demo that allowed players to walk through some woods. CAPY/Superbrothers decided to submit this demo to the

Independent Games Festival, and also showed it off on the show floor. Response from players was extremely positive, but Piotrowski says that he and the other developers were "kind of freaked out" after they realized that most players walked away from the demo not realizing that that's all there was to the game. "We got the sense that players thought the demo was just a small fraction of the overall experience," says Piotrowski. "In all honesty, we were not really sure what the game was going to be."

This posed an interesting challenge for the CAPY/Superbrothers team. If the "walk through the woods" demo was expanded into a full game, what would it be? They had no clear narrative to guide them, but they did have ideas. Lots of them. "We started off with a high-level approach, and it took us a very long time to 'find the game' and crystallize the design and bring everything together," Piotrowski says. "We wasted a lot of time feeling our way through the darkness, trying to find the shape of the project we were working on."

Piotrowski says that the team soon began to lose morale—and thus the reason to continue working on the game. He remembers the time spent in that confusing period "nearly sank the ship." He adds, "I honestly feel like the only reason the project didn't totally explode in our face was because we all trusted each other's instincts, talent, and sensibilities. We had a lot of faith in the end goal, and that things would eventually come together." The team's faith was not misplaced. As *Sword and Sworcery* inched closer and closer to its eventual release date, gaming media outlets began to pick up the story and the game started getting a lot of attention.

Meanwhile, *S&SEP*'s developers were busy creating a game world with far more scope than the demo they had shown at GDC. This world was very much like what its creators had dreamed of. "The way it all came together was pleasantly surprising even to us," says Piotrowski.

With a healthy dose of hype leading up to the game's release, CAPY/Superbrothers were in good hands on release day. *S&SEP* launched to critical acceptance and commercial success. It sold hundreds of thousands of copies, and was lauded for its originality and plot. Piotrowski thinks these things are what made the game so successful. "The App Store is still primarily dominated by a very specific type of game: free or 99 cents with simple, casual mechanics," says Piotrowski. "Our game was the exact opposite, and in a way, that's kind of why we thought it may actually do well."

Piotrowski was right. *Sword and Sworcery* may not have caught on with the regular *Cut the Rope* crowd of casual gamers, but the audience that the game did find was big enough to make up for that. The game sold over a quarter-million units in its first six months. Piotrowski calls it "mind boggling."

Fun Facts

- The ten-digit number given to players at the end of *S&SEP* is a working phone number. Yes, you should call it.
- Jim Guthrie (the game's sound guy) sells the beautiful *S&SEP* soundtrack on his website. It costs $7.99 but is absolutely worth it.

Sword of Fargoal

Platform: iPhone/iPod Touch (iPad version available separately)
Price: $2.99
Developer: Fargoal LLC
Released: December 1, 2009

What Is It?

Although I've already introduced you to *100 Rogues* (a sort of arcade derivation of the roguelike genre), *Sword of Fargoal* is worth taking a look at because it's an excellent example of a more traditional, slow-paced roguelike. Everything about the game reeks of 1980s design philosophy, and that's in part because the game is actually a remake of one of the first roguelikes ever created, which came out under the same name in 1982.

The goal in the game is to get to the 20th floor of a dungeon and snag the legendary sword of Fargoal. Once you do that, you'll have exactly 2,000 seconds to climb all the way back to the surface and escape the lair before the entire dungeon collapses and traps you forever. This feat is made more difficult by the fact that the lower you go, the bigger and scarier enemies

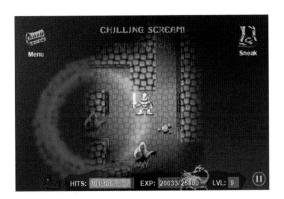

become. If you want to be able to survive 20 floors deep, you're going to need to do a lot of leveling up.

Sword of Fargoal is fundamentally a game about dealing with the unknown. Until you explore areas, they'll appear as nothing more than fog on your map. That fog can conceal an impressive variety of enemies—from thieves who steal your precious items (or worse, the sword itself, if you've already collected it) to incredibly powerful dragons that'll take all of your energy to conquer. The knowledge that this could happen at any moment can be genuinely scary, because if you die once, *your character will be gone forever.*

In *100 Rogues*, that's not such a big deal, but when you've invested half-a-dozen hours into your character in *Sword of Fargoal*, the fear of virtual death becomes very real. Once you've put more than a couple of hours into the game, every battle becomes incredibly intense, and it goes from being a lighthearted action RPG into an intense fight for survival that can really get your blood going.

They just don't make games like *Sword of Fargoal* any more. For better or worse, a game that deletes your save file every time you die is a rarity in the 21st century. Because of this, *Sword of Fargoal* is worth experiencing for any hardcore gamer.

Behind the Game

Like many children growing up in the 1970s, Jeff McCord was immersed in the fantasy worlds created by *The Lord of the Rings* and *Dungeons and Dragons*. Tales of orcs and dwarves and massive adventures were the hallmarks of his childhood.

The young McCord was also exposed to programming at an early age. His father worked as a computer-science professor at the University of Kentucky, and was thus able to get McCord access to top-of-the-line computers. As a result, McCord spent countless hours playing with modems and other cutting-edge toys. "Ninety percent of the time I spent solving the famous text-based game, *Adventure*," says McCord. "I got to the point that I could type ahead about 200 commands or more to get through the game to the last place that I had died, until I solved all of the puzzles and made it through the game with a perfect score."

While he was still in high school, McCord's father purchased and brought home a Commodore PET (the first ever full-featured computer created by Commodore). McCord began experimenting with programming his own games using the PET. Soon after he had a working version of a game he called *Gammaquest II*, which would later become *Sword of Fargoal*. McCord wrote everything—monsters, traps, treasures, spells, and even relatively complex aspects of the game like randomly-generating levels—using the BASIC programming language. This was in late 1979 and early 1980, months before *Rogue* had even been released.

By 1981, McCord was a freshman in college at the University of Tennessee. He heard from a friend about another student his age, who had created his own game (on a brand new computer from a start-up tech company called Apple) and had actually gotten it published. This was inspirational for McCord, who had continued working on *Gammaquest* in his free time. "I had never thought of actually publishing my game, but it sure sounded fun to try," says McCord.

McCord sent an application for a copyright to the Library of Congress, then submitted his game to a handful of publishers. A couple of publishers—including a small company called Epyx—wrote back expressing interest in McCord's game. Epyx won the bidding when they offered McCord a $2,000 advance (worth about $5,000 in 2012).

Using his advance money, McCord moved to Palo Alto, California, where he lived for months in a camper behind the Epyx offices. McCord spent his time translating his game to run on the VIC-20, a new computer from Commodore intended to be more economical than the PET. McCord worked hard on his game, and *Sword of Fargoal* was released in 1982. Less than a year later, McCord also ported a slightly enhanced version of *Fargoal* to the powerful and incredibly popular Commodore 64.

By 2003, *Sword of Fargoal* was well known and respected for being an innovative piece of PC gaming history. It had even been recognized as one of the 150 "greatest games of all time" in 1996 by *Computer Gaming World* magazine (later renamed *Games for Windows: The Official Magazine*).

Paul Pridham and Elias Pschernig were big fans of McCord's decades-old RPG. The two decided to make an updated tribute game for the PC, which they successfully created in fewer than two weeks. Satisfied with their work, Pridham found a way to contact McCord and let him know about the remake. "I took a look and was extremely impressed by the attention to detail in how they reproduced the look and feel of the original," says McCord. "They did their own pseudo-perspective dungeon tiles as the main look, but they also made it so other people could create their own dungeon 'skins,' and they made one skin that matched the original C64 tiles."

McCord was so impressed with their remake that he put a download link for their game on fargoal.com, his official *Sword of Fargoal* website. It became an officially endorsed remake, and was distributed for free to whoever wished to download it (Pschernig also created a Mac port later).

McCord kept in touch with the pair for the next few years, and according to McCord the possibility of creating another version of the game was discussed more than once. Finally, in 2007, McCord heard about the announcement of the iPhone. He contacted Pridham and Pschernig and suggested

---

Statistics

- Development time (iOS version): 1 year
- Amount of memory the first *Fargoal* used: 15 kb
- Times downloaded (including free promotions): 100,000

Fun Facts

- The VIC-20 was the first computer to sell over a million units.
- *Fargoal* was originally spelled *Fargaol*, a reference to the Middle-English word gaol, which means "jail." Epyx talked McCord into changing the title.
- McCord was a *Dungeons and Dragons* "dungeon master" in high school. He says one of those *D&D* games inspired the story behind *Fargoal*.
- Other apps by Jeff McCord include *Wizard Hex* and *Cargo Runners*.

that the group work together to create an iPhone version of *Fargoal*. For *Fargoal*'s iOS debut, McCord allowed Pridham to do the majority of the coding and design work, with Pschernig pitching in on the code and UI. Meanwhile, McCord acted as the public face of the game, making contacts at Apple, speaking to gaming media outlets, and occasionally helping out with the game's art and music direction.

Sales of the game's iPhone and iPad versions (and the updated, universal app *Sword of Fargoal Legends*) have been good, but McCord admits that the money hasn't been good enough for the team to buy an office and create a real business. Still, McCord is extremely satisfied with the positive reaction his creation has received nearly three decades after its initial release. "We've come to realize that the *Fargoal* franchise is really an 'evergreen' in many ways," he says. McCord and his team are now hard at work on a sequel—*Sword of Fargoal 2*.

Tilt to Live

Platform: iPhone/iPod Touch (iPad version available separately)
Price: $2.99
Developer: One Man Left
Released: February 24, 2010

What Is It?

As you may already know from reading the entry on Chaotic Box's *Silverfish* (pp. 196–198), *Tilt to Live* is an arena survival game in which you attempt to take out enemies by tilting your way into on-screen weapons that randomly appear. It's a lot like *Geometry Wars*, in that enemies spawn in waves, but *Tilt to Live* has two big things going for it: an incredibly accurate tilt-based control scheme and some of the most creative, fun weapons ever created for a game in this genre.

First, I've got to address the controls. These are the most accurate tilt controls I've ever seen. Seriously, it makes me sad, because now I want to know why every other iOS game can't use tilt this well. It doesn't even use the gyroscope that's in newer devices, and players can safely and consistently slip between enemies that are less than a millimeter apart.

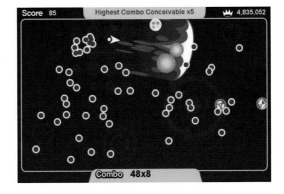

Those weapons: man, are they fun! The game's Saturday-morning-cartoon art style makes explosions and other attacks look awesome. Each pick-up is good for only one use, and it'll activate automatically once you grab it. One example of an early weapon, the purple laser, charges up for a moment and then sends a massive purple shockwave of doom in the direction you're facing at the moment of launch. All of this is topped off with a wonderful system for unlocking and achieving weapons that's designed to keep you playing.

Behind the Game

Alex Okafor had less than one semester to go before he would finally be done with college, and he was bored. He and his friend Adam Stewart had begun creating simple game prototypes in their spare time as a hobby. "At that time we were working with Xbox XNA and things like that," says Okafor. "I ended up getting my hands on an iPhone—the *Tilt to Live* prototype was created in one or two nights, and he [Stewart] had a triangle running around the screen killing red dots by hitting explosions."

Okafor says that in the beginning, Stewart wasn't sold on the idea of creating and selling an iPhone game. Stewart was running a graphic-design business and trying to keep clients happy, so he saw *Tilt to Live* as just one more thing to do.

The two members of One Man Left describe their work relationship in the initial stages of *Tilt to Live*'s development as "disjointed." That all changed when the game began to come together and Stewart became more interested in putting his time and effort towards the project. "I got to see that I could give Alex some input, and he would actually put it together," said Stewart. "Then I could see the idea that we talked about running around on the screen, and I got super excited about it."

All of this was happening while Okafor was still attending college, and he was able to use equipment provided by a game-design professor to work on the game. The professor told Okafor that so long as he was doing something game-related that could help the professor's class, he had free reign to do what he wanted. This resulted in Okafor having the time to create a prototype of *Tilt to Live* using a Wii remote connected to a PC. The prototype was used in a few of the labs in the game-design professor's class. Toying with the Wii controller taught Okafor how accelerometers worked, letting him take what he learned and transfer it to the iPhone prototype of the game.

From February 2009 to February 2010, when the game was finally released, Okafor balanced work on *Tilt to Live* with a full-time job as a federal contractor in Washington, DC. "It was your typical nine-to-five job and I'd come back, and I'd try to put in like two, three, four hours per night to try to get work done," he says. "It went on like that for a year, putting in 60-hour weeks with work and *Tilt to Live* combined."

Statistics

- **Development time:** 15 months
- **Number of players who purchased the *Viva La Turret* expansion:** 64,000
- **Times downloaded:** 500,000

Stewart was aware of the stress Okafor was under, and did his best to work around it. "I was scared to give him feedback," he jokes. "So I'd be like, no, that's fine, I know what you went through to make that." Okafor says that at certain points in *Tilt to Live*'s development, he began to become pretty discouraged by how long the process was taking. "Wow, this is still going on," he remembers thinking.

In early February of 2010, Washington was paralyzed by a massive blizzard that shut down roads and left hundreds of thousands of residents without electricity. For a few days, Okafor was stuck in his home with nothing to do but work on *Tilt to Live*. He calls it his first taste of working as a full-time indie developer. He loved it. "A lot of the finishing touches and final polishes came in during that week, because I was getting uninterrupted time to work on the game instead of doing bits and pieces," he says.

Once the first version of *Tilt to Live* was released, Stewart was able to gradually stop taking in new clients and begin to focus on working more on the game, developing new modes and pushing out updates to keep the game fresh.

Tilt to Live got lots of press, and it sold so well that cheap clones started appearing on the App Store; the most notable example is a game called *Tilt to Fly* by Water Planet Development. Stewart describes it as "*Angry Birds* mixed with *Tilt to Live*." Stewart laughs, "I was like, that is the most beautiful thing I've ever seen in my life. We did a blog post, we told everybody to go buy it." Stewart says he even considered sending Water Planet a *Tilt to Live* T-shirt.

Why reward a cheap clone by promoting it? I asked Stewart and Okafor this seemingly obvious question, and their answer blew me away. "I was hoping that it would take off so that everybody would see the complaints of, it's just like *Tilt to Live*!" Stewart explains. "We could ride the coattails of the rip-off." One Man Left's surprising and hilarious counterstrategy worked: almost all of the reviews on the App Store page for *Tilt to Fly* mention *Tilt to Live* and explain to readers that One Man Left's title is the better game. Now THAT'S creative marketing.

A side note: when I interviewed Okafor and Stewart, I had already spoken to Frank Condello, creator of *Silverfish* (who nearly cancelled his game because of perceived similarities between it and *Tilt to Live*). I asked Okafor and Stewart what they thought about his story, but they were entirely unaware of the impact their game had had on Condello. "I played the game and I liked it," Okafor says. "And I told him that I liked it, and that was the extent of it. I thought it was different enough."

Tiny Tower

Platform: iPad/iPhone/iPod Touch (universal app)
Price: Free
Developer: NimbleBit
Released: June 22, 2011

What Is It?

There aren't many "freemium" games in this book, and there are several reasons for that. First and foremost, many freemium games on the iPhone and iPad aren't much more than

shallow rip-offs of Zynga's *Farmville* (which itself is a rip-off of another game). Look to every game ever released by iOS developers TeamLava if you want to see a shockingly sad example of that.

Secondly, many (but not all) freemium games are designed to take your money rather than provide a fun experience. Neither of those reasons holds true for *Tiny Tower*, a wonderful little tower construction simulator that also happens to be free to play.

In *Tiny Tower*, your goal is to build and fill up as many floors on your tower as possible. Each floor is dedicated to a single type of activity, like recreation, food, retail, etc. You also want to build apartments so you can have "bitizens" (adorable little pixel people) come to live in your tower, as they'll act as a workforce to keep all of your floors up and running. Ultimately, your job as the player is to make sure that stores stay stocked with goods and customers stay happy. There are a few extra layers of interactivity like helping visitors onto the elevator and reading Bitbook status updates from your bitizens, but for the most part the fun of the game comes from watching your tower grow as you earn more coins.

There is, of course, a way to pay to get ahead in *Tiny Tower*—you can spend cash on tower bux (a rare form of currency that's more valuable than coins)—but *Tiny Tower* by no means requires it.

Behind the Game

Unlike most games, *Tiny Tower*'s art style was created before the game itself even existed. Twin brothers Ian and Dave Marsh were contemplating creating a restaurant-management game (like *Diner Dash*), and in the process Dave had developed a cutesy 8 bit–inspired art style that both men really fell in love with. "We decided it would be a waste if we didn't apply it to a game that had more environments than a single restaurant," says Ian.

From there, the duo began thinking about the success behind some of their past releases. *Pocket Frogs* became a major hit partly because of the incredible amount of customization options offered, and the Marsh brothers wanted to apply that to some sort of building simulation or other type of management game. "The other big consideration was to create a world that seemed natural and at home inside your iPhone," Ian explains. "A vertically scrolling side view of a tower seemed to be a perfect fit."

> ### Statistics
> - **Development time:** 4 months
> - **Average session length for a *Tiny Tower* player:** 10.7 minutes
> - **Times downloaded:** 6,000,000 and counting

This became the theme of the game that would become *Tiny Tower*—what would happen if tiny digital people could live in your phone? Giving the characters engaging personalities became a top priority for NimbleBit, so it added the ability to dress characters up, give them their dream jobs, and see what they posted on Bitbook.

By the time NimbleBit began work on *Tiny Tower*, it had long since established itself as a great App Store developer. Games like *Dizzypad* and *Mega Panda* had already gotten major exposure on big sites, so NimbleBit was confident that *Tiny Tower* would be a success.

They were right.

In the weeks after its release, *Tiny Tower* was given glowing reviews by dozens of major websites. It was featured as Game of the Week by Apple and quickly shot to the top of the charts on the App Store. Within just a few weeks the game had been picked up by nearly four million people. "I think

> ### Fun Facts
> - Nearly 4% of *Tiny Tower* players buy tower bux with their money.
> - A few of the business floors in the game are inspired by places the Marsh brothers have worked in the past.
> - Other apps by NimbleBit include *Pocket Frogs* and *Dizzypad HD*.

consumers and reviewers alike were refreshed and happy to see a freemium game that didn't take a heavy-handed approach in trying to monetize the players," muses Ian.

He's right. *Tiny Tower*'s clever but unobtrusive implementation of the tower-bux system allows players to pay cash to get ahead in the game, but this function is never pushed on players and isn't required to see all that the game has to offer. It's subtle but effective, and should be a lesson that freemium games don't have to work like *Farmville* to be successful.

Toki Tori

Platform: iPhone/iPod Touch (iPad version available separately)
Price: $2.99
Developer: Two Tribes
Publisher: Chillingo
Released: May 22, 2009

What Is It?

Toki Tori is a small yellow bird that *really* wants eggs. In the game, each level is a small, closed-off ecosystem filled with enemies, traps, and (of course) eggs. At the start of each level, you're handed a limited number of tools to navigate those environments. That might include things like bridges that you can use to plug gaps, a freeze ray gun that can turn enemies into useful platforms, or even a teleporting ability that allows you to pass through thin walls. Often you'll need to use the tools in specific places, and it's up to you to examine the situation and figure out the best approach.

It's a very different type of puzzle platformer because, instead of just running around and solving things through trial and error, players must usually stop and take a minute to examine what's happening on the screen. Often you'll want to look at the parts of the level that can't be traversed without a particular item, and the

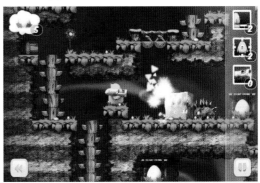

paths that enemies are moving in, then use that information to determine which route Toki Tori might take to collect all of the eggs in one go. A lot of times you can mess up and get trapped in a hole or lose access to one side of the level, but a post-release update to the game added an incredibly helpful rewind button that allows you to immediately undo any mistake you make.

One thing to note is that iPad owners will get to enjoy graphics that are much better than those on the older iPhone version of *Toki Tori* (the iPad edition uses assets from the PC version of the game, which was released after the iPhone edition). The game really looks great on the iPhone too, but iPad owners end up getting a better overall experience.

Behind the Game

Colin Van Ginkel has been making *Toki Tori* games for a long time.

It all began in 1994, when a little company called Fony released a game called *Eggbert* for the MSX2 home computer. *Eggbert* would be immediately recognizable to anyone who ever played one of the many versions of *Toki Tori*—the puzzles are the same, the environments are the same, and *Eggbert's* main character is a squat yellow bird. Five years later, some of the former employees of Fony (including Van Ginkel) formed Two Tribes, a new studio targeting the Game Boy Color. According to Van Ginkel, the Game Boy Color was roughly comparable to the MSX2, so he was interested in seeing if they could get *Eggbert* rereleased on the GBC platform.

Van Ginkel didn't actually know how to get a game published on a Nintendo platform, but he gathered together a small team of developers interested in working on the game and began importing flash carts from Hong Kong. For a full year Two Tribes worked on fleshing out its new version of *Eggbert*, with no guarantee that the game would ever see the light of day. "We talked to a lot of companies and people in the Netherlands, most of whom told us there was no money to be made with Game Boy Color games," says Van Ginkel.

> ### Statistics
> - **Development time:** 9 months
> - **Copies sold (Game Boy Color version):** 40,000
> - **Times downloaded on iOS:** 200,000

Two Tribes kept searching, and eventually got in contact with someone who said he would take the game to E3 and show it to publishers. Despite having never met this person, Two Tribes sent him a build of its game in good faith. The move paid off. The contact came back from E3 with not one but two offers for Two Tribes to consider—both Capcom and Konami were interested in publishing the game. "This was the start of a rather surreal period for us," says Van Ginkel. "We had sent our game unsecured, without any agreement in place, to a guy we did not really know, and he told us two big publishers wanted our game."

Van Ginkel and his team continued working on the game, and at one point in the process decided to change the name to *Toki Tori*. He says he didn't truly begin to believe "this was all happening" until the company received a five-figure deposit from Capcom, their publisher. All of the members of Two Tribes were students at the time, so this was a very big deal.

Toki Tori was one of the last great games to ever be released for the Game Boy Color. Critics praised its intelligent puzzle design and graphics (it was hailed as being "nearly as pretty as a Game Boy Advance game"), but the game didn't sell very well due to the Game Boy Advance being released a few months prior.

By 2009, Two Tribes had become a full-fledged company with a proper office and much bigger staff. After experimenting with some client work (including a couple of *Worms* games and a *Monkeyball*-branded minigolf game for mobile phones), the company had gone back to *Toki Tori* once again to deliver an enhanced remake for the WiiWare service. The vastly improved and graphically superior Wii version served as the basis for *Toki Tori*'s subsequent iPhone port.

Van Ginkel says that after meeting representatives from Chillingo at GDC 2009, he was persuaded to let them publish the game. Chillingo later published the iPad port of the game as well (which was based on the even higher resolution PC/Mac version).

The iPhone and iPad versions of *Toki Tori* have been a success, but Van Ginkel is wary of putting all of his faith in the platform. "We always go for high-quality games with an original design and high-production values, and it seems that this, in combination with the 99 cents–mentality, makes it almost impossible to sell to iPhone customers and make a profit," he remarks. "We consider iOS to be an important part of our strategy going forward, but we will not target it exclusively for our future games."

> ### Fun Facts
>
> - Players who beat all 40 of *Toki Tori*'s levels will learn the real reason Toki Tori is collecting all those eggs. The truth is a bit disturbing.
> - You can download the original version of *Eggbert* for free from file-hunter.com/eggbert.html.
> - The Game Boy Color version of *Toki Tori* never had more than two enemies on screen at once due to hardware limitations.

Words With Friends

Platform: iPhone/iPod Touch (iPad version available separately)
Price: $1.99
Developer: Newtoy Inc.
Publisher: Zynga
Released: July 19, 2009

What Is It?

Words With Friends is Scrabble for the 21st century. If you're not already one of the millions of connected gamers who have been enjoying the game since it was first released in

2009, I'll explain how it all works: *WWF* uses something called asynchronous online multiplayer, which basically allows you to take a turn and then put your iDevice aside. Your opponent can play you back when he or she gets the time, and you'll be alerted via push notification that it's once again your turn to play. A single game of *WWF* can take an hour or two or stretch over several days, depending on how busy each of you are. The game is flexible, conforming to the lifestyle and schedule of whoever is playing it.

The asynchronous online aspect of *Words With Friends* is just one reason it's so popular; the other big reason is that its reach is massive. The game can be played using iPhones, iPads, Android devices, and even Facebook. Unless you didn't successfully make the transition into the 21st century, there's a pretty good chance that you (and most of the people you know) have access to *Words With Friends*. Plus, it's Scrabble! What game has more universal appeal than Scrabble? Kids, teenagers, adults, and grandparents around the world love Scrabble, so pick up *Words With Friends* and invite some folks to join you. It could become a bonding experience.

Behind the Game

Words with Friends may be one of the most popular casual games ever published on a mobile platform, but its creator got his first big break working on one of PC gaming's most legendary franchises.

Paul Bettner joined Ensemble Studios right after the original *Age of Empires* game shipped. He remained with the studio for the next ten years, building numerous games and expansion packs in the *Age of Empires* series and occasionally working on prototypes that never evolved into full games (he references the *Halo* MMO in particular).

In mid-2008, Ensemble was in the midst of working on *Halo Wars* when Microsoft announced that the studio would be shutting down as soon as work on the game was complete. Apple had just launched the App Store, and knowing that he'd soon be out of a job, Bettner began to look seriously at the App Store for his next source of income. "My brother [David] and I had always talked about opening our own studio at some point, and we realized this was the perfect opportunity to take the leap," says Paul. "So in August of 2008 we left Ensemble, bought some MacBooks, and started working out of our local public library."

> **Statistics**
> • **Percentage increase of daily *WWF* players after Zynga acquired Newtoy:** 200%

According to Paul, the transition from working on massive games like *Age of Empires* to independent games was liberating. "Those big games end up taking years to complete, and it's easy to get burnt out after a while. But when developing for the iPhone, those years turn to months. To be able to have a vision for a game and see it fulfilled just a short time later is very satisfying."

By November of the same year, the newly formed Newtoy had released *Chess With Friends* on the App Store. It was moderately successful, but it was in no way a phenomenon. Despite this, Newtoy wasn't ready to pull out of the App Store just yet; the fledgling company was looking to create another *With Friends* title that capitalized on the biggest thing that *Chess With Friends* did right—approachable asynchronous multiplayer. *Words With Friends*, a Scrabble-style take on their first game, was released in mid-2009, and soon became far, far larger than the Bettner brothers and their growing staff could ever have hoped.

Right after releasing *Words With Friends,* Newtoy began work on *We Rule* for ngmoco. The company had accepted the contract work as a way to make some money—it was hurting for cash, and *Words With Friends* hadn't taken off in the first few months following its launch.

By October, *Words With Friends* had begun to enjoy a slight improvement in sales, but few would dispute that it was a single tweet sent out on October 5 that launched *Words With Friends* into the top sales charts and kick-started the game's popularity. The CW33, a Dallas-based broadcast news station, summed up events that followed with its headline "John Mayer Saves Texas Gaming Company with a Tweet."

Yes—*that* John Mayer. The blues-pop icon sparked a sales surge that propelled *Words With Friends* into the spotlight when he tweeted that *Words With Friends* "is the new Twitter." Neither the Bettners nor anyone else knew exactly what he meant by that, but Mayer's millions of Twitter followers took it as an endorsement and bought the game in droves, making it into the sensation it has since become.

In late 2010 Newtoy was purchased by Zynga, the goliath social-games company responsible for Facebook hits like *Farmville* and *Zynga Poker*. Newtoy was rebranded as Zynga With Friends and has since produced another *With Friends* title, based on the classic pen-and-paper game Hangman.

Fun Facts

- *Words With Friends* was one of the first games to support cross-platform multiplayer between the Android, iPhone, iPad, and Facebook platforms.
- John Mayer has since deactivated his Twitter account (he says he had become a "tweetaholic").
- Other apps by Newtoy include *Chess With Friends* and *Hanging With Friends*.

Zen Bound

Platform: iPhone/iPod Touch
Price: $2.99
Developer: Secret Exit
Released: February 25, 2009

What Is It?

Zen Bound is the gaming equivalent of sitting down and playing with Play-Doh. It's borderline therapeutic.

Each level in the game centers on a wooden sculpture. You have a limited amount of rope at your disposal, and the goal is to completely cover the sculpture by slowly turning the object and stretching the rope tightly around it, which you do by dragging one or two fingers across the screen. Whenever rope touches any part of the sculpture that segment becomes painted and a percentage counter in the upper-right corner of the screen increases, allowing you to keep track of how much of the sculpture has been covered and which areas remain.

As you play, you'll need to look for nicks and grooves on the sculpture to identify the best places to wrap the rope. The rope itself behaves just like a real rope would, so if you're not careful about wrap-

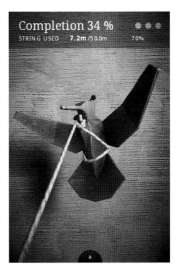

ping it tightly around the sculpture it may come unraveled, and then all of your work will have been for nothing. Once you've covered the sculpture in rope, you finish the level by finding the nail that juts out of each object and touching it with your rope. Then you're graded based on what percentage of the structure is painted.

Much of the experience of playing *Zen Bound* involves visualizing each object in your mind and thinking several steps ahead to determine the path you should take. The game has been designed to provide a slow-paced, thoughtful experience, and as you play you'll hear the creaks and groans of the rope as it twists and stretches around the object. Those sounds merge with the background music (which sounds like something you'd hear in a massage therapist's office) to create an incredibly peaceful mood. There's a good reason *Zen Bound* won the Audio Achievement award in the IGF Mobile 2009 competition.

Behind the Game

In 2005, Mikko Mononen released a free-to-download PC game about wrapping rope around wooden sculptures. Tuukka Savolainen created the soundtrack under the alias "Ghost Monkey," and even contributed some art to the game.

Jani Kahrama of Secret Exit saw Mononen's creation and was extremely impressed by it. He tried to recruit Mononen to make a full-fledged game out of his original prototype, but he had taken a job as the AI lead working on Crytek's landmark PC game *Crysis*. "Tugging his sleeve to join Secret Exit was only possible a couple of years later," he says.

Kahrama was finally able to get both Mononen and Savolainen to join him, and the three set out to remake Mononen's free game. The first order of business was to change the name, which originally was *Zen Bondage*. Secret Exit quickly settled on *Zen Bound*, and Kahrama notes with some humor that changing the game's name helped the design document pass through publishers' email filters.

Mononen's prototype provided a good start for the three-person team, but it lacked structure: players could wrap things in rope but they weren't really given a reason to do so. "The real challenge was building the game rules on top of the core gameplay and finding a structure that provided a sense of progression and elevated the game from being just a collection of levels," Kahrama notes.

The team also wanted to create an experience that felt tactile. "Not just responsive, but as close to touching a real surface as it could feel," Kahrama says. "We wanted to capture the essence of materials like brown cardboard, unpolished wood, and natural stone."

Perhaps the biggest problem facing Secret Exit was that throughout much of development, it had no idea which platform its game would end up on. It first considered the

Statistics

- **Development time:** 12 months
- **Number of Secret Exit employees who worked on *Zen Bound 1*:** 3
- **Number of Secret Exit employees who worked on *Zen Bound 2*:** 6
- **Combined units for *Zen Bound 1* and *2*:** 500,000

PS3, but decided that budgeting would be too difficult. It looked at Nintendo's WiiWare channel also, and didn't end up settling on the iPhone until months had gone by. "Much effort was wasted during the platform evaluations," Kahrama laments.

Even once the team had discovered a way to add structure and rules to the game, selected a platform, and honed their art and sound to create a tactile experience, the day-to-day work on *Zen Bound* was constantly interrupted with debates among team members about small details. "All three of us are stubborn perfectionists and adjusting the tiny details to the satisfaction of each was not easy, but we were all very proud of how the game was shaping up," says Kahrama. "One of the hardest lessons to learn after that is how to kill your darling and release something when it's good enough and nobody else is going to see the difference, much less appreciate it."

Eventually Secret Exit was able to overcome its perfectionism and put a product out. On November 11, 2010, *Zen Bound* was introduced to the App Store, where it quickly became a massive critical success. TouchGen.com called it "one of the most immersive games ever." IGN claimed that the game redefined what could be considered a video game, and Gamespot called it "a masterpiece." The accolades kept flowing in, and it rapidly became one of the most beloved iPhone games ever produced. *Zen Bound* never reached *Angry Birds'* levels of popularity, but it sold well enough to warrant a sequel.

> **Fun Facts**
>
> - Other apps by Secret Exit include *Zen Bound 2* and *Stair Dismount*.
> - *Zen Bound 2* has all of the original game's levels, along with improved graphics and an expanded soundtrack. If you're going to download a version of *Zen Bound*, the sequel is your best bet.
> - Kahrama says that the paper-sculpture work of artist Jen Stark was a big influence on *Zen Bound*'s aesthetic.
> - One *Zen Bound* fan told Secret Exit that playing *Zen Bound 2* on his iPad helped him to recover the use of his arm after losing control of it due to a stroke.

For Secret Exit, the most rewarding thing was hearing back from people who enjoyed the game. "We've noticed that people approach the game on many different levels. Some simply perceive the levels as spatial obstacles and approach them strictly as a puzzle," says Kahrama. "Others are instantly bored because nothing explodes in the game. However, there is also the minority who take the time to interpret each level as a singular art piece, and reflect on the emotions that may be evoked when performing the action of wrapping the rope around the sculpture. It's the comments from this minority that are very rewarding. The levels do contain subtle messages and themes, and it's wonderful to see people respond to them."

Acknowledgments

Creating this book took a lot out of me, but my parents and sister, Kelly, were there to encourage and support me throughout the entire experience. Mom gets a special shout-out for working tirelessly to help me edit the book into perfect shape in its final hours. I love you guys.

Much appreciation is also owed to the rest of my (ever-growing) family for its interest in what I do and cheering me on whenever I need encouragement. Uncle Clyde and I may never finish our garage projects, but at least I wrote a book!

I also owe much to all of the kind people in my hometown—Poplarville, MS—who have supported me with their thoughts and prayers. Y'all seriously don't know how much it means to me. Every time I get stopped by someone on the street who has a kind word to say, I'm reminded how blessed I am to have grown up among such good people.

Many, many thanks to Steve Seal for taking his precious time and donating far too much of it to younger people like me. Few teachers ever inspire someone the way he inspired me.

I can't forget the scores of people whom I interviewed for this book: without their participation, this book wouldn't exist. Each and every one of you has my immense gratitude. Thanks also to John Davison, for utilizing his time and unparalled understanding of mobile gaming to write the book's introduction.

Special thanks to all the people from GamePro for facilitating my insane obsession with iOS games by allowing me to write a weekly column and countless reviews about them. I'm willing to bet that Will Herring hopes to never again have to edit another piece of text from me.

And most importantly:

"In all your ways acknowledge him, and he will make your paths straight."
—Proverbs 3:6